Dr Monika Marie-Ilse von Zitzewitz-Lonmon was born in Zitzewitz, Pomerania (Prussia) between the wars. She studied Italian History and Culture and the History of Art at Freiburg University (Germany). She has had three books previously published. In 1965 she was appointed Cultural Correspondent in Italy for the distinguished German newspaper 'Die Welt'.

Dr von Zitzewitz's husband Ted Lonmon an ex-8th Army Officer was the first Civil Affairs Officer (Military Governor) of Florence City. She has lived in Italy (Florence, Como, Varese) for the past 25 years. They have a daughter and a son.

Dr von Zitzewitz lives a rural life in Varese Province, "Surr-ounded by animals" she says. She broods race-horses and greatly enjoys riding them at early morning training gallops.

Florence &Tuscany

Monika von Zitzewitz

Roger Lascelles, Cartographic and Travel Publisher
47 York Road, Brentford, Middlesex TW8 0QP Telephone: 01-847 0935

Publication Data

Title	Florence & Tuscany
Typeface	Phototypeset in Compugraphic Times
Photographs	By courtesy of the Ente Provinciale de Turismo, Firenze where indicated, others by the Publisher.
Printing	Kelso Graphics, Kelso, Scotland.
ISBN	0 903909 63 4
Edition	First June 1982, Second Mar 1988
Publisher	Roger Lascelles
	47 York Road, Brentford, Middlesex, TW8 0QP.
Copyright	Original text by LN Verlag, Lubeck.
	This English text by Roger Lascelles

Distribution

Africa:	South Africa —	Faradawn, Box 17161, Hillbrow 2038
Americas:	Canada —	International Travel Maps & Books, P.O. Box 2290, Vancouver BC V6B 3W5.
	U.S.A. —	Boerum Hill Books, P.O. Box 286, Times Plaza Station, Brooklyn, NY 11217, (718-624-4000)
Asia:	Hong Kong —	The Book Society, G.P.O. Box 7804, Hong Kong 5-241901
	India —	English Book Store, 17-L Connaught Circus/P.O. Box 328, New Delhi 110 001
	Singapore —	Graham Brash Pte Ltd., 36-C Prinsep St.
Australasia	Australia —	Rex Publications, 413 Pacific Highway, Artarmon NSW 2064. 428 3566
	New Zealand —	David Bateman Ltd. P.O. Box 65602, Mairangi Bay, Auckland 10 (9-444-4680)
Europe:	Belgium —	Brussels - Peuples et Continents
	Germany —	Available through major booksellers with good foreign travel sections
	GB/Ireland —	Available through all booksellers with good foreign travel sections.
	Italy —	Libreria dell'Automobile, Milano
	Netherlands —	Nilsson & Lamm BV, Weesp
	Denmark —	Copenhagen - Arnold Busck, G.E.C. Gad, Boghallen, G.E.C. Gad
	Finland —	Helsinki — Akateeminen Kirjakauppa
	Norway —	Oslo - Arne Gimnes/J.G. Tanum
	Sweden —	Stockholm/Esselte, Akademi Bokhandel, Fritzes, Hedengrens. Gothenburg/Gumperts, Esselte Lund/Gleerupska
	Switzerland —	Basel/Bider; Berne/Atlas; Geneve/Artou; Lausanne/Artou; Zurich/Travel Bookshop

Contents

Part 1 Practical Information for Visitors to Italy
On entering Italy   6
Tips for motorists   12
Some useful phrases   15

Part 2 Tuscany — A Background
Introduction   17
Practical Information   19
Tuscan Cooking   23
Tuscan Wines   25
Tuscany's Varied Landscape   28
Famous Tuscans
    Painting, Sculpture & Architecture   31
    Notes on a few types of painting   34
    Notes on architectural styles   35
    Literature and Science   36
    Music   37
Postscript   38

Part 3 Florence
Florence — An Introduction   39
Hotels, pensioni and locande   44
Eating out in Florence   54
Galleries, museums and gardens   88
Florence A-Z   94
A tour of Florence   106
Fiesole   144

Part 4 The Provinces of Tuscany
Arrezzo and Province   147
Grosseto Province   155
    The Etruscans in Tuscany   158
    Elba and the Islands   165
Livorno   169
Lucca and Massa Carrara   170
Prato to Pistoia & Pisa   179
Siena   193
    Excursions from Siena   200

Bibliography   209

Index   212

PART ONE

Practical Information

On Entering Italy

The information in this guide is accurate at the time of going to press, but exchange rates and certain regulations may alter at short notice. Exact prices have therefore been omitted, but indications as to level of expense are given throughout.

The Italian State Tourist Office (ENIT), 1 Princes Street, London W1R 8AY, Tel: 01-408 1254 produces an excellent booklet (free) entitled *Italy: Traveller's Handbook* which has much detailed information on different aspects of travelling in Italy.

Arriving:

By Air: There are direct flights daily to Milan from major European airports and a connecting flight to Pisa twice daily. There is a frequent rail service from Milan to Pisa. From 1st April to 31st October there are flights direct to Pisa from London, flying time 2 hours. Alternatively you may fly to Rome and either take the connecting flight to Pisa or the fast train service to Florence.

By Rail: Trains to Florence leave Victoria Station every day at 10.30 a.m. and 14.00 p.m. and reach Florence some twenty-four hours later at 10.36 and 16.00; the first of these is direct to Florence from Calais and you must have a couchette booking. The second involves a change at Milan.

By Road: The approach to Florence from Britain by car may be made as follows:-
From France: By the Autoroute du Sud to the Riviera and into Italy via Nice and Monaco. There is an Autostrada along the Ligurian Coast which joins up with the Pisa—Florence Auto-strada not far from Lucca.

By the Lyon-Chambery Autoroute (E13) to Lanslebourg Mont-Cenis where one drives over the pass and down to Susa.

Alternatively one can take the 12.9km Tunnel du Frejus (toll) leaving the E13 a short distance west of Modane. One then travels by way of Turin where one has the alternatives of driving via Piacenza and Bologna or via Genoa and La Spezia.

The third road by France is by way of Chamonix and the Mt Blanc road tunnel. Here again one has the alternatives mentioned above.

From Switzerland: From Geneva one can drive via Sallanches and Chamonix to the Mt Blanc Road Tunnel — see under the second French option above. (At Aosta you can stay in a pleasant, modestly priced hotel, the Cavallo Bianco).

Other routes into Italy from Switzerland are via the St Bernard Pass, the Simplon pass or car-train, the St Gothard Pass or road tunnel or the San Bernadino Pass via Lugano. All converge on Milano whence travel via Bologna is the shortest route.

From Austria There are three main approaches viz from Landeck via the Resia Pass to Merano and Bolzano; from Innsbruck via the Brenner Pass to Bolzano; and in the east via Villach and Udine.

Currency: Visitors are not permitted to bring into or take out of the country coins or notes in excess of 400,000 lire in Italian currency. The importing of foreign currency is unrestricted, but complete a V2 form on entry if you will want to take out again more than 1,000,000 lire. This form declares the amount of currency you are bringing in.

Lire coins (10, 20, 50, 100, 200 and 500 lire pieces) are almost always in short supply. Tram and bus tickets, sweets, chewing gum, stamps, etc. are often accepted as change. The bank note denominations are: 500, 1,000, 2,000 (N.B. it is very like the 5,000 note), 5,000, 10,000, 20,000, 50,000 and 100,000. The two latter are legal tender only in Italy, so you must exchange them at a bank before leaving the country.

The exchange rate (1987) is about 2,150 to the pound.

Customs: Visitors from EEC countries may bring in 300 cigarettes or 75 cigars duty free. The limit for other countries is 200 cigarettes or 50 cigars. The following are allowed per person: two cameras, one pair of binoculars, one television set, one transistor radio, one record player, one portable typewriter, one musical instrument, sports equipment (tennis, golf or skiing equipment, etc.), camping equipment, one boat up to 5.5m (18 ft) and one moped. It is advisable to have a list of items of this sort stamped by the customs official on entry.

Customs payable on alcohol:
3 litres of still wine and 3 litres of sparkling wine or 1.5 litres (2.6 pints) of spirits per person may be taken out of the country duty free. Perfume 75g (3 fl ozs). In addition presents and souvenirs up to a value of 120 pounds sterling. These figures apply to goods obtained duty and tax paid within the EEC.

Doctors: Ask at the Reception Desk in your hotel or obtain the recommended list from your nearest consulate. As Italy is in the EEC there is a reciprocal health service treatment but to take advantage of it British Visitors must obtain Form E111 from their Social Security Office before they go. To take advantage of the Italian Health Service this form will have to be produced at the nearest I.N.A.M. Office (*Istituto Nazionale per l'Assicurazione contro le Malattie*).

Holidays (National): January 1st, 6th, Easter Monday (not Good Friday or Whit Monday), 25th April (Liberation Day), May 1st, August 15th, November 1st, December 8th, 25th, and 26th. Ascension Day and Corpus Christi are the only remaining religious holidays, but there are local holidays as well — e.g. S. Giovanni, (patron saint of Florence), June 24th. August 15th, *Ferragosto*, is officially the one-day state holiday but in practice many restaurants and shops are closed for part or the whole of August, traditional holiday month for the Italians as for the English. It is a terrible time to be a tourist anywhere, but especially in Italy.

Hotels and Motels: The AGIP motels are very good and most reasonably priced. If you use one AGIP hotel, they will supply a list of all the others. The Italian State Tourist Office will supply a complete list of hotels in Tuscany (*Annuario Alberghi D'Italia*) on request.

Information: Italian State Tourist Office (ENIT) 1 Princes Street, London W1R 8AY, Tel: 01-408 1254. In Italy, at the *Ente di Turismo* is the local office of the Ministry of Tourism. Complaints and problems may be raised with them. For bookings and detailed advice, see local agencies. Smaller towns may only have a '*pro loco*' (tourist information office) run by the municipality. [*See also A-Z of Florence*].

Museums: As from 1980 the concessionary rate entry cards for State museums have been abolished. Opening times vary a lot, so check with the local tourist office who will have an up-to-date list of museum opening times. Many museums are closed on Mondays.

Newspapers: Major European morning newspapers are generally available on the afternoon of publication in all major cities and resorts. Newsagents (usually large kiosks on main squares) are plentiful and the Italian word for one is *'edicola'*.

Opening times: *Grocers:* Frequently from 7 a.m. till 12.30 p.m. and from 3.30 p.m. (in southern Tuscany from 5 p.m.) till 7.30 p.m. or 8 p.m. *Other shops* from 8.30 or 9 a.m. till 12.30 p.m. and from 3 or 3.30 p.m. till 7.30 p.m. Shops on the coast generally remain open longer.

Police: In principle, charm is to be recommended in all dealings with the police. There is a specific law in Italy against 'insulting' the police, or the state. So don't try it. A smile (preferably from a female) works better than aggression. There seem to be innumerable different types of police in Italy but you will encounter three basic varieties.

The *Vigili Urbani* are something between traffic wardens and policemen on the beat, being the municipality's own force. They wear black or, in summer, all-white uniforms (on traffic duty).

The *Polizia* or Public Security Police are less visible and much-suspected, because of their origins in the Fascist period, though they do struggle against crime on low pay and in bad conditions.

The *Carabinieri* are a para-military force whom you will see dealing with public disturbances of any kind. They wear a grey-green uniform and look more like soldiers than police. Off-duty many can be seen walking the streets on Sunday dressed in their smart navy-blue ceremonial dress. There are also the *Guardia di Finanza* who deal with customs matters and are a branch of the Polizia. If you need help and want the nearest Police Station ask for the 'questura' or ring the Carabinieri. *See also Emergency Telephone numbers in Florence A-Z.*

Motorists in Florence may be intrigued by the glamorous female traffic wardens who look more like Gucci models than wardens. They are to be seen blending elegantly with the architecture in the centre of town.

Religious Services: Ask for consulate or hotel porter for information on Roman Catholic and Protestant religious services. Times of Mass (*'ore di messe'*) are posted near the entrance of churches. *See also Florence A-Z.*

Shopping: Department stores (*Upim, Standa, MS, S-Lunga, Rinascente,* etc.) and most shops have fixed prices. One should try to bargain a little in markets and small shops. Eurocheques and Travellers' Cheques are accepted in all large hotels and shops. Access, American Express, Barclaycard and Diners Club will be accepted in the more expensive shops and restaurants.

Signore is the plural of signora and not to be confused with *signori* (gentlemen). *NB* for public toilets.

Snakes: Since the snakes' natural enemies, the porcupine and birds of prey, have been decimated by 'sportsmen' in Tuscany the number of poisonous snakes has increased enormously. It is advisable to wear long trousers and sturdy shoes and to carry a stick when out walking in the countryside. Take with you some serum for snake bites (stocked by all chemists) if you embark on a long walk.

Telephones: You must use the *gettoni,* the special discs available from the Post Office or in bars with telephones. One *gettone* is sufficient for a local call. Several (at least 6) are needed for trunk calls depending on distance and the duration of the call. International calls are best made from the Central Post Office of the town. When making a trunk call, dial the numbers *slowly* or you will not get a connection. (*See also Florence A-Z.*)

Time: Summer Time lasts from the 6th April till 28th September. Clocks go forward one hour from British Time.

Tips: Are included only in 'inclusive prices', (*prezzi compresi*). Waiters, porters and chambermaids do expect an appropriate tip (approximately 10% — but not less than 500 lire). Usherettes in theatres and cinemas are customarily tipped as well.

Voltage: In general 220 volts a.c. Adaptors are necessary because of the difference in sockets which are usually for two round pins.

Water: Almost every Italian will order a bottle of water with his wine. There are many excellent brands of gassy or still mineral water of which *San Pellegrino* is probably the best. In principle, you should always inquire if the local water is safe to drink (*"L'acqua é potabile?"*) Fruit should always be washed or peeled.

Weights: The standard measurements of weight are the *"Chilo"* (1 kilo = 2.2 lbs.) (*un chilo, due chili*), the *"etto"* (100 g = 3.5 ozs. — *un etto, due etti*) the *"quintale"* (100 kilos = 220 lbs.) and the *"tonnellata"* (one ton = 1000 kilos).

Youth Hostels: Information is available from the Italian Youth Hostel Association (*Associazione Italiana Alberghi per la Gioventu*) *Palazzo della Civiltà del Lavoro, Quadrato della Concordia, 00144 E.U.R. Roma, Tel: 591 3702.* There are hostels in the ski resort of *Abetone* (*Pistoia Province*), in *Arezzo, Florence, Lucca, Marina di Massa, Massa-Carrara, Pisa* and *Tavarnelle Val di Pesa* (*Florence Province*).

The Youth Hostels Association, 14 Southampton Street, London, WC2. (Tel: 01-836 8541) deals with membership, travel enquiries and provides a list of hostels in Italy. (*See also Florence A-Z*).

Tips for Motorists

It used to be mostly in Naples that unlocked cars were broken into or stolen. Nowadays, unfortunately, it happens everywhere in Italy. The huge number of tourists, many of whom appear wealthy to Italians suffering from soaring inflation and unemployment, has produced a generation of hit and run thieves. Never leave cars unlocked or windows partially open. As far as theft of cars is concerned it is some, but not much, consolation to know that the record for theft is held by the Fiat 500, an outdated model seldom driven by tourists. It is much in demand for spare parts.

Should you have the misfortune to have your car stolen, consult your nearest Consulate, especially if you speak little Italian. Italian bureaucracy is even more unnerving when official and customer cannot understand each other.

Where possible leave your car in an attended garage.

Parking meters are checked constantly in the cities. If they run out, local police usually turn a blind eye in the case of foreign cars. But they never do if it is otherwise unlawfully parked: the car will probably be towed away. Reclaiming it from one of the municipal compounds is time-consuming and expensive.

Translation of words on Italian road signs:

Senso unico   one way street
Vietato ingresso veicoli   no entry for vehicles
Sosta autorizzata   parking permitted (times will be indicated)
Divieto di sosta   no parking
Passaggio a livello   level crossing
Rallentare   slow down
Svolta   bend
Incrocio   crossroads
Uscita   exit
Entrata   entrance
Lavori in corso   road works ahead
Caduta massi   beware falling rocks

Automobile Club: The Italian Automobile Club (ACI) has an office in all provincial capitals and can also be contacted on the emergency breakdown service number 116. By joining ACI at the border, you become eligible for assistance in the event of a breakdown; and you will be given road maps, lists of hotels and special reductions etc.

Car Rental: Hired cars are available at the airports, main railway stations or through your hotel porter. The weekly rates are better value. Fully comprehensive insurance is advisable. (*See also Florence A-Z*)

Driving Licence: British driving licences are valid but should be accompanied by an Italian translation obtainable at an ACI office.

Motorway Tolls: There are tolls on all *Autostrade*. Cumulatively they can be quite expensive. Milan to Florence costs Lire 9,600 for cars of less than 774cc, Lire 18,000 for cars of 775-1372cc, Lire 20,950 for cars of more than 1372cc, Lire 8,200 for motorcycles. There are extra charges for caravans. Full details of Italian motorway tolls are given in the free booklet available from the Italian State Tourist Office (see page 6).

Petrol: Tourists who take their own car to Italy are entitled to a 15% discount on the pump price (supergrade only). Discount vouchers are used and must be purchased in advance. The AA, RAC or CIT (50 Conduit St, London W1, tel. 01-434 3844) can supply various petrol coupon packages which include motorway vouchers towards the payment of tolls.

Petrol stations: Attendants are generally friendly and helpful, and, unlike those in Britain, will clean your windscreen, test the oil, check the tyres etc. in the motorway stations. A modest tip is usual. Use *Super* petrol as *Normale* is low quality.

Registration Book, Insurance: The car log-book must be carried. A Green Card is no longer obligatory for insurance, but you must be fully insured, especially as there are many people driving around in Italy who are not. Consult the A.A. before you start your holiday.

Speed limit in built up areas is 50 km/30 miles per hour, 110 km/70 miles per hour on country roads, although vehicles with less than 1300 c.c. capacity have a lower speed limit. On motorways the same applies with the 1300 c.c. upwards limit being 140 km (85 miles per hour).

NOTE: In many towns traffic lights are hanging on wires over the middle of the street. They are *very* easy to miss.

Some useful Phrases

Good morning	*buon giorno*
Good evening	*buona sera*
Goodnight	*buona notte*
Goodbye	*arrivederci*

Please	*per favore*
Thank you	*grazie*
Yes	*si*
No	*no*
Excuse me, sorry	*mi scusi* (sorry) *or permesso* to get out of a crowd, etc.

January	*gennaio*	one	*uno*
February	*febbraio*	two	*due*
March	*marzo*	three	*tre*
April	*aprile*	four	*quattro*
May	*maggio*	five	*cinque*
June	*giugno*	six	*sei*
July	*luglio*	seven	*sette*
August	*agosto*	eight	*otto*
September	*settembre*	nine	*nove*
October	*ottobre*	ten	*dieci*
November	*novembre*		
December	*dicembre*		

Monday	*lunedi*	left	*sinistra*
Tuesday	*martedi*	right	*destra*
Wednesday	*mercoledi*	above	*sopra*
Thursday	*giovedi*	below	*sotto*
Friday	*venerdi*	straight ahead	*diritto*
Saturday	*sabato*		
Sunday	*domenica*		

I would like something to eat   *Vorrei mangiare qualcosa*
I would like something to drink   *Vorrei bere qualcosa*

Please bring me some (beer, water, lemonade, fresh lemon or orange juice)
Per favore, mi porti un po di vino (birra, acqua, limonata, spremuta di limoni/aranci)

I would like to pay   *Vorrei pagare*
That is too expensive   *E troppo caro*

Please give me a room for one (two) with bath or shower
Mi dia per favore una camera per una (due) persona (persone) con bagno o doccia.

How much is it?   *Quanto costa?*
Where is the nearest hotel? (the nearest garage, petrol station, bar?)
Dove trovo il prossimo albergo? (la prossima autorimessa? Il distributore de benzina? Il bar?)

Please fill up with Super *Mi dia il pieno di Super, per favore.*

Please check the air, the water, the oil.
Le prego di controllare l'aria, l'aqua, l'olio

I would like some bread, butter, cheese, salami, an egg (two), a bottle of mineral water, red wine, white wine —
Vorrei pane, burro, formaggio, salame, un uovo (due uova), una bottiglia di acqua minerale, vino rosso, vino bianco.

An ice, please   *Un gelato, per favore*

What time is it?   *Che ore sono?*

Where can I find a doctor, dentist?
Dove posso trovare un medico, dentista?

Goodnight! Sleep well!   *Buona notte! Dorma bene!*

I will certainly be back next year!
L'anno prossimo tornero senz'altro!

PART TWO

Tuscany — A Background

Introduction

Using the Guide

The aim of the guide is to enable readers to acquaint themselves rapidly with the beauty and pleasures of Florence and Tuscany. It cannot hope to point out every detail of scenic or artistic interest, and some will have their own interests to pursue in greater depth. For them there is a bibliography further on in the book listing further reading on various topics. For the general readers the guide will provide a concise factual *vade mecum* for a stay of a few weeks enabling them to use the transport services efficiently, find places to stay, see the sights of likely interest, eat well and/or cheaply and get the most out of a visit.

Tuscany: a survey

The 24,000 square kilometres covered by the former Grand Duchy of Tuscany, since 1860 a central region of modern Italy, present the traveller with some of the finest art treasures, the most enchanting countryside and the most delightful people to be found anywhere. It is a region which is an historic entity, bounded by Emilia-Romagna in the north and north-east, by Umbria and the Marches in the east, Latium (Lazio) in the south, the Tyrrhenian Sea in the west and Liguria in the north west .

A modern internal division of historic Tuscany has produced nine provinces:

Arezzo	Livorno	Pisa
Florence	Lucca	Pistoia
Grosseto	Massa-Carrara	Siena

Tuscany is mostly hilly or mountainous, with a long flat coastal area in the west, originally disease ridden marsh, which is known as the Maremma.

The People and the Region

In a country characterised by diversity the Tuscans, and especially the Florentines, are perhaps the most individualistic of all. Hard-headed and hard working as much today as ever, their literature, architecture and incomparable painting reflect the minds of a lively, inquisitive and rational people who, for a while, were able to create conditions in which the pursuit of excellence could flourish.

Though Florence dominates we shall see as we visit them that other centres of artistic activity such as Pisa, Siena and Arezzo produced their own geniuses who developed their own vision.

The countryside provides a vivid contrast to urban sophistication. This is the landscape of laboriously cultivated terraced plots, punctuated by olive groves and sentinel cypresses. The centuries old *'mezzadria'* system is now all but dead — a feudal arrangement whereby the peasant pays his landlord, partially, in kind. More modern methods of agriculture and viticulture produce, on the one hand, the meat of the magnificent Florentine *'bistecca'* (beefsteak) from the Charolais bulls of the Val di Chiana near Arezzo, and on the other the prized Chianti wine from the Sangiovese grape without which no meal in Tuscany is complete. This wine is produced in the region stretching from Pontassieve, on the outskirts of Florence, down towards Siena.

The great names of the Florentine past and present appear also on the labels of bottles of Chianti wine - Ricasoli, Antinori, Frescobaldi and others. But beware of imitations! Your guarantee that you are getting the product produced under controlled conditions, and not some indifferent blend of wines from the surrounding region, is the 'Black Rooster' printed on a strip round the neck of the bottle - the imprint of *'chianti gallo'*, or the little cherub, *chianti putto*, which is less distinguished but still reliable wine.

18

Practical Information

Camping: There are over twenty camping sites on the Tuscan coast (Information from the Italian Government Tourist Office, 201 Regent Street, London, W1R 8AY, Tel: 01-439 2311, or local tourist information centres); there are five on Elba, one on the Isola del Giglio. A list of camp sites may be obtained from *Centro Nazionale Campeggiatori Stranieri, Casella Postale 649, 50100 Firenze,* or from the *Italian State Tourist Office in London.*

Climate: Generally mild. Frost and snow are unusual in the lowlands. Florence has an average of seventy-five days of sunshine annually; the maximum and minimum air temperatures in August are 31°C/88°F and 17°C/61°F. Most years one can swim in the sea at Elba from April (water temp. 19°C, 66°F) till October (water temp. 24°C, 75°F) and on the coast from May 19°C, 66°F) till October (19.5°C, 67°F). The main rainy seasons are November and February but there are heavy showers at other times.

Clothing: Casual. Only Forte dei Marmi, Viareggio, Punta Ala and Monte Argentario are more elegant. Diving goggles are recommended for the rocky coast. For protection from sea urchins, the painful spines of which are difficult to remove, bathing shoes should be worn. Take some strong shoes for walking. Sun hats are advisable.

Farm Holidays: 'Agriturismo' or Holidays on the Farm: :
This type of holiday, which has long been popular in Northern Europe, is slowly beginning to gain ground in Italy. The addresses of the *'cascine'* which take in paying guests, and, in some cases, expect help with the harvest, are available from the Associazione Regionale Toscana Agriturist, Via del Proconsolo 10, Firenze. Tel: 055/28 78 38. (The same agency arranges villa tours). This is one quite new — and probably very pleasant — way of getting to know Tuscany and its way of life.

19

Festivals in Tuscany (Arts)

Apr-Jun	— Lucca - Sacred music festival in the town's churches.
Jun	— Pietrasanta - Concerts in the town's churches - 'Estate Musicale Pietrasantese'
Jul to mid-Aug	— Barga (Province of Lucca) - Opera Barga. Marina de Pietrasanta - Drama and Ballet in the open air theatre 'La Versiliana'.
Aug	— Siena - Music Festival.
Aug	— Torre del Lago Puccini (Province of Lucca) - Puccini operas in open-air theatre.

February - Viareggio — *'Carnevale';* colourful carnival floats.

June 16 - 17 - Pisa — *San Ranieri* __ Illumination of buildings and historical regatta.

July 2 and August 16 - Siena — *'Il Palio';* traditional bare-back horse race round city square.

September (1st Sun) - Arezzo — *'Giostra del Saracino',* joust of the Saracens with armoured knights. Festival dates from 13th century.

September (2nd Sun) - Sansepolcro (Province of Arezzo) — *'Palio Balestrieri',* crossbow *Palio* (contest) between Sansepolcro and Gubbio.

September 13 - Lucca — *Luminaria di S. Croce* on the eve of the Holy Cross. Illuminated buildings and torchlight procession.

See also Florence A-Z. (Page 97)

Holiday Apartments: On request, Cuendet S.p.a., 1-53030 Strove (Siena) will send you a most informative colour brochure of their properties in Tuscany. You may also obtain details at the local *Azienda Autonoma di Soggiorno* (Tourist Office) in resorts.

Holiday Villages: *Villagi Turistici:* Particularly suitable for large families, these are common in Tuscany. ENIT (Italian Government Tourist Office) in London and local information offices will supply details.

Mining: Tuscany is rich in minerals. Marble is quarried in the Apuan Alps, the hinterland between La Spezia and Viareggio, and the most famous quarries are at Carrara. Alabaster is mined in the Volterra area. In Volterra itself, alabaster ornaments may be purchased, though only a few are in good taste. Piombino is the centre of the iron and steel industry of the region. Limestone and iron ore come from the hills near the coast and from Elba. Mercury is mined on Monte Amiata and lignite in the Arno valley.

Swimming: If you are travelling with children you will want the sandy beaches - but the water is dirty in most places. Along the rocky stretches the water at least looks crystal clear. But do not be deceived by appearances, for, in terms of pollution, the Mediterranean comes a close second to the Baltic. Avoid swallowing it.

Generally speaking, the Tuscan coast has plenty of wide, sandy beaches from the *Ligurian* border in the north to *Livorno* for divers and more adventurous swimmers, it is only interesting in those places where rocky breakwaters have been built e.g. at Marina di Pisa near the mouth of the Arno, or off the islands. From Livorno south, the picturesque rocky coastline extends to *Rosignano Solvay,* where the sand starts again, though swimming is not advisable because of the local chemical plant. With a few interruptions (for example just south of Punta Ala) the southern coastline is sandy and wide, down to the border with Latium.

Topography: Tuscany is mainly green and hilly. The highest peaks of the Apennines are *Monte Giove* (1991 m/6532 ft.) in the north and *Monte Amiata* (1734m/5689 ft.), an extinct volcano, in the south (above *Grosseto*). The rugged Alpine character of the Apuan Alps in the north-west where marble has been mined since antiquity, is in sharp contrast to the features of the Apennines. *Monte Pisanino* (1750m/5742 ft.) is the highest peak. In the coastal areas, the once extensive pine forests and evergreen scrub have given way to agriculture on the one hand, and development of coastal resorts on the other.

Villa Tours: From April to June, Agriturist organises daily coach excursions to the most beautiful villas in the Florence area, including the *Villa I Tatti* which belonged to Bernard Berenson, the *Villa La Pietra* owned by scholar and writer Harold Acton, which has one of the most beautiful 18th century gardens in Tuscany, and the *Villa Petraia,* favourite residence of

King Victor Emanuel II, which has magnificent gardens in the Florentine manner. (See pp 66)

During the grape harvest, in September and October when the autumn colours are at their best, the company offers longer excursions ('*Arte e Campagna*') including a visit to a vineyard and a winetasting on the spot.

Agriturist, Via del Proconsola 10, Firenze. Tel. 055/28 78 38

The Province of Tuscany

Tuscan Cooking

Even an expertly and correctly prepared meal never tates as good at home as on that evening in ... The aromas of the foreign country are missing. That is particularly true of Tuscany because the cuisine, as we have said already, is very simple and its excellence depends on the fresh ingredients: the oil, in particular that from Lucca, which is said to be the best in the world: The good meat, the fresh vegetables. In addition to wine, you should try to take a few bottles of oil back home with you — do not buy it from a shop but from the farmers.

Here are three simple recipes (for six): you can dream of Tuscany as you prepare them and savour them.

Fagioli "All'Uccelletto"
Ingredients: 400g (14 ozs.) fresh haricot beans; 1 glass of oil; 2 cloves of garlic, crushed; 1 piece of sage; 400g (14 ozs.) fresh tomatoes, cut into pieces, or two tablespoons of tomato purée; pepper and salt.
   Cook the beans in boiling salted water. Drain well. Fry garlic in the hot oil till golden. Remove from pan. Cook the beans, sage, tomatoes (or the tomato purée dissolved in a little boiling water), salt and pepper for roughly 20 minutes in the hot oil, till the sauce has reduced.

Fegatelli alla Toscana (Liver Tuscan style)
Ingredients: 1 kg (2.2 lbs) of pigs' liver cut into small pieces; 300g (10.5 ozs.) caul (the outer skin of the liver); pinch of fennel seeds; salt, pepper, breadcrumbs, bay leaf, croûtons.
   Soak the caul till it is easy to open. Cut into pieces. Sprinkle pieces of liver with salt, pepper, fennel seeds and breadcrumbs and wrap each piece individually in a piece of caul. Push the pieces on to skewers, alternating them with bay leaves and croûtons. Grill for 10 minutes over a wood fire or deep fry. Serve hot.

Pollo alla fiorentina (*Chicken Florentine style*)

Ingredients: 1 large chicken; 2 rashers of bacon or ham, chopped finely; ½ onion chopped finely; clove garlic, crushed; ½ glass oil; small glass of Marsala or dry white wine; 40g (1.4 ozs.) dried mushrooms; 300g. (10.5 ozs.) tin of tomatoes, peeled; small bunch of parsley, chopped.

Cut the chicken into 16 pieces. Wipe and dry carefully. Brown in oil on a low heat together with the garlic, bacon and onion. Remove the garlic when golden and add the Marsala or wine to the chicken. Season to taste and add the mushrooms which have been soaked in warm water, and the tomatoes, chopped into pieces. Adjust seasoning and simmer for 30 minutes. Add a little hot chicken stock if necessary. Serve hot with sauce.

Tuscan Wines

The Land of the Black Rooster: Florence to Siena

The best-known wine of Italy is *Chianti,* coming from the region of that name near Florence. It is lively and fruity and mostly drunk young, but the best of it ages well. *Chianti Classico* is senior wine from the central area and some of its *Riservas* (a wine of more than 3 years of age) have the bouquet of having been aged in oak casks. The sign of quality chianti is the famous 'Black Cock' label affixed to the neck of the bottle *(Chianti Gallo).*

Cosimo III, Grand Duke of Tuscany, set out in a decree in 1716 the limits of the area within which Chianti should be produced. Simultaneously, he forbade the export of all wine produced in the plains, since the best grapes grow on the dry, stony ground below the pine-covered hills. These limits still apply to the area in which *Chianti Classico* is produced. The name first appears in a deed dated 1398 and is said to derive from the Etruscans.

Just beyond the ring of hills around Florence towards Siena, you enter the domain of the Black Cock; the trademark was originally the crest of the Medieval *'Liga del Chianti'.*

The countryside between Florence and Siena — or rather the countrysides, since the scenery changes constantly from gentle olive groves to slopes of dark firs to light coloured woodland mainly of oaks — has in general changed little from what we see in Renaissance paintings.

The castles and villas of the statesmen, writers and patrons of the arts, whose descendants often still live here and produce wine, guarantee that a tour of the Tuscan vineyards is also a study of the culture and history of the area.

If you are an enthusiastic wine-taster and are looking for precise information about the Chianti country, or if you do not have the time for a leisurely tour but would like to sample the wines and buy some to take home, you should contact the

"*Consorzio del Vino Chianti Classico*" in Florence, Via *Valfonda 9,* near the main station, or the "*Enoteca del Chianti Classico*", in *Greve* (approx. 20km, 12.4 miles south of Florence on Road 222) where a picturesque Wine Fair is held every year from September 12th—15th. In the back room of the *Enoteca,* you can admire the oldest and finest of all Chiantis, stored like religious relics behind glass.

2.6km (1.5 miles) from Greve along the charming road to *Lamole* is the *Villa di Vignamaggio,* which is said to have been the birthplace of Mona Lisa dei Gherardini, Leonardo di Vinci's famous model.

Monastery wines and 'roof' wines

Castellina in Chianti (Road 222, 20km from Greve towards Siena) stands on a hill overlooking three river valleys: the churches, palaces and castle are hidden behind the huge grape silos. It is worth taking a trip from here towards *Montevarchi* (Road 408) if only for the fine scenery. As you leave the village, there are three huge Etruscan tombs on the left (look for the yellow sign).

Take the road through *Radda in Chianti* to the 11th century *Badia* (abbey) *a Coltibuono,* which is now a vineyard producing excellent wines (here as everywhere else in Chianti country, it is best to buy wine direct from the producer). The food and wines in the rustic restaurant next to the abbey are excellent. The priest will be glad to show you the Romanesque monastery church, which was altered to the Baroque style — and even more delighted to show you his horses.

Approximately 12km (7.4 miles) further on is the most splendid of all the domains in Chianti, the *Castello di Brolio* which has belonged to the Ricasoli family since 1141. Visits are permitted to part of the castle, in particular, the dining hall with its Gobelin tapestries and coats of armour. The *Brolio* wine, which can be tasted in the *Cantina Ricasoli* at the foot of the castle, is one of the most famous in Tuscany.

For further investigation of the *Chianti Classico* territory, you must turn back past Castellina to take the Florence—Siena motorway towards Poggibonsi. Stop briefly in the walled village of *Monteriggioni,* to the left above the road, which was mentioned by Dante. The only restaurant in the village, "*Il Poggio*", is to be recommended.

Not far from Monteriggioni is *Cusano.* If you feel like a fine white wine after the classic red Chianti, try the *Vernaccia di San Gimignano* here, the only wine in Italy which is allowed to

26

mature for up to 40 years. The president of the Vernaccia consortium. Prince Strozzi-Guicciardini, lives in Cusano in the villa built by his ancestor, Francesco Guicciardini, the 16th century historian and moralist.

At *Castello di Poppiano,* two kilometres from Cusano, a descendant of the Hapsburg Duke of Tuscany produces, in addition to the classic Chianti, the strangest wine in the country, the *"Tegolato"*. *'Tegola'* is the word for the characteristic curved roof tile on Italian houses. The wine, which is produced from the best vintages (wines of lesser quality would not survive such barbaric treatment) is first matured for four years in oak casks, then bottled and left for a year on the roof of the castle, exposed to rain, sun and cold. One half explodes, but the bottles that survive are quite priceless — and delicious. Take the Cassia (Road 2) or the Florence road (but stop off to see the altar paintings in *S. Casciano in Val de Pesa* and the reliefs in the *della Misericordia* church) then turn off the road another 800m (875 yards) further along, pass the 18th century Villa Antinori and continue till you reach the village of *S. Andrea in Percussina.* If you like neither Machiavelli nor garlic, then drive on: both bring me here ....

S. Andrea in Percussina (Prov. Firenze)
Dismissed from the service by the Florentines in 1512, Niccolo Machiavelli, the greatest and most misunderstood political thinker Italy has ever produced, came to live in S. Andrea in Percussina. On December 10th, 1513 he wrote a letter which has gone down in literary history. In it he told his friend, Francesco Vittori, of his miserable day-to-day existence in exile, of how he passed the time of day in the local tavern and spent princely evenings "dressed in fine robes at the courts of the great men of the day" — meaning with his books.

You will be given a copy of this letter along with the excellent wine and delicious *'fettunta'* in the cleverly decorated, rustic restaurant opposite Machiavelli's villa. *'Fettunta'* is bread toasted over a wood fire then rubbed with garlic and brushed over with oil and salt.

Tuscany's Varied Landscape

Tuscany is not majestic like some of the other regions of Italy, - the Northern Italian lakes, the Roman Campagna or the picturesque splendour of the Amalfi coast. Apart from the endless cornfields in the former marsh lands of the Maremma in the south-west and on the coast, it consists mainly of hills which have been transformed by man into a landscape of gardens and terraces. The coast with its sandy beaches and rocky coves, the gentle hills of the Apennines and the rugged screes of the Apuan Alps and the islands, tall mountain forests, vineyards and olive groves, the remnants of the pine forests and the evergreen scrub of the Macchia with its sweet smelling bushes and trees, all go to produce a diversity of scenery scarcely matched by any other region of Italy.

Hot springs, which are still exploited in many spas, point to the existence of extinct volcanoes. The most important spas are *Montecatini, Monsummano, Saturnia* and *Chianciano:* in some places where the hot steam from the *soffioni* (gas) rises out of the ground, it is harnessed to provide a geothermal source of energy. The biggest of these, *Larderello,* in Pisa province on Road 322, provides Florence with electricity.

The Futa Pass

You could begin or end your visit to Tuscany by a route avoiding the *Autostrada del Sole* which is often under repair in summer causing endless traffic jams. The old mountain road to Bologna through the wild, lonely Apennines enters Tuscany through the *Futa Pass (900m/2,953 ft).* You can also reach it from the *Pian del Voglio* exit of the motorway. The road slows but is scenically exciting and it is worth all the hairpins to round a corner, perhaps in the evening, and find the twinkling lights of Florence set out below you, and to descend past Fiesole on the Via Bolognese into the heart of the city.

On the way you can make a detour to the left at *Ponte Ghierto* to visit *Borgo San Lorenzo, Scarperia* and *Santa Agata* in the Mugello - an enchanting drive.

The Mugello

The Mugello, a very beautiful, hilly region of vineyards, woods and arable land, was, until a few years ago, seldom visited by tourists. The Arno rises near its highest peak, *Monte Falterona* (1654m, 5,426 ft) which spans the border with Emilia. Many Northern Europeans have bought and renovated abandoned farmhouses in the area. Some years ago the Tuscan regional government laid out the largest road racetrack in Europe for cars on a network of local roads near Borgo San Lorenzo. The major race meeting is in June.

Borgo San Lorenzo

This is the principal town of the Mugello: the town has some interesting Mediaeval palaces. The same is true of the neighbouring town, Scarperia, which possesses a miniature 'Palazzo Vecchio'.

On the way to Vicchio, the birthplace of *Fra Angelico* (7k, 4.3 miles) from *San Lorenzo,* is the Cimabue bridge. A memorial plaque tells of the memorable encounter between the great *Cimabue* and the young *Giotto di Bondone,* who was drawing a sheep on a rock and was later taken by the famous painter to his workshop in Florence. 1 km (0.6 miles) further on, in the tiny village of *Vespignano,* stands the house which is said to have been Giotto's birthplace: it was partially destroyed by an earthquake in 1919.

The Mugello was once reputed to be the most charming region of Tuscany. If you visit it, you will not be surprised that it inspired painters and poets. Next to the *Romanesque church of S. Agata* (3.5km, 2.2 miles from *Scarperia*), we found a haven for travel-weary children. In a section of the cloisters behind the church is a *papier mâché* model of the everyday world of peasants and craftsmen long ago. Everything moves mechanically: the knife sharpener is sharpening, the blacksmith is hammering, the women are weaving, the threshing machine is rattling. The man who built this model village still sells oil and cheese in the shop next to the church and he will escort visitors enthusiastically to his masterpiece.

We encountered a strange procession in the pine and chestnut forests above *S.Agata.* Ten mules, each loaded with firewood, made their way down a steep path, nose to tail and occasionally emitting a loud sigh. Mules have become quite rare in Italy, although until the last war they were bred for the crack Alpini regiment.

Continuing on Road 65 from Scarperia towards Florence, you will see to your left the turrets and towers of the *Villa Cafaggiolo,* originally a fortress for Florence, which was converted by *Michelozzo* into a summer residence for Cosimo the Elder, the first great Medici. (To visit it see details on P. 20)

Alternatively you can go via *Borgo San Lorenzo* on the *Faentina* (302), the road from Faenza (where faience was invented) to Florence: the road is particularly attractive. In a tiny monastery to the left of the road, there is a huge neo-classical organ; it is almost bursting out of the church. Napoleon removed it from the Badia Fiesolana but abandoned the attempt to take it to France because of its size.

At the next junction, take the left turn to *Santa Brigida* to the beautifully restored *Castello del Trebbio* (visits by appointment only). Produce from the castle is on sale next door - excellent wine and olive oil.

You continue past Fiesole on steep roads between historic Renaissance villas, down to Florence. On the way you can drive from Fiesole via *Coverciano* and visit the turreted *Villa di Poggio Gherardo* which is one of the places claimed as the setting for the first three days of Boccaccio's *Decameron.* In those days it was called *Il Palagio del Poggio,* The Palace on the Hill. The description that Boccaccio gives certainly fits this villa as well as its rivals : "A Palace on the brow of a hill with a fine and spacious courtyard in the centre and with loggie and halls and rooms ornamented tastefully with jocund paintings; surrounded with grass plots and marvellous gardens, and with wells of coldest water, and cellars of rare wines, a thing more suited to curious topers than to sober and virtuous women". There is still a well in the garden known as Boccaccio's well.

Continuing on the *Via del Ponte a Mensola* you pass, and would not be wasting time if you visited, the Church of *S.Martino a Mensola.* Then proceeding to the next village, *Settignano,* a stop should be made at the *Villa Gamberaia.* Near here is one of the best restaurants of the area, *"Le Cave di Maiano"* where in summer you can eat *al fresco.*

Famous Tuscans

Painting, Sculpture and Architecture

Fra Angelico, known also as *Beato* ("Blessed") *Angelico:* born circa 1400, died 1455. Painter, Dominican friar. Altar paintings and frescoes. When his order took over the convent of *San Marco* in Florence, he decorated it with a series of some fifty frescoes, most of them in the cells of the friars and intended as aids to contemplation. His works may be seen in the *Museo di S. Marco, Florence.*

Sandro Botticelli: 1445—1510. Painter of allegorical, mythological and religious subjects. His most important works - *Primavera ("Spring"), La Nascita di Venere ("The Birth of Venus"),* and others, are in the *Uffizi,* Florence.

Filippo Brunelleschi: 1377—1446. Architect and sculptor. Designer of the largest dome since Antiquity (*Duomo - Florence*).

Giovanni Cimabue: born circa 1240, died circa 1302. Dante called him the most famous painter of his generation. Florence: Panel painting of the *Santa Trinita Madonna* (*Uffizi*), *"Crucifixion"* (*Santa Croce* - badly damaged in the 1966 flood disaster). He is thought to have been the teacher of Giotto.

Donatello de'Bardi: circa 1386-1466. Greatest sculptor of the early Renaissance. He created the first free-standing sculptures since Antiquity. Principal works in Florence: *"San Marco"* and *"San Giorgio"* (*Orsanmichele*), *"David"* (*Bargello*), choir stall (*Duomo*), *"Judith and Holofernes"* (*Loggia dei Lanzi*). *Crucifix* (*S. Croce*). In Padua: *Gattamelata equestrian monument* and the *high altar* in the church of *Sant Antonio.*

Piero della Francesca: born circa 1420—1492. Painter and theoretician of the early Renaissance. Principal works: *La Leggenda della Croce* ("Legend of the Cross") in the choir of *S. Francesco* (Arezzo), *"Resurrection"* (*Borgo San Sepolcro*), *Federigo da Montefeltro* and *Battista Sforza* (*Uffizi*) *"The Flagellation of Christ"* (*Urbino*).

Lorenzo Ghiberti: 1378—1455. Sculptor and goldsmith. His famous work is the *Porta del Paradiso* (Door of Paradise) — so called by Michelangelo) of the *Baptistery* in *Florence,* a commission he won in competition with *Brunelleschi, Iacopo della Quercia* and others.

Domenico Ghirlandaio: 1449—1494. Painter sometimes in collaboration with his brother David; historical frescoes depicting the citizens of Florence in Bible stories. (*Florence; S. Maria Novella* and *S. Trinita. San Gimignamo*).

Giotto di Bondone: circa 1267—1337. Painter and architect (Design for the *Campanile* in *Florence*), pupil of *Cimabue* and said to have been discovered by him at the age of ten drawing a lamb on a flat stone at his home at Vespignano near Florence. Principal works in *Florence* include frescoes in *Santa Croce.* In *Padua,* the *Arena Chapel.* In *Assisi,* the frescoes in *San Francesco.* In 1334 he was appointed Master of Works of *Florence Cathedral.*

Benozzo Gozzoli: 1420—1497. Painter, pupil of *Fra Angelico.* One of the most colourful observers of the early Renaissance. Main works: frescoes showing members of the Council of Florence in the *Medici-Riccardi palace, Florence; S. Agostino* in *San Gimignano; Camposanto* in *Pisa.*

Fra Filippo Lippi: born between 1406 and 1409, died 1469. Early Renaissance painter of gentle Madonnas. Main frescoes are in the Cathedrals at *Prato* and *Spoleto.* His son, *Filippino* (1457—1504), pupil of *Botticelli,* painted his most important frescoes in Florence and Rome. He finished the famous frescoes begun by *Masaccio* in the *Brancacci chapel of the Basilica del Carmine* in *Florence.*

Masaccio: 1401 to circa 1428. Painter, one of the founders of the Renaissance; famous for the plasticity of his figures, the spiritual quality of their expression and the boldness of his perspectives. Among his main works are the frescoes in the Brancacci Chapel of the *Basilica del Carmine, Florence.*

Lippo Memmi: dates of birth and death are unknown. Son-in-law of Simone Martini (whose works may be seen in S. Gimignano), Main work: *The Maestà* in the *Pallazza Comunale* of *S. Gimignano.*

Michelangelo Buonarroti: 1475—1564. Sculptor, painter, architect, poet. With *Leonardo da Vinci* the greatest all round genius of the Renaissance. His main works in *Florence* are: The *David,* (the Accademia) the *Medici tombs in S. Lorenzo* and the *Pietà* in the Cathedral. In *Rome:* the frescoes on the ceilings of the *Sistine Chapel* in the *Vatican* commissioned by Pope Julius II, and the dome of Saint Peter's.

Michelozzo Michelozzi: 1396—1472. Architect and sculptor. Colleague of *Donatello.* Main works: villa at *Cafaggiolo (Mugello), tabernacle* in *San Miniato al Monte (Florence).*

Andrea Orcagna: circa 1308—1368. Architect, sculptor and painter. With *Giotto,* one of the leading *trecento* (14th century) painters. Main works in Florence: *Tabernacle* in *Orsanmichele, (Death and Assumption of the Virgin), polyptych* in the *Strozzi Chapel* in *S. Maria Novella.*

Nicola Pisano: born circa 1225, died after 1278. Sculptor. He combined the Romanesque — Gothic and Classical elements to form a new style. His main works: *Pulpits* in the *Baptistery* in *Pisa* and *Siena.* His sons: *Giovanni,* (born circa 1250, died after 1314) perfected the style of his father and teacher. Main works: *Pulpits* in *Pistoia* and in *Pisa Cathedrals. Madonnas* in *Pisa, Prato* and *Padua. Andrea,* (born circa 1290, died 1348), sculptor and goldsmith. Main works: *Bronze door* for the *Baptistery* and reliefs for the *Campanile* of *Florence Cathedral. His* son, *Nino,* (born circa 1315, died before 1368), architect, sculptor and goldsmith.

Iacopo della Quercia: circa 1371—1438. Sculptor. Main works in *Lucca, Siena (Fonte Gaia)* and *Bologna (Doorway for S. Petronio).*

Luca della Robbia: 1400—1482. Sculptor. Famous for his glazed *terra cotta* reliefs, mainly white Madonnas on a blue background. *Andrea,* Luca's nephew, carried on his thriving business. He was the creator of the relief of the babes in swaddling clothes on Florence's orphanage in the *Piazza SS Annunziata.* Andrea's sons *Giovanni* and *Girolamo* continued the tradition. *Della Robbia* family works can be seen in the *Bargello, Florence* and in *Pistoia.*

33

Andrea Sansovino: 1460—1529. Sculptor and architect. His pupil *Iacopo Sansovino,* 1486—1570, was responsible for sculptures in *Venice* (Library and other buildings).

Luca Signorelli: circa 1441—1523. Main work: *Fresco cycle* of the *End of the World,* the *Coming and Fall of Anti-Christ* and *The Last Judgement* in *Orvieto Cathedral.*

Paolo Uccello: 1397—1475. Early Renaissance painter noted for the originality of his perspectives. The *Battle of San Romano* in the *Uffizi,* and the battle scenes in the *Louvre* and in *London.* Main frescoes in *Florence: painting of Sir John Hawkwood* in the *Cathedral* and the *Deluge* in the *Chiostro Verde of S. Maria Novella.*

Andrea del Verrochio: 1435—1488. Sculptor and painter. The teacher of *Leonardo da Vinci.* Main works in *Florence: David (Bargello),* and the *Group with Thomas (Orsanmichele).* In *Venice: Equestrian statue* of *Bartolommeo Colleone.*

Leonardo da Vinci: 1452—1519. Painter, sculptor, architect and engineer. Most famous works are *The Last Supper* (1498) in Milan and the *Mona Lisa* (1504) in the Louvre. His ideas were revolutionary and he must be one of the most intelligent men who ever lived; amongst his projected inventions were outlines for both aeroplanes and submarines. He was also a prolific writer and his works, apart from the writings of the *Codice Atlantico* in Milan include his celebrated treatise *'On Painting'* (*Trattato della Pittura*).

Notes on a few types of painting

Oil painting, which is realized on panel, canvas, etc., derives its name from the soluble element (oil) of the colouring substance (pigment in powder form).

Fresco is painted directly on fresh (fresco) plaster and especially prepared with colours extracted from pigments in their powder form, dissolved in water.

Tempera is a particular type of painting using soluble (eggyolk) which mixes readily with water thus obtaining assimilation and unity in the various strata of colour spread on the painting.

Notes on Architectural Styles

The **Romanesque style** prevails in Italy from the XI-XIII cent.; in Florence, it achieves such spatial clarity and harmony in the disposition of its building components as to be considered a Proto Renaissance. A characteristic of the Florentine Romanesque, besides the elements which normally distinguish it — semicircular arch, pilasters, columns, piers —, is the marble decoration — white, dark-green — arranged in geometrical patterns according to pure architectural laws. The Baptistery S. Miniato, the Fiésolana Abbey are its most representative monuments.

The **Gothic style** becomes established in Italy in the 2nd half of the XIII cent. but yields, above all in Florence, to the Romanesque tradition which diminishes its impetus and verticality, transforming the final results. Its distinctive elements are: pointed arch (ogee), columns, piers, buttresses and pinnacles; walls greatly relieved of their weight-bearing function, open in ample windows; the entire construction elastic and taut. Some of the city's most remarkable edifices bear its characteristics. S. Croce, S. Maria Novella, S. Maria del Fiore, Giotto's Camp anile

The **Renaissance,** born in Florence in the XV cent. is a spiritual movement spurred by a never entirely forgotten classical tradition. Bent on the study of classical proportions, it is materialized by the artist in his work, directed on a perspective plane. It is characterized by all the elements of the classical style — semicircular arch, columns, vaults — but arranged according to strict laws of perspective and functionalism. The Foundling Hospital S. Lorenzo, S. Marco Cloisters, are some of the constructions animated by its spirit. The Renaissance is the glory of Florence.

The **High Renaissance** follows, and finally the **Baroque** which, with its light effects, stimulates the proper elements of the Renaissance to extreme ends.

Literature and Science

Dante Alighieri: 1265—1321 - Poet
His most famous works are *La Vita Nuova* in which the poet
relates how he first set eyes on the woman who became the
object of his Platonic love ever after — Beatrice Portinari; and
La Divina Commedia his great visionary masterpiece of
Medieval thought, a sort of spiritual and historical travelogue of
Hell. Purgatory and Heaven.

Pietro Aretino: 1492—1557. Poet. Evidently Aretino was good
company and he certainly needed to be; for although he secured
patronage from the Pope, Giovanni de'Medici and assorted
bishops and noblemen, his scurrilous, and occasionally obscene
writings inevitably caused a rapid turnover in patrons. Indeed
he earned the nickname *'The Scourge of Princes'.* His best
known work is *'I Ragionamenti'* (*The Dialogues*), sexually
explicit discussions about current sexual mores by a group of
splendidly witty and outspoken Renaissance characters.

Giovanni Boccaccio: 1313—1375 - Writer. The illegitimate son
of a Certaldo merchant, Boccaccio lived alternately in Florence
and Naples until 1350. Besides being a professional diplomat
he was an accomplished poet; but his greatest work is the
Decameron (1358) in which seven ladies and three gentlemen
taking refuge from the plague in Florence, while away ten days
by each in turn telling a story. The stories (there are 100 in all)
run the gamut from the frankly licentious to the poetical and
serious.

Leonardo Bruni: 1369—1444 - Humanist writer from Arezzo.
Bruni wrote a History of Florence and gave impetus to the
Renaissance with his translations (into Latin) of the great Greek
writers. He also wrote lives of Petrarch and Dante in Italian.

Galileo Galilei: 1564—1642 - Astronomer born at Pisa. He made
or perfected numerous inventions including a thermometer, a
proportional compass, and a reflecting telescope. Unfortunately he became convinced that the Copernican system of
astronomy was correct, which brought him into conflict with
the Church. He was brought before the Inquisition in 1632 and
imprisoned, eventually being permitted to end his days in
Florence.

Francesco Guicciardini: 1483-1540. Historian. After a long and distinguished career in the Papal diplomatic service he returned to Florence and helped secure Cosimo de'Medici as Duke. Disappointed not to receive preferment he retired to the village of Arcetri and wrote his famous *Storia d'Italia,* a dispassionate account of Italy from 1494 to 1532.

Niccolò Machiavelli: 1469-1527 - Statesman and Philosopher. Machiavelli was exiled from Florence when the Republic fell in 1512. His work *The Prince,* a treatise on the arts of statesmanship, though often abused as a work of typically Italian cynicism and amorality, would nevertheless appear to be a perceptive account of the political mind.

Francesco Petrarca: 1304—1374 - Poet. Together with Dante the greatest poet of his age. He himself was most proud of his great works in Latin, the language of scholarship and learning as he saw it; but his popular fame rests on his *Canzoniere* (1470), (Sonnets, Lyrics, and Madrigals) inspired by his unrequited passion for Laura (possibly Laura de Noves). His work influenced the English sonnet writers of the early Elizabethan period, Sir Thomas Wyatt and Henry Howard, Earl of Surrey.

Angelo Poliziano (Politian): 1454—94 - Humanist scholar. Born at Montepulciano, Poliziano tutored the sons of Lorenzo the Magnificent. He was a brilliant classical scholar and translated (into Latin) a large body of the Greek authors, besides writing many original works in Latin

Music

Guido d'Arezzo (or *Guido Aretino*): circa 990—1050. A Benedictine monk who invented the modern system of musical notation.

Luigi Boccherini: 1743—1805. Composer of chamber music and symphonies. Main work *Cello Concerto in B Flat Major,* and also his celebrated *Minuet* which occurs in one of the 125 string Quintets he wrote. He was himself a fine cellist. He was a native of *Lucca.*

Giacomo Puccini: 1858—1924. Composer of operas, the best known of which are *La Bohème, Tosca, Turandot, Madame Butterfly, Manon Lescaut* and *The Girl of the Golden West.*

Postscript

Tuscany without the cypresses?

In August 1978, every local mayor in Tuscany was requested in a Ministry of Agriculture and Forestrics' circular to examine every cypress tree in their district, and to fell them if necessary. Disease has struck the cypresses which so typify the Tuscan landscape, and which were sacred even in Etruscan times. One quarter of the twelve million trees in the area (of which four million alone are in the Province of Florence) show signs of the disease which is killing them, even to the unpractised eye. It is a result of pollution - rusty spots appear on the dark trunks; the dead branches look as though they have been struck by lightning - and is known locally as "the plague".

The cypresses are suffering from two maladies. Firstly an infectious form of cancer which causes a fungus. Secondly a disease transmitted by an insect which, however, can be cured. The problem now is finding experts fast enough to keep the two dieases apart and cut down immediately any trees which can no longer be saved. C.N.R., the National Research Institute, and the University of Florence are engaged in the search for a new type of cypress which would be immune to the disease. Provided everything goes according to plan, their results will be available in four to five years time.

And in the meantime who could imagine Tuscany without cypresses? Without these dark green "exclamation marks" which punctuate the landscape, and provide, along with the silvery green of the olive trees, the natural hues of the landscape? Who would recognise Tuscany without these slim, black silhouettes which define its horizons? · Thanks to them and the olive trees, the countryside in the hills around Florence has remained as it was in Giotto's day; around Siena too the landscapes of the *quattrocento* painters survive. Anthologies of poetry and scores of paintings celebrate these "dark flames" which still stand, solemn and stately in that superb light, as though placed there by Giotto, Duccio or Lorenzetti.

PART THREE

Florence

An Introduction

When to Visit

Spring or Autumn, besides being pleasant times for their mild
temperatures and balmy air, are also when the crush of tourists
abates (though it never ceases); but bring a raincoat! At
Easter Florence is crowded — but delightful — with some
exciting events such as the *Scoppio del Carro* (see p. 118) and
much religious activity. Winter can be cold and certain places
have restricted visiting hours (e.g. the Boboli Gardens - see
p. 64). Mid-summer (July-August) can be unbearably hot and
many Florentines very sensibly depart for the mountains or the
coast.

Whenever you come there is quite a lot of walking involved in
seeing places (it is often not worth the hassle of getting a taxi or
struggling onto a crowded bus for a short distance); so children
may become tired or footsore — and so may adults! There are
ice-cream parlours and pleasant cafés which you will find
indicated in the guide; take advantage of them! The most
beautiful picture becomes just another boring Madonna to the
jaded eye.

Florence at first sight

Many have commented on the disappointment experienced by
first time visitors as they struggle into modern Florence. By car
it *is* a struggle, for, once off the swishing *Autostrada del Sole*,
the motorist passes through an apparently shapeless jumble of
dull suburbs before arriving without warning in the confined,
almost claustrophobic centre of old Florence clustered round the
four central bridges of the Arno. He will probably be in a traffic
jam. And the approach by rail on the main line down from
Bologna or up from Rome, or in the airport bus from Pisa, is
hardly more edifying. He must not despair; a short time with
the guide, a street plan and a talk to the Travel Agents listed
below will soon set him right. (See page 104).

Soon he will feel, seeping into him, the atmosphere of the city, described thus by the modern writer Giovani Papini; "Giotto painted its churches, Dante wrote its decrees, Machiavelli wrote its letters, it won Savonarola for Christianity and had its battlements secured by Michelangelo". This is the city once designated the 'new Athens on the Arno'. Even if you have never been to Italy and know nothing about Florence, what happened here in the 14th, 15th and 16th centuries will probably have influenced your native culture, and hence you, more than you imagine.

From the Boboli Gardens looking down to the rear of the Uffizi Palace.

Florentia or Fiorino?

Scholars cannot agree whether the name Firenze (Florence) comes from "florentia", a bloom, or from "Fiorino", the name of the Roman officer who thwarted the plot to murder Cataline at Fiesole. However, it is known that Florence was founded as a Roman encampment in 63 B.C., at the foot of Etruscan Fiesole, in the unhealthy marshlands between the Arno and the Mugnone. Fiesole itself had been settled from pre-historic times and finds from the area can be seen in the Florence Museum of Archaeology, the second best such museum in the country after the Villa Giulia in Rome. (*Museo Archeologico, Via della Colonna 36*).

In the reign of the Emperor Henry III (1017-56), Florence was made an Imperial City and thus became part of the Holy Roman Empire. But the city had no great love for either Empire or Emperors and its real history does not begin until the 12th century when it became a City State, governed by the wealthy craftsmen's guilds.

40

The Republic

No sooner had the Republic been founded than it split into two rival factions: the Ghibellines, the supporters of the Emperor, and the Guelphs, the supporters of the Pope. The names derive from the Germanic tribal names, Welf and Waibling. The warring families were united only when attacking neighbouring cities.

As soon as the conquest of Pisa, Lucca, Siena, Arezzo (or whoever might challenge Florence's claim to supremacy in Tuscany) was complete, the Florentines went back to fighting each other; so violently in fact, that it is perhaps this city's greatest miracle that so much brilliance, beauty and harmony could emerge amidst so much murder and intrigue. To understand the reasons, one must get to know the character of the Florentines. The typical characteristics of the Tuscans are at their most exaggerated in the Florentines. Indro Montanelli, one of Italy's leading journalists, himself a Tuscan, describes his compatriots as follows: "They are the most civilised, most greedy, most wicked and most intelligent inhabitants of the peninsula".

In Renaissance times, noblemen and guilds were fiercely competitive, acutely aware if a neighbour's palazzo, or a rival's church, was larger or contained more works of art than their own. This competitiveness stimulated artistic activity — and spilled over into the attitudes of the artists themselves. Thus Florence abounded with glory and art, and towns like San Gimignano bristled with towers competing with their neighbours in height; the richer the owner, the higher the tower.

Personal and political quarrelling were the hallmarks of Tuscan and Florentine life. Once the disputes between Guelphs and Ghibellines were finally over, the victorious Guelphs split into right and left factions, the "white" and the "black," and continued to fight and banish each other according to which party was in power. Those banished temporarily or for life included Petrarch's father, Dante Alighieri, (a supporter of the "Whites"), and Machiavelli who passed the time snaring thrushes and dicing at the local inn by day; at night he dressed up in his finest clothes and entered his study to commune with 'the great men of the past'. The results of this communing included in his great work *The Prince,* a seminal and unendingly controversial work on statecraft.

In 1443 Florence banished its first great statesman, Cosimo de Medici, fearing, justifiably, that he could upset the jealously guarded Republican balance. After ten years exile, he returned however. His wisdom brought peace to the city and saw in an era of artists and humanists; the city honoured him after his death by inscribing *"Pater Patriae"* on his tombstone in front of the altar in *San Lorenzo.*

Another plaque may be found of a very different kind on the *Piazza della Signoria* where the stern preacher, Savonarola, was burned on May 2nd, 1498, after a revulsion against his puritanical regime, which had, however, begun with great popular support. The inscription refers to an "unjust sentence". On the anniversary of his death a wreath of flame-coloured roses is placed on the stone. And in modern times, the eccentric visionary Mayor of Florence in the 60s, Giorgio La Pira, has been remembered with a characteristically opaque inscription scrawled on the stone terrace of the Forte di Belvedere.

Florence knows how to honour its dead. A splendid marble sarcophagus for Dante was erected in *Santa Croce,* Florence's Pantheon but it remains a gesture and Florentines still burn with indignation that it should stand empty. The fight for possession of the remains of Italy's greatest poet (who died in Ravenna, his final exile, in 1321) lasted for centuries: Princes and Popes, and in particular, the two Medicis, Leo X (1513—1521) and Clement VII (1523 — 1534), tried in vain to persuade the Franciscan Brothers in Ravenna to hand them over. When the pleas turned to threats, the Franciscans concealed the remains in a crack in the monastery wall and were not to "discover" them again until the Unification of Italy (1860). After 500 years the creator of the "Divine Comedy" was finally given a resting place in the original sarcophagus in Ravenna.

Lorenzo and the Renaissance

Lorenzo il Magnifico, the most gifted of the Medicis, and himself a poet, gave his family and Florence many of its finest monuments. Under his rule artists and humanists produced great works of the Renaissance. His patronage encouraged all talents. His humanist friends debated with him in the Platonic Academy, dispelling with their words and ideas the remnants of the spirit of the Middle Ages. The list of great artists and humanists who flourished at this time is impressive: Politian, the poet, and painters such as Botticelli, Gozzoli, the Ghirlandaio brothers, the young Michelangelo; architects such as Giuliano da Sangallo and many others.

The Christian dignitaries of the 1438 Oecumenical Council who had visited Florence in the reign of Cosimo to attend the Council, (some of them are featured in Benozzo Gozzoli's colourful fresco in the *Chapel of the Palazzo Medici-Riccardi*) returned in 1451 seeking refuge on the Arno and bringing with them rich gifts. More importantly, scholars rescued the writings of Antiquity, as Constantinople fell to the Turks, and brought them to Florence. Thus, thanks to Lorenzo's hospitality in giving them a new home the expansion of the Renaissance was provided with new impetus.

The post-Renaissance history of the city is of less interest to most visitors. The main branch of the Medici family, whose glory diminished as their titles increased (the last Medicis were Grand Dukes) along with the number of bullets on their coat of arms (five became seven), ended with the death of Ludovica, Princess of the Palatinate in 1743. In her will, she bequeathed to Florence two of the city's greatest buildings: the *Uffizi* and the *Pitti Palace.* Her successors, the Grand Dukes of Hapsburg-Lorraine, were removed from the throne by Napoleon and then finally by the *Risorgimento,* the movement for the unification of Italy masterminded by Cavour, Mazzini and King Victor Emmanuel of Savoy. Italy's last foreign ruler, the last Grand Duke, Leopold II, a friendly though rather foolish gentleman known locally as the *"Grand-oca"* (the big goose), rolled out of the city in his coach, flanked by lines of cheering ex-subjects in 1859.

From 1865 — 1871, Florence was the capital of the new kingdom of Italy and the House of Savoy was installed in the Palazzo Pitti. Today Florence is the seat of the regional government for Tuscany and its nine provinces, an international centre of study and the home of the European University.

Hotels (Alberghi), Pensioni and Locande

Two factors govern the choice of accommodation — location and price.

With so many visitors who resort to their feet to see the great sights of the city, the strategic situation of a hotel becomes a matter of some importance.

Rather than pick a few hotels and run the risk that they will be filled by other users of this guide when the reader arrives there, we have elected to present a comprehensive listing of hotels, pensioni and locande in Florence by area.

This is based on the official hotel guide to the city. We have analysed the alphabetical list of hotels (in order of price) into one based upon areas within the city. These areas are the grid squares of a map of the city inside the back cover. We have added brief descriptions as to the area of location.

Most *'Pensioni'* will offer full or half board at an inclusive price; the most economic way of staying in the city with everything provided but with the option of the occasional good meal out is half board residence at a *Pensione*.

You will need to book in advance - certainly in the high season and usually at other times - if you are to be sure of staying in the place of your choice. Certain travel packagers from Britain - e.g. Magic of Italy, Russell Chambers, Covent Garden, London W.C.2. - have arrangements with individual hotels and it is worth shopping around amongst travel agents to see what is on offer. Many smaller *'Alberghi'* (Hotels) have no dining facilities (except for breakfast).

What you will pay

Italy may give the impression of happy spontaneity, but when it comes to hotels which play such a vital part in helping the tourist revenue of the nation, there is a highly organised system of classifications.

Here is what you can expect to pay for the various *categoria* classified hotels. Prices are quoted for a **double room** with bathroom where applicable.

Accommodation	Lire
	(000's)
Hotel: five star	215-522
Hotel: four star	77-205
Hotel: three star	50-100
Hotel: two star	41-62
Hotel: one star	27-40
Pension 1	60-120
Pension 2	25-60
Pension 3	13-25
Locande (without bath/shower in room)	Mostly 11-13

Rooms without bath/shower are generally about 20% cheaper than those with them. Single rooms are about a third cheaper than double rooms.

Youth Hostels in Florence:
Villa Camerata, Viale Augusto Righi 2-4 (city outskirts below Fiesole) Tel: 601 451.
Casa dello Studente, Piazza Indipendenza 15 (not far from the station) Tel: 496 629.
Tavarnelle Val di Pesa (Chianti) - Tel: 827 009.

Sq	Cat	Hotel	Rms/Beds	Street & No	Tel

The northern edge of the city (NE of the Ex Fortezza da Basso)

Sq	Cat	Hotel	Rms/Beds	Street & No	Tel
1I	H3	Astor	23-29	Viale Milton 41	483 391
1L	P2	La Favorita	15-29	Via Lorenzo il Magnifico 2	490 047
1M	H4	Residenza Universitaria	57-105	Viale Don Minzoni 25	576 552
1N	Loc	Lea	13-26	Via Fra Bartolomeo 21	575 301
1O	Loc	Sogg Emma	5-9	Via Pacinotti 20	575 901
1R	P3	Ungherese Stadio	13-24	Via G.B. Amici 8	587 039

East of the Fortezza da Basso

Sq	Cat	Hotel	Rms/Beds	Street & No	Tel
2H	P3	Fedora	10-20	Viale S. Lavagnini 45	480 013
2I	H3	Rapallo	31-35	Via Sta Caterina d'Alessandria 7	472 412
2I	H3	Royal	29-51	Via delle Ruote 52	483 287
2I	Loc	Florise	5-10	Viale Lavagnini 8	489 056
2L	H3	Tirreno	20-29	Via Lupi 21	490 695
2L	P3	Mia	14-28	Via Cavour 85	486 621
2L	Loc	Elia	10-15	Via B. Lupi 7	471 989
2L	Loc	Giovannini	12-21	Via B. Lupi 14	470 992
2L	Loc	Sogg Tina	5-7	Via S. Gallo 31	483 519
2M	H2	De La Pace	44-68	Via Lamarmora 28	577 343
2M	P2	Genzianella	10-17	Via Cavour 112	572 141
2M	P3	Benvenuti	14-21	Via Cavour 112	573 909
2M	P3	Cordova	23-31	Via Cavour 96	587 948
2M	P3	Graziella	10-15	Via P. Capponi 87	572 807
2M	P3	Savonarola	16-29	Viale Matteotti 27	587 824
2M	Loc	Becattini	7-11	Via Lamarmora 38	573 810
2M	Loc	San Carlo	5-9	Viale Matteotti	588 473
2M	Loc	Sogg. Laura	5-9	Via Lamarmora 26	577 875
2O	P3	Flora	13-22	Via Buonvicini 50	50132

West of North end of Station

Sq	Cat	Hotel	Rms/Beds	Street & No	Tel
3E	H1	Michelangelo	138-253	Viale Fratelli Rosselli 2	278 711
3E	H2	Golf	39-70	Viale Fratelli Rosselli 56	293 088
3E	H2	Villa Azalee	20-37	Viale Fratelli Rosselli 44	260 353
3F	H2	Leonardo da Vinci	33-61	Via G. Monaco 12	474 352
3F	Loc	Sogg. Aurora	8-15	Via L. Alamanni 5	210 283

West of the Piazza Independenza

Sq	Cat	Hotel	Rms/Beds	Street & No	Tel
3H	H3	Boston	16-25	Via Guelfa 68	470 934
3H	H3	Corallo	23-35	Via Nazionale 22	496 645
3H	H4	Arianna	16-26	Via D. Barbano 12	496 742
3H	H4	Augustea	10-18	Via Guelfa 87	262 658
3H	H4	Casa dello Studente 'G. Salvanini'	62-95	Piazza Indipendenza 15	471 581
3H	P3	Andrea	13-20	Piazza Indipendenza 19	483 890
3H	P3	Edelweiss	20-36	Via Ridolfi 2	489 844
3H	P3	Independenza	10-17	Piazza Indipendenza 8	496 630
3H	P3	Mary	11-21	Piazza Indipendenza 5	496 310
3H	Loc	Casa Cristina	5-9	Via della Fortezza 6	496 730
3H	Loc	La Rosa Tea	10-15	Piazza Indipendenza 24	474 316
3H	Loc	Piera	4-7	Via Guelfa 110	471 177
3H	Loc	Sogg. Caterina	7-11	Via Di Barbano 8	483 705
3H	Loc	Sogg. Delle Camelie	9-14	Via Di Barbano 10	490 467
3H	Loc	Sogg. Monica	7-11	Via Faenza 66	283 804

Sq	Cat	Hotel	Rms/Beds	Street & No	Tel
East of the Piazza Independenza					
3I	H2	Castri	56-94	Piazza Indipendenza 7′	496 412
3I	H3	Capri	51-95	Via XXVII Aprile 3	215 441
3I	P2	Splendor	30-50	Via San Gallo 30	483 427
3I	P3	Cellai	31-47	Via XXVII Aprile 18	489 291
3I	P3	Righi	9-16	Via S. Zanobi 89	486 350
3I	P3	Roxy	9-16	Via Piazza Indipendenza 5	472 928
3I	P3	Souvenir	13-14	Via XXVII Aprile 9	472 194
3I	P3	Vienna	9-17	Via XXVII Aprile 14	483 256
3I	Loc	Enza	7-9	Via S. Zanobi 47	490 990
3I	Loc	Sampaoli	5-10	Via San Gallo 39	480 316
3I	Loc	Sogg. Rudy	12-18	Via San Gallo 51	475 519
North of Piazza San Marco					
3L	P2	Panorama Angelico	28-48	Via Cavour 60	214 243
3L	P3	Asso	11-16	Via Lamarmora 27	587 595
North of Piazza Donatello					
3N	P2	Il Granduca	16-24	Via Pier Capponi 13	572 803
3O	H4	Veneto	22-37	Via Santa Reparata 33	294 816
East of Piazza Vittoria Veneto (West of South end of Station)					
4D	H1	Jolly Carlton	140-249	Piazza Vit. Veneto 4-A	27-70
4D	P3	Garden	16-29	Piazza Vit. Veneto 8	212 669
South of the Porto Al Prato (West of South end of Station)					
4E	HL	Villa Medici	105-193	Via Il Prato 42	261 331
4E	Loc	Gori	6-11	Via Montebello 49	212 086
West of the Station					
4F	H1	Londra	104-184	Via Iacopo da Diacceto 16-20	262 791
4F	H2	Caravel	59-103	Via L.Alamanni 9	217 651
4F	H3	Delle Nazioni	129-132	Via Alamanni 15	283 575
4F	P3	Giselda	7-13	Via L.Alamanni 5	211 145
4F	P3	Grazia	12-21	Via L.Alamanni 5	211 145
4F	P3	Hermes	9-18	Via L.Alamanni 11	293 420
4F	P3	La Scala	8-13	Via della Scala 21	212 629
4F	Loc	Sogg. Elite	4-5	Via della Scala 12	215 395
4F	Loc	Sogg. La Romagnola	20-24	Via della Scala 40	211 597
4F	Loc	Sogg. Gigliola	15-23	Via della Scala 40	211 597
Round South End of Station/Via Fiume					
4G	H2	Ambasciatori	102-183	Via Alamanni 3	287 421
4G	H3	Nord Ovest	30-55	Via Cennini 9	212 753
4G	P3	Beatrice	20-35	Via Fiume 11	216 790
4G	P3	Desiree	14-24	Via Fiume 20	262 382
4G	P3	Fiorita	11-20	Via Fiume 20	283 693
4G	P3	Fiume	8-13	Via Fiume 14	282 506
4G	P3	Joly	9-18	Via Fiume 8	292 079
4G	P3	Lombardi	12-19	Via Fiume 8	283 151
4G	P3	Tamerici	10-15	Via Fiume 5	214 156
4G	Loc	Marilena Tourist House	5-10	Via Fiume 20	261 705
4G	Loc	Medicea	7-13	Via Fiume 14	283 910
4G	Loc	Petrarca	8-14	Via Fiume 20	260 858
4G	Loc	Sogg. Adua	6-10	Via Fiume 20	287 506
4G	Loc	Sogg. Erina	7-13	Via Fiume 17	284 343
4G	Loc	Sogg. Mariella	6-12	Via Fiume 11	212 302
4G	Loc	Stella Mary	6-11	Via Fiume 17	215 694

Sq	Cat	Hotel	Rms/Beds	Street & No	Tel
4G	Loc	Sogg. Satellite	7-13	Via Fiume 14	294 796
4G	Loc	Tourist House Serena	6-12	Via Fiume 20	213 643

Near Mercato Centrale (Central Market) Faenza/Nazionale

4H	H2	Corona d'Italia	92-149	Via Nazionale 14	215 330
4H	H3	Ascot	33-42	Via Nazionale 8a	284 171
4H	H3	Atlantico	67-108	Via Nazionale 12	213 031
4H	H3	Basilea	49-90	Via Guelfa 41	214 587
4H	H3	City	16-30	Via San Antonino 18	211 543
4H	H3	Nuova Atlantico	106-174	Via Nazionale 10	216 622
4H	H3	Nuova Italia	20-31	Via Faenza 26	287 508
4H	H3	Rex	31-49	Via Faenza 6	210 453
4H	H3	Sempione	33-48	Via Nazionale 15	212 462
4H	H3	Victoria	20-36	Via Chiara 22 rosso	287 019
4H	H4	Globus	23-35	Via St Antonino 24	211 062
4H	P1	Embassy House	25-43	Via Nazionale 23	262 266
4H	P2	Le Cascine	22-40	Via Nazionale 6	211 066
4H	P3	Apollo	9-17	Via Faenza 77	284 119
4H	P3	Berna	8-15	Via Nazionale 5	287 701
4H	P3	Derby	9-13	Via Nazionale 35	260 804
4H	P3	Eden	15-29	Via Nazionale 55	483 722
4H	P3	Kursaal	9-15	Via Nazionale 24	496 324
4H	P3	Maggiore Sovrana	14-19	Via Nazionale 6	210 309
4H	P3	Ausonìa E Rimini	9-17	Via Nazionale 24	496 547
4H	P3	Merlini	9-16	Via Faenza 56	212 848
4H	Loc	Anna	6-12	Via Faenza 56	298 322
4H	Loc	Armonia	8-12	Via Faenza 56	211 146
4H	Loc	Azzi	10-18	Via Faenza 56	213 806
4H	Loc	Bellavista	7-12	Via Nazionale 6	284 528
4H	Loc	Daniel	5-9	Via Nazionale 22	260 267
4H	Loc	Ester	8-14	Via Nazionale 6	212 741
4H	Loc	Etrusca	5-7	Via Nazionale 35	213 100
4H	Loc	Giovanna	5-8	Via Faenza 69	261 353
4H	Loc	Marcella	7-12	Via Faenza 58	213 232
4H	Loc	Marini	9-17	Via Faenza 56	284 824
4H	Loc	Mario's	9-17	Via Faenza 89	212 039
4H	Loc	Medea	6-9	Via Nazionale 8	217 227
4H	Loc	Mia Cara	20-37	Via Faenza 58	216 053
4H	Loc	Nella	6-10	Via Faenza 69	284 256
4H	Loc	Paola	6-11	Via Faenza 56	213 682
4H	Loc	Pina	5-8	Via Faenza 69	212 231
4H	Loc	Sogg. d'Errico,	6-10	Via Faenza 69	214 059
4H	Loc	Tony's Inn	8-15	Via Faenza 77	217 975

North East of Piazza San Lorenzo (2 blocks N. of Duomo)

4I	H3	La Terrazza	37-48	Via Taddea 8	294 322
4I	H4	Imperia	27-51	Via Rosina 7	294 322
4I	P3	Casci	14-26	Via Cavour 13	211 686
4I	P3	Cristallo	17-28	Via Cavour 29	287 651
4I	P3	Europa	8-14	Via Cavour 14	210 361
4I	P3	Gioia	20-34	Via Cavour 25	282 804
4I	P3	Il Magnifico	18-33	Via Ginori 7	284 840
4I	Loc	Fabio	6-10	Via Ginori 24	260 775
4I	Loc	Casa Florida	6-9	Via Ginori 17	283 139
4I	Loc	Guelfa	6-11	Via Guelfa 28	215 882
4I	Loc	House for Tourists Aglietti	6-9	Via Cavour 29	287 824
4I	Loc	San Gallo	4-6	Via Ginori 33	295 390
4I	Loc	Sofia	10-17	Via Cavour 21	283 930
4I	Loc	Sogg. Colomba	9-18	Via Cavour 21	263 139

Sq	Cat	Hotel	Rms/Beds	Street & No	Tel
4I	Loc	Sogg. Colorado	10-18	Via Cavour 66	217 310
4I	Loc	Sogg. La Noce	5-9	Borgo La Noce 8	213 519
4I	Loc	Sogg. Magliani	6-7	Via S. Reparata 1	287 378
4I	Loc	Sogg. Montecarlo	9-16	Via Ginori 17	293 472
4I	Loc	Sogg. San Lorenzo	8-13	Via Rosina 4	284 925
4I	Loc	Villa Medidiana	7-13	Via Cosimo il Vecchio 30	410 098

Piazza Annunziata

Sq	Cat	Hotel	Rms/Beds	Street & No	Tel
4L	H4	Morandi	24-45	Piazza SS Annunziata 3	212 687
4L	P3	Le Due Fontane	9-14	Piazza SS Annunziata 14	210 185
4L	P3	Le Due Font.(Dipendenza)	10-13	Piazza SS Annunziata 14	210 185
4L	Loc	San Marco	10-16	Via Cavour 50	284 235

Piazzale Donatello

Sq	Cat	Hotel	Rms/Beds	Street & No	Tel
4N	H3	Liana	20-36	Via Vit Alfieri 18	587 608
4N	P3	Donatello	8-12	Via Alfieri 9	587 521
4N	P3	Losanna	9-17	Via Alfieri 9	587 516
4N	Loc	Sogg. Alfa	6-12	Via Alfieri 9	571 652

North Bank East of Ponte Vittorio

Sq	Cat	Hotel	Rms/Beds	Street & No	Tel
5D	P2	Ariele	15-29	Via Magenta 11	211 509
5D	P3	Crocini	17-27	Corso Italia 28	212 905

North Bank-Via Palestro

Sq	Cat	Hotel	Rms/Beds	Street & No	Tel
5E	Hi	Anglo American	118-202	Via Garibaldi 9	282 114
5E	H1	Executive	41-53	Via Curtatone 5	217 451
5E	H1	Kraft	66-124	Via Solferino 2	284 273
5E	H1	Principe	21-38	Lungarno Vespucci 34	284 848
5E	H3	Argentina	32-53	Via Curtatone 12	215 408
5E	P2	Casa de Lago	16-28	Lungarno Vespucci 58	216 141
5E	P2	Consigli	11-20	Lungarno Vespucci 50	214 172
5E	P3	Cosy Home	14-22	Via Solferino 5	296 818

SW of Station-Via Finiguerra

Sq	Cat	Hotel	Rms/Beds	Street & No	Tel
5F	H2	Adriatico	108-204	Via Maso Finiguerra 9	261 781
5F	H3	Albion	23-39	Via del Prato 22 rosso	214 171
5F	H3	Byron	50-72	Via della Scala 49	216 700
5F	H3	Melegnano	20-38	Via Maso Finiguerra 1	214 013
5F	H3	Primavera	18-25	Via Maso Finiguerra 12 rosso	287 072
5F	H4	Bastia	9-16	Via Sta Caterina da Siena 1	213 635
5F	P3	Cosmopolitan	13-25	Borgognissanti 8	284 080
5F	P3	Dino	9-14	Borgognissanti 70	287 072
5F	P3	Pagnini	20-33	Via Montebello 40	261 238
5F	P3	Patrizia	16-27	Via Montebello 7	282 314
5F	Loc	Ida	5-10	Borgognissanti 31	287 614
5F	Loc	Madrid	15-25	Via della Scala 59	282 776
5F	Loc	Palazzuolo	7-11	Via Palazzuolo 71	284 883
5F	Loc	Sarah	6-9	Via della Scala 59	282 776
5F	Loc	Sogg. Lucia	5-8	Borgognissanti 67	214 079

South of Station/Santa Maria Novella

Sq	Cat	Hotel	Rms/Beds	Street & No	Tel
5G	H1	Croce di Malta	100-188	Via della Scala 7	282 600
5G	H1	Grand Hotel Minerva	112-199	Piazza Santa Maria Novella	284 555
5G	H2	Rivoli	61-101	Via della Scala 33	216 988
5G	H2	Roma Pietrobelli	38-67	Piazza Santa Maria Novella	210 366
5G	H3	Alba	24-45	Via della Scala 22	211 469
5G	H3	Aprile	30-51	Via della Scala 6	216 237

Sq	Cat	Hotel	Rms/Beds	Street & No	Tel
5G	H3	Universo	53-90	Piazza Sta Maria Novella 20	211 484
5G	P3	Cely	12-20	Piazza Sta Maria Novella 24	218 755
5G	P3	La Mia Casa	13-23	Piazza Sta Maria Novella 23	213 061
5G	P3	Margareth	11-19	Via della Scala 25	210 138
5G	P3	Montreal	9-15	Via della Scala 43	262 331
5G	P3	Nettuno	19-32	Piazza Sta Maria Novella 24	294 449
5G	P3	Palmer	12-20	Via degli Avelli 2	262 391
5G	Loc	Giacobazzi	5-8	Piazza Sta Maria Novella 24	294 679
5G	Loc	Sogg. Florentino	9-13	Via degli Avelli 8	212 692
5G	Loc	Sogg. Iris	9-14	Piazza Sta Maria Novella 22	296 735

South East of Piazza dell'Unita Italiana

Sq	Cat	Hotel	Rms/Beds	Street & No	Tel
5H	H1	Astoria	90-163	Via del Giglio 9	298 095
5H	H1	Grand Hotel Baglioni	195-359	Piazza Unita Italiana	218 441
5H	H1	Grand Hotel Majestic	103-183	Via del Melarancio 1	264 021
5H	H2	Bonciani	65-114	Via Panzani 17	210 039
5H	H2	Laurus	54-76	Via Cerretani 8	261 752
5H	H2	Milano Terminus	85-146	Via Cerretano 10	283 372
5H	H3	De la Gare e Lorena	14-22	Via Faenza 1	282 785
5H	H3	Martelli	44-85	Via Panzani 8	217 151
5H	H3	La Gioconda	29-45	Via Panzani 2	213 150
5H	H3	Lombardia e Rebecchino	14-26	Via Pan zani 19	215 276
5H	H3	Nizza	17-32	Via del Giglio 5	296 897
5H	H3	Paris	60-108	Via dei Banchi 2	263 690
5H	H3	Polo Nord	17-29	Via Panzani 7	287 952
5H	H3	Romagna	25-29	Via Panzani 4	211 005
5H	H3	San Giorgio	57-55	Via Sant'Antonino 3	284 344
5H	H3	Spagna	22-32	Via Panzani 9	211 860
5H	H4	Stazione	14-18	Via dei Banchi 3	283 133
5H	H4	Varsavia	9-13	Via Panzani 5	215 615
5H	P2	Centrale	18-35	Via dei Conti 3	215 216
5H	P3	Accademia	16-22	Via Faenza 7	293 451
5H	P3	Belletini	8-12	Via dei Conti 7	213 561
5H	P3	Burchianti	10-18	Via del Giglio 6	212 796
5H	P3	Il Perseo	11-20	Via Cerretani 1	212 504
5H	P3	San Giovanni	9-16	Via Cerretani 2	213 580
5H	Loc	Banchi	6-8	Via de'Banchi 1	294 450
5H	Loc	Cerretani	7-13	Cia Cerretani 1	212 504
5H	Loc	Concordia	12-19	Via dell'Amorino 14	213 233
5H	Loc	Diana's Guest House	13-22	Via Panzani 10	216 730
5H	Loc	Giada	6-12	Via Canto dei Nelli 2	215 317
5H	Loc	Sogg. Alesandri	6-12	Via Cerretani 1	212 504
5H	Loc	Sogg. delle Rose	4-8	Canto dei Nelli 2	296 373
5H	Loc	Sogg. Giappone	7-11	Via dei Banchi 1	210 090
5H	Loc	Sogg. Parodi	14-18	Piazza Madonna 8	211 866
5H	Loc	Sogg. Stefy	5-9	Piazza S. Lorenzo 1	217 077

North of Piazza Duomo

Sq	Cat	Hotel	Rms/Beds	Street & No	Tel
5I	H3	Fenice	61-112	Via Martelli 10	210 087
5I	P2	Duomo	15-22	Piazza Duomo 1	219 922
5I	P3	California	12-22	Via Ricasoli 30	282 753
5I	P3	Canada	9-14	Borgo San Lorenzo 14	260 209
5I	P3	Manuelli	9-16	Via Martelli 6	210 893
5I	Loc	Sogg. Versailles	7-11	Via Martelli 3	287 575

NE of Duomo

Sq	Cat	Hotel	Rms/Beds	Street & No	Tel
5L	P3	Florentia	25-49	Piazza Brunelleschi 10	213 138
5L	P3	Margherita	11-19	Via dei Servi 8	287 695
5L	P3	Sally	11-19	Via dei Servi 3	284 519

Sq	Cat	Hotel	Rms/Beds	Street & No	Tel
South of University					
5M	P1	Monna Lisa	21-35	Borgo Pinti 27	296 213
5M	Loc	Mirella	5-8	Via degli Alfani 36	283 070
5M	Loc	Sogg. Chiazza	13-23	Borgo Pinti 3	213 263
5M	Loc	Sogg. Ideale	5-7	Via Alfani 27	284 867
Piazza d'Azeglio					
5N	H1	Regency Umbria	31-56	Piazza M D'Azeglio 3	577 728
5N	H4	Arizona	16-22	Via Farini 2	211 940
5O	P3	Geneve	12-21	Via della Mattonaia 43	666 923
5O	P3	Rita Major	27-45	Via della Mattonaia 43	678 294
Piazza Ognissanti					
6F	HL	Excelsior Italie	207-348	Piazza Ognissanti 1	294 301
Piazza Goldoni					
6G	H3	Amsterdam	29-47	Via de Fossi 27	287 313
6G	P3	Ferretti	14-20	Via delle Belle Donne 17	261 328
6G	P3	Fiorentina	11-21	Via dei Fossi 12	219 530
6G	P3	Ottaviani	19-32	Piazza degli Ottaviani 1	296 223
6G	P3	Toscana	9-14	Via del Sole 8	213 156
6G	P3	Vigna Nuova	11-16	Via Vigna Nuova 17	213 506
6G	Loc	Sogg. Mio Sogno	7-12	Piazza Ottaviani 1	213 877
6G	Loc	Sogg. Sirena	5-10	Piazza Rucellai 1	298 768
West of Piazza della Repubblica					
6H	H1	De La Ville Florence	71-129	Piazza Antinori 1	261 805
6H	H2	Helvetia E Bristol	88-153	Via dei Pescioni 2	287 814
6H	H4	Esplanade	28-42	Via Tornabuoni 13	287 078
6H	P1	Beacci Tornabuoni	29-46	Via Tornabuoni 3	212 645
6H	P2	La Residenza	18-30	Via Tornobuoni 8	284 197
6H	P2	Pendini	34-62	Via Strozzi 2	211 170
6H	Loc	Scoti	6-9	Via Tornabuoni 7	292 128
6H	Loc	Venere	12-20	Via Monalda 1	210 369
South of Duomo					
6I	HL	Savoy	94-173	Piazza della Repubblica 7	283 313
6I	H2	Cavour	96-171	Via dei Proconsolo 3	287 102
6I	H4	Firenze	48-81	Piazza Donati 4	214 203
6I	P2	Chiari	17-26	Vicolo Adimari 2	216 086
6I	P2	Medici	26-42	Via dei Medici 6	216 202
6I	P3	Bigallo	9-18	Vicolo Adimari 2	298 995
6I	P3	Costantini	9-11	Via Calzai oli 13	215 128
6I	P3	De Lanzi	16-26	Via delle Oche 11	296 377
6I	P3	Esperanza	10-15	Via dell'Inferno 3	213 773
6I	P3	Gentile	9-15	Via del Presto 2	292 019
6I	P3	Maxim	16-30	Via de'Medici 4	217 474
6I	P3	Olimpia	21	Piazza della Repubblica 2	262 860
6I	Loc	Aldini	11-20	Via Calzaiuoli 13	214 752
6I	Loc	Casa Grossi	6-7	Piazza de'Giochi 1	211 235
6I	Loc	Costantini	7-9	Via Calzaioli 13	215 128
6I	Loc	Elisa	12-20	Via delle Oche 11	296 451
6I	Loc	Sogg. Brunori	7-14	Via del Proconsolo 5	263 648
6I	Loc	Sogg. Diva	5-10	Via dei Medici 4	294 518
6I	Loc	Sogg. Rina	7-8	Via Dante Aligheri 12	
6I	Loc	Sogg. Taiuti	5-7	Piazza San Giovanni 1	295 143

Sq	Cat	Hotel		Rms/Beds	Street & No	Tel

West of Piazza Salvemini (2 mins E of Piazza Repubblica)

Sq	Cat	Hotel	Rms/Beds	Street & No	Tel
6L	P3	Antica	10-15	Via Pandolfini 27	296 644
6L	P3	l'Orologio	9-17	Via dell'Oriuolo 17	294 019
6L	P3	Zurigo	9-18	Via del Oriuolo 17	296 144
6L	Loc	Orchidea	4-7	Borgo degli Albizi 11	296 646
6L	Loc	Rosy	6-10	Via Pandolfini 22	263 083
6L	Loc	Sogg Bavaria	6-10	Borgo degli Albizi 26	211 024
6L	Loc	Sogg. S. Egidio	9-15	Via S.Egidio 6	282 280

East of Piazza Salvemini

Sq	Cat	Hotel	Rms/Beds	Street & No	Tel
6M	H4	Certini	23-39	Via Fiesolana 40	214 260
6M	P2	Bodoni	17-21	Via Martiri del Popolo 27	240 741

Ponte S. Trinita   Bank

Sq	Cat	Hotel	Bank	Rms/Beds	Street & No	Tel
7G	P2	Bretagna	N	16-25	Lungarno Corsini 6	263 618
7G	P3	Bartolini	S	16-25	Lungarno Guicciardini 1	296 452
7G	P3	Adria	S	-13	Piazza Frescobaldi 4	215 029
7G.	P3	Bandini	S	10-20	Piazza S.Spirito 9	215 308

Between Ponte Trinita & Ponte Vecchio

Sq	Cat	Hotel	Rms/Beds	Street & No	Tel
7H	H1	Augustus & Dei Congressi	67-134	Vicolo dell'Oro 5	283 054
7H	H1	Lungarno (S. Bank)	71-138	Borgo S.Jacopo 14	260 397
7H	H2	Berchielli	78-134	Lungarno Acciaiuoli 14	211 530
7H	H2	Continental	63-124	Lungarno Acciaiuoli 2	282 392
7H	H2	Della Signoria	27-46	Via delle Terme 1	214 530
7H	H3	Porta Rossa	71-130	Via Porta Rossa 19	287 551
7H	P2	Hermitage	14-22	Vicolo Marzio 1	287 216
7H	P3	Alessandria	25-43	Borgo SS Apostoli 17	283 438
7H	P3	Norma	10-20	Borgo SS Apostoli 8	298 577
7H	P3	Te-Ti e Prestige	16-27	Via Porta Rossa 5	298 248
7H	Loc	Archibusieri	5-7	Vicolo Marzio 1	282 480
7H	Loc	Cestelli	6-12	Borgo SS Apostoli 25	214 213
7H	Loc	Davanzati	8-12	Via Porta Rossa 15	283 414
7H	Loc	Tarvisio	5-9	Borgo SS Apostoli	284 583

Uffizi-Signoria

Sq	Cat	Hotel	Rms/Beds	Street & No	Tel
7I	H3	Columbia Parlamaneto	96-162	Piazza S.Firenze 29	213 400
7I	P2	Quisisana Ponte Vecchio	37-63	Lungarno degli Archibusieri 4	216 692
7I	Loc	Aily Home	5-10	Piazza S.Stefano 1	296 505
7I	Loc	Cristina	6-12	Via Condotta 4	214 484
7I	Loc	Sogg. Por Sta Maria	7-11	Via Calimaruzza 3	212 718
7I	Loc	Sogg. Quercioli	5-10	Piazza Signoria 3	219 259

West of Piazza S. Croce

Sq	Cat	Hotel	Rms/Beds	Street & No	Tel
7L	H4	Santa Croce	10-12	Via Bentaccordi 3	260 370

North of Sta Croce

Sq	Cat	Hotel	Rms/Beds	Street & No	Tel
7M	H3	Dante	10-20	Via S.Cristofano 2	241 772
7M	P3	La Locandina	10-20	Via dei Pepi 7	240 880

South of Piazza Beccaria

Sq	Cat	Hotel	Rms/Beds	Street & No	Tel
70	H2	Capitol	88-141	Viale Amendola 34	675 201

East of Piazza Beccaria

Sq	Cat	Hotel	Rms/Beds	Street & No	Tel
7P	H3	Bologna	20-33	Via Orcagna 50	672 685
7P	H3	Jane	28-44	Via Orcagna 56-58	660 939
7P	H3	Orcagna	18-36	Via Orcagna 57	675 959

Sq	Cat	Hotel	Rms/Beds	Street & No	Tel
South Bank (Oltrarno)					
NE of Pitti Palace					
8H	P1	Pitti Palace	17-32	Via Barbadori 2	282 257
8H	P3	La Scaletta	11-19	Via Guicciardini 13	283 028
North Bank					
Ponte Alle Grazie					
8L	H2	Balestri	49-86	Piazza Mentana 7	214 743
8L	H2	Jennings Riccioli	20-35	Lungarno delle Grazie 2	244 751
8L	P2	Rigatti	28-47	Lungarno Diaz 2	213 022
North Bank East of Ponte Alle Grazie					
8M	H1	Plaza E Lucchesi	100-180	Lungarno della Zecca Vecchia 38	264 141
8M	H2	Ritz	32-58	Lungarno della Zecca Vecchia 24	671 651
North Bank					
West of Ponte S. Nicolo					
8N	H3	River	45-76	Lungarno della Zecca Vecchia 18	666 529
8N	H3	Villa Michelangelo	23-40	Piazza Piave 3	268 533
8N	P3	Norchi	15-26	Lungarno della Zecca 8	666 451
North Bank					
East of Ponte San Nicolo					
80	H2	Mediterreneo	335-668	Lungarno del Tempio 44	672 241
As above-running North					
8P	H4	Lido	12-20	Via dell Ghirlandaio 1	678 887
East of Ponte da Verrazzano					
8R	H2	Columbus	101-156	Lungarno C.Colombo 22A	677 251
8R	H2	Ville Sull'Arno	36-70	Lungarno C.Colombo 1	670 971
8S	H3	Da Verrazzano	24-40	Via di Bellariva 18	660 669
South Bank					
SW of Palazzo Pitti					
9G	P2	Annalena	11-22	Via Romana 34	222 402
9G	P3	Boboli	13-21	Via Romana 63	227 169
SE of Ponte alle Grazie					
9L	P2	Silla	25-40	Via dei Renai 5	284 810
9M	H3	San Remo	17-31	Lungarno Serristori 13	213 390
90	H2	David	27-43	Viale Michelangelo 1	681 696
10R	Loc	Sogg. Goffredo	10-18	Via di Ripoli 169	687 924
10S	H4	Gavinana	11-21	Via Uguccione della Faggiola 25	687 659
11E	H3	Villa Betania	15-26	Viale Poggio Imperiale 23	220 532
11E	H4	Sul Ponte	8-13	Via Senese 315/A Galluzzo	2049 056
11E-	FH2	Villa Belvedere	27-50	Via Castelli 3	222 501
11E-	FP2	Villa Carlotta	26-44	Via Michele di Lando, 3	220 530
11E-	Floc	Sogg. Belvedere	5-9	Via B.Castelli 7	222 501
11M	H1	Park Palace	26-52	Piazzale Galileo 5	222 431
11T	H1	Crest Hotel	92-184	Viale Europa 205	686 841
11G	H1	Grand Hotel Villa Cora	56-97	Viale Machiavelli 18	229 84 51

Eating Out in Florence

Definitions of Eating Establishments

In theory, there are clear distinctions to be made between the various eating establishments in Florence. Nevertheless, the visitor dining out will encounter any number of misnomers and blurred identities. The following is an attempt at general definitions:

The **Ristorante** aims to be the grandest of all from its freshly laundered linen to its extensive menu, containing classical dishes from all the well known culinary regions.

Waiters in a ristorante tend to put on airs — and not variably to the benefit of the customer. Don't be discouraged. It may be counted as one of Italy's charms that in a country renowned for its cuisine, the table service can be haphazard.

The **Trattoria** evokes something of the spirit of country life. In Florence this may translate into the casualness of a 'neighbourhood' spot. The menu will be more compact, offering typical Tuscan dishes (some of which have only recently been revived after disappearing from the scene during the 'modern' 1970's.)

In a trattoria you may be asked to share a long refectory table with strangers. Adding to the festive feel are the straw covered 'fiaschi' of chianti wine standing on the tables. You will be billed for the wine according to consumption.

The waiters in a trattoria are likely to be of carefree disposition which may just produce service both quicker and cheerier than that in a ristorante. The standards in the kitchen of a Florentine trattoria can be quite high — with prices to match.

An **Osteria** is an inn and once upon a time provided roadside lodging for travellers as well as refreshment. An osteria ought certainly to be rustic with perhaps shoulders of ham (prosciutto) hanging from the rafters and/or game included in the menu. Many of the characteristics of a trattoria will be found in an osteria.

A **Pizzeria** specialises in pizza, but almost surely offers pasta and meat dishes as well — at economy prices.

A **Birreria** is where you will find beer — on draught from Britain. You will also usually find something to eat whether pizza, pasta or panini (sandwiches). The birreria serves as a pub where one can sit drinking without the obligation of dining.

A **Rosticceria** supplies the Italian version of fast-food, with ready made dishes available to take away. Roasted chickens predominate. Rosticcerie are extremely useful (1) for a quick inexpensive lunch (2) for stocking picnic baskets (3) when all other establishments are shut. Prices will fall within the one-star level.

Rest Days
Most eating establishments are open during the weekend and generally have a 'giorno de riposo' (rest day) during the week — often Monday or Tuesday.

Meal Times
Lunch is generally served between 12 and 12.30pm and dinner from 7.30 to 10pm — or perhaps later in the city centre.

Menu Turistico
This is a cheaper meal at an all-in price including service.

Some suggested restaurants by area.

South of station F-5
Sostanza, Via del Porcellana 25. Authentic Tuscan Fare. Here everything is cooked over a wood fire. Great value.

S.E. of station — *Near Piazza Santa Maria Novella H-5.*
Sabatini, Via Panzani 41. Once considered the last word in Florentine dining, this warhorse still offers perhaps the most formal and elegant ambience in town. Classical menu. Expensive.

West of Via Tornabuoni (W of Centre) G-6
Buca Mario, Piazza Ottaviani 16 (opposite Cinema) G-6. This serves excellent food, particularly game in season. Large and bustling premises below stairs. Credit Cards taken.

Coco Lezzone, Via del Parioncino 26. The modest facade conceals an interior where is to be found some of the best and most imaginative Florentine cooking and it has to be said that prices are those of a middle priced London restaurant with main dishes costing at least Lire 8,000. Unlike a London restaurant at this level, however, the food is top class, the service efficient if a little pushy, and the ambience in the small, crushed interior, quite pleasant. Anyone who has tried the *'farfalline'* with truffles and garlic, or the delicious rare roast beef will not feel that he has been more than a little overcharged.

Latini, Via Palchetti 6. A Florentine institution for decades. At Latini you eat well at a good price. Its four rooms hold upwards of 200 people, yet often you'll find a queue waiting to be seated. The atmosphere of bustle and good cheer is much more Roman than Florentine.

La Cantinetta, Piazzo Antinori 3 (North end of Via Tornabuoni) H-6
The house of Antinori, who produce much of the better Chianti, maintain this excellent and elegant wine bar in the courtyard of the ancestral home. Besides offering the full range of their wines by the glass or by the bottle, they also do excellent meals and salads. A good place to go when the first figs are available to have a glass of wine with a piece of ripe Brie to accompany it. Quite expensive unless you sit at the bar and confine yourself to glasses of wine. Very congenial ambience.

North of Duomo Baptistery
Ristorante Self Service Giannino in San Lorenzo, Borgo San Lorenzo 35. I-5
Of all the self-service establishments in Florence this is the only one to combine a wide range of dishes with a standard of quality that is far higher than can be found in supposedly quite good English restaurants. There is also a wide choice of wine and other drinks. Canteen food at its very best.

Central area
La Bussola, Via Porto Rosso 58. H-6
Open till 2 a.m., this colourful restaurant has an open brick oven where you can watch your pizza being made. The sea food is a speciality. It is expensive if you sit at a table, less if you sit up at the counter.

N of Piazza della Signoria. I-6
Ganino Osteria, Piazza Cimatori 4. This small osteria in the centre of town was placed first in a local newspaper survey of favourite restaurants. It is fully deserving of its popularity on the basis of its bill of fare, never mind the added attraction of the professional soccer players who have made it a hang-out. Try Carpaccio (veal tartare with shavings of parmagiano cheese and the superb semi-bitter lettuce rugeta). Not cheap.

North of Ponte Vecchio
Queen Victoria, Via Por S. Maria 32. H-7
Spotless and reasonably priced self service lunch. Wide plate selection.

Near Piazza Santa Croce (East of Centre) L-6
This is a low income area of the city and accordingly there are a lot of cheap places to eat and drink in the vicinity. A few suggestions are:
Mr Hang, Via Ghibellina 134. Recently there has been an influx of Chinese in Florence and rumour has it that in the coming months there will be an explosion of Chinese restaurants here. Chinese is the only ethnic food to be found in Florence, perhaps because it offers Chinese 'Spaghetti'. Mr Hang has an excellent reputation and moderate prices. Unfortunately, seating is limited.

Santa Croce (SE of centre) L-7
Quinto, Piazza dei Peruzzi 5. The only place in town where you'll hear live opera and Neapolitan songs, near the end of the evening

sung by Quinto himself. The food is of a consistently higher quality than the music. A good choice for a special evening. Not cheap.

East of the Duomo Area M-5
Da Noi, Via Fiesolana 46. Fully booked weeks in advance, Da Noi is small, first rate and an in place for Florentines to dine and to be seen. Pricey.

Piazza San Ambrogio, (East of Centre) N-6
Il Cibreo, Via de'Macci 118. This unique new place has vaulted to the head of the list. Refusing to serve any pasta dishes, the owner chooses instead to refresh the local palates with innovative soups and souffles. More radical still, the restaurant is divided into two sections, rich and poor. The poor section enjoys much of the same fare as the rich, only on a reduced scale — of portions, comforts and prices. In only a few years the young owner has become so sure of Cibreo's appeal that his menu posted on the street bothers to list only the following information: Appetizers 8,000, Firsts 10,000 and Main Dishes 18,000. Top wines.

Oltrarno (South of Ponte Vecchio)
The best place, despite invasions of tourists and some inevitable rise in prices, remains *Angiolino, Via Santo Spirito 36.* A family concern in which all the waiters have a stake, this is the friendliest trattoria in town and you will be well looked after by Carlo. Severino and the rest. In winter it is especially congenial when they light the huge iron stove in the centre of the room and a warm glow pervades the restaurant. The food is dependable, the vegetables being especially good and fresh, and none should fail to try the speciality for dessert, a meringue cake known as Cavour.

Camillo, Borgo San Jacopo 57/r.
Highly respected. Like Sabatini in terms of atmosphere, only pitched a tone lower. Expensive.

Cinghiale Bianco (White Boar Inn), Borgo San Jacopo 43 (red)
Englishman Stephen Tobin married an Italian wife and started this congenial eating place. The restaurant is a beautifully restored 12th century building and serves medieval Florentine dishes in candle-lit surroundings.

> N.B.   The Italian Government has passed a law under which you can be prosecuted if you do not have a *ricevuta fiscale* (tax receipt) on leaving a restaurant, shop, or hotel. This is designed to stamp out evasion of the I.V.A. (Value Added Tax), and although prosecution is not very likely, it is best to make sure you have a receipt.

Around Florence:

Cave di Maiano   Not too cheap. Situated north of the church at *Maiano* (near *Fiesole*). Open-air eating at wooden tables with fine views towards John Temple Leader's dramatic architectural folly, the *Castello di Vincigliata.*

Foresteria di Artimino   Beside Medici villa of *Artimino.*   A beautiful part of Tuscany. Modestly priced.

Zocchi, Via Bolognese (near *Pratolino*). Fine view of Fiesole, and marvellous at night. Not very cheap.

Centanni Just above *Bagno a Ripoli* on the road to *S. Donato in Collina.* Not very cheap but excellent.

Tea-rooms, cafés and bars in Florence:

Partly because of long standing British influence on Florentine fashion the habit of taking tea does exist, but it is a sorry affair consisting of people sitting in expensive and fashionable *Giacosa* (V. Tornabuoni 83) drinking tea made from tea-bags. However, *Giacosa* has good cakes and sandwiches (*tramezzini*).

Rivoire on Piazza della Signoria is especially congenial in winter where you can huddle over a cup of their piping hot chocolate (home-made) and watch the goings-on outside the *Palazzo Vecchio.*

In the *Piazza della Repubblica* there are several cafés, all tourist traps, but *Donnini* (in front of the Banca Nazionale delle Communicazioni) and *Gilli* offer good, though expensive, snacks, breakfasts, cocktails etc.

Near the station in *Piazza San Maria Novella* there is a pleasant outdoors cafe.

In *Fiesole* there is the Bar-Tea Room *S. Francesco, Via S. Francesco 18.*

The above are naturally the ones in prime locations; they charge accordingly and their customers will reflect the nature of their business. But all over Florence there are hundreds of little corner bars, often with only one or two tables outside, a pin-ball machine, bar-football or jukebox inside, where the real flavour of the city may be enjoyed. *Oltrarno* is a particularly pleasant area for a drink or cup of coffee, in *Piazzo Santo Spirito* or off the *Borgo San Frediano*. The *Cennini* family run a delightful bar and bakery in *Borgo S. Jacopo* (near *Ponte S. Trinita*). They have excellent fresh *'paste'* (cakes and pastries).

Food Stores:

Procacci, Via Tornabuoni 64 (red) are famous for their *panini tartufati* (truffle sandwiches).

Calderai, Via dell' Ariento 31 (red) have a good selection of Tuscan specialities and there is a good cheese shop in *Via dell' Oriuolo* where whole cheeses such as the ewe's milk *Pecorini* may be bought.

Ice Cream Parlours

Gelataria Vivoli is, as we go to press, the top establishment for ice cream in Florence. It is located near the Piazza Santa Croce, opposite the Astro Cinema. There is always a crowd here enjoying their superb gelati.

Perche No? (Why not?), Via dei tavolini close to the Piazza della Signoria also has a good choice of ice creams.

Restaurants

How to select an eating place:

This chapter incorporates a system for choosing an eating place suitable for your taste, purse and convenience. Here is how it works:

From the 'A' listing, select the TYPE of establishment you fancy and determine the PRICE ranking you would like.

Star rating by price (approx)

Stars	*****	****	***	**	*
In 000's of Lire	40 +	25-40	15-30	10-20	5-15

From the resulting selection and by reference to the pull-out map inside the back cover of this book, choose the establishment in the GRID SQUARE which is most convenient for you.

Then from the 'B' listing, ascertain the **address,** and make sure that the chosen establishment is **not closed** on the day on which you want to eat there. Check the **details.**

'A' Listing

EATING PLACES IN FLORENCE by type in alpha order

Birreria (2)

**Tally Ho	I-7
**Il Boccale	H-7

Fast Food (2)

**Money Money	I-4
**Italy Italy	G-4

Osterie (9)

****'l' Rosso	G-6
****Ganino	I-6
****Pepolino	0-9
****Quinto, Da	L-7
***Baldovino	L-7
***Barcaccia, La	L-7
***Cinghiale Bianco Osteria	H-7
***Gatto e la Volpe, Il	L-6
***Osteria Della Bistecca	I-5

Pizzerie (15)

***Capanna, La	I-4
***Clara	L-7
***Cotton Club	I-7
***David, Il	I-7
***Follie, Le	0-8
***Nuti	H-5
***Porta Gialle, La	L-6
***Scala Pizzeria, La	N-6
***Yellow Bar Pizzeria	I-6
**Marchigiana, Alla	I-6
**Piezzo	I-7
**Rosy, La	E-3
**San Gallo	L-1
**Spuntino, Lo	I-5
**Tarocchi, I	

Ristorante
5-star (6)

Barrino, Il	1-5

Capannina di Sante, La	
(Piazza Ravenna)	R-9
Cibreo	N 6
Corsini	G-6
Enoteca Pinchiorri	L-7
Harry's Bar	F-6

4-star (38)

Antico Crespino — Poggio	
Imperiale (off map south of	
Boboli Gardens)	
Bargello, Il	P-4
Bussola, La	H-6
Caffe Concerto	Q-8
Cammillo	H-7
Campidoglio, Al	I-6
Cantinetta Antinori	H-6
Coccodrillo, Il	G-5
Cuscussu, Il	N-5
Da Noi	M-5
Danny Rock	L-6
Don Chisciotte	H-3
Eito	L-7
Fagiano, Il	I-7
Greppia, La	P-9
Loggia La	M-9
Lume di Candela, Al	H-7
Maremma, La	L-7
Martinicca, La	G-6
Mister Hang	L-6
Monnalisa	H-4
Murate, Alle	L-6
Nandina, La	H-7
Narciso	O-7
Oliviero	H-7
Omero	Arcetri:N-10
Otello	F-4
Ottorino	I-6
Paiolo	I-6
Perseus	M-1
Rampe, Le	M-10

Rose's Café	G-6	Giglio Rosso	H-5
Sabatini	H-5	Golosi, I	L-6
Silvio	G-6	Gourmet, Il	E-4
Vien	L-7	Griglia, La	G-4
York	H-7	Grotta Guelfa, La	H-6
Zi Rosa, Da	G-6	Lampada, La	N-7
Zodiaco, Lo	N-7	Lampara, La	H-4
		Latini	G-6
3-star (79)		Leo in Santa Groce	L-7
Acquerello	L-6	Lorenzaccio	F-4
Alfredo sull'Arno	H-8	Macelleria, La	I-3
Baccus	I-6	Mamma Gina	H-7
Baldini	H-5	Mandarino, Il	I-7
Barbano, Di	H-3	Mario, Da	F-6
Barile, Il	B-2	Maximilian	M-5
Barone	E-10	Montecatini	I-7
Barroccio	I-7	Nanchino	I-6
Battistero	I-5	Nannoni	I-5
Beppa La	M-9	Natale	H-7
Bibo	L-7	Nuova Campana, La	H-5
Birreria il Boccale	H-7	Nuova Cina	G-5
Borghesi	I-6	Orcagna	I-7
Bronzino	I-3	Paoli	I-6
Bruno, Da	F-4	Peking	H-4
Buca Lapi	G-6	Pennello, Da	L-6
Buca Mario	G-6	Pentola d'Oro	M-7
Buca Poldo	I-7	Pepe Verde	H-4
Buca San Firenze	L-7	Pino & Bambu	G-7
Buca San Giovanni	I-5	Pit-Stop Pizza	
Cantine, Le	I-5	(North of station off map)	
Casa del Vin Santo	H-7	Pizzeus	0-6
Cavallino	I-7	Posta, La	I-6
Celestino	I-7	Profeta, Il	F-5
Corona	H-4	Pro-Polis 80	M-4
Dino	F-5	Renard, Le	I-6
Drago Verde	F-7	Sacrestia, La	H-8
Fagioli, Del	L-8	Sasso di Dante	I-6
Federigo	I-6	Shangai	M-1
Fior di Loto	L-4	Sorelle, Le	0-9
Fonticine con		Spada, La	G-6
Gigarrosto, Le	H-4	Tirabuscio, Il	L-7
Fortunato	G-5	Toto	H-7
Galleria, La	H-8	Vecchia Bettola	E-7
Ghibellini, I	L-6	Vecchia Carlino	F-3
Gigi, Da	H-5	Vecchia Firenze	L-6

2-star (2)

Apriti Sesamo	F-7
Pinnochio, Da	G-5

Rosticcerie (5)

**Alisio	F-7
**Giannino in San Lorenzo	I-5
**Pacini	I-7
**Spada, La	G-6
**Vargas	M-7

Self-Service (8)

***Don Burger	M-7
***Giovacchino Self Service	H-6
**Cancelli d'Oro	F-4
**Queen Victoria	H-7
**Self Serv in San Lorenzo	P-2
**Self Serv Leonardo	H-6
**Self Serv Nazionale	H-4
**Self Serv Old Bridge	H-8

Trattorie
4-star (7)

Cave di Maiano, Le	Fiesole/Maian
Coco Lezzone, Trat	G-6
Club pippo poppo	M-6
Garga Trattoria	G-6
I Che c'e c'e, Trat	L-7
Quatro Stagioni, Trattoria le	G-8
Strettoio, Lo	Careggio

3-star (62)

Acqua al Due	L-7
Dell'Agnolo	M-6
Alfredo	I-7
Angiolino	I-4
Angiolino	G-7
Anita	L-7
Antichi Cancelli	H-4
Antico Fattore	I-7
Armando	F-5

Baldini	E-4
Benvenuto, Da	L-7
Boboli	F-9
Bordino	H-8
Borgo Antico	G-8
Buca dell'Orafo	H-7
Buzzino	I-7
Cafaggi Giancarlo	I-4
Caminetto, Il	I-6
Campane, Le	L-7
Carabaccia, La	G-5
Carlo	L-7
Carmine, Del	F-7
Cesarino	M-7
Cinque Amici	I-6
Conca D'Oro, La	H-3
Cosimo, Da	L-6
Croce al Trebbio	H-5
Enzo & Piero	H-4
Falterona	H-4
Firenze	L-1
Francescano, I	M-7
Gabriello	I-7
Di Gennaro	I-7
Giardino	G-5
Guido, Da	H-4
I due 'G'	G-3
Luna, La	P-6
Marino, Da	I-6
Mario	H-4
Mario, Da	I-4
Mossacce	I-6
Natalino	L-7
Nello	F-7
Oreste	G-7
Palo d'Oro	I-3
Pasquini	H-6
Quattro Leoni	G-8
Rinaldo	F-8
Robertino	L-7

San Agostino	F-8
Santosuosso Giovanni	I-4
San Zanobi	I-3
Scala, La	G-5
Serragli, I	F-9
Silio, Da	I-4
Sostanza	F-5
Spada, La	G-6
Teatro, Il	L-5
Tito	L-3
Tittup	L-7
Tredici Gobbi	F-5
Verandina, La	H-6

2-star (7)

Cantinone del Mallo Nero	G-8
Carretto	H-4
Edo La Gratella	I-4
Marione	H-6
Nella	H-7
Nello	M-5
Santa Croce	L-7

'B' Listing'

Eating Places in Firenze in alphabetical order

Acqua al Due
Via dell'Acqua 2
Tel 284170   GS L-7
Trattoria   DC Mon
Spec: Mixed plate of Pastas
Res: Desirable

Acquerello
Via Ghibellina 156/r
Tel 0340554 GS L-6
Ristorante   DC Tue
Spec: Tuscan
Res: Desirable

Agnolo, Dell'
Via dell'Agnolo 21r
Tel 240971   GS M-6
Trattoria   DC Tue
Not necessary

Alfredo
Via dei Leoni 14
Tel 294912   GS I-7
Trattoria   DC Thu
Res: Not Necessary

Alfredo sull'Arno
Via dei Bardi 46/r
Tel 283808   GS H-8
Ristorante   DC Sun
   & Sat evening
Res: Desirable

Alisio
Via Serragli 75
Tel 225192   GS F-7
Rosticceria   DC Mon

Angiolino
Via Guelfa 138
Tel 475292   GS I-4

Trattoria   DC Thu
Res: Not Necessary

Angiolino
Via Santo Spirito 36
Tel 298976   GS G-7
Trattoria   DC Sun
      evening/Mon
Res: Not Necessary

Anita
Via del Parlascio 2
Tel 218698   GSL-7
Trattoria   DC Sun
   + Wed evenings
Res: Not Necessary

Antichi Cancelli
Via Faenza 73
Tel 218927   GS H-4
Trattoria   DC Mon
   + Tue lunch
Res: Not Necessary

Antico Crespino
Largo Enrico Fermi 15
Tel 221155   GS Poggio
Imperiale (off map south)
Ristorante   DC Wed
Spec: Internat & Tuscan
Res: Desirable

Antico Fattore
Via Lambertesca 1
Tel 261215   GS I-7
Trattoria   DC
               Sun/Mon
Spec: Toscana
Res: Not Necessary

Armando
Borgo Ognissanti 140
Tel 216219   GS F-5
Trattoria   DC Tues
             eve/Wed
Res: Not Necessary

Apriti Sesamo
Via dei Serragli 4
Tel 298804   GS F-7
Ristorante   Open only Thu
Fri Sat nights
Spec: Macrobiotic,
Vegetarian

Baccus
Via Borgo Ognissanti 45r
Tel 283714   GS F-6
Ristorante   DC Sun
Res: Not necessary

Baldini
Via Panzani 57/r
Tel 283331   GS H-5
Tistorante   DC Wed
Res: Not necessary

Baldini Trattoria
Via Il Prato 96/r
Tel 287663   GS E-4
Trattoria   DC Sat
Res: Desirable

Baldovino
Via San Giuseppe 22
Tel 241773   GS L-7
Osteria   DC Tue
Res: Not necessary

Barbano, Di
Piazza della Indipendenza 3
Tel 486752   GS H-3
Ristorante   DC Wed
Spec: International
Res: Not Necessary

Barcaccia, La
Via de'Levatoi 3
Tel 283958   GS L-7
Osteria   DC
             Mon/Tue
Res: Desirable

Bargello, Il
Piazza della Signoria 4r
Tel 214071   GS I-7
Ristorante   DC Mon
Res: Desirable

Barile, Il
Viale dell'Aeronautica 4
Tel 352563   GS B-2
Ristorante   DC Mon
Res: Not Necessary

Barone
Via Romana 123/r
Tel 220585   GS E10
Ristorante   DC Sun
Res: Desirable

Barrino, Il
Via de'Biffi 2
Tel 215180   GS I-5
Ristorante   :DC Sun
Spec: American Bar +
Grill/Nouvelle Cuisine
Res: Essential

Barroccio
Via della Vigna Vecchia 31/r
Tel 211503   GS I-7
Ristorante   DC Wed
Spec: Tuscan
Res: Desirable

Battistero
Via Ricasoli 5/7/r
Tel 292124   GS I-5
Ristorante   DC Mon
Res: Not Necessary

Benvenuto, Da
Via Mosca 16
Tel 214833   GS L-7
Trattoria   DC
            Wed/Sun
Res: Not Necessary

Beppa, La
Via dell'Erta Canina 6
Tel 296390   GS M-9
RistoranteDC Wed
Res: Not Necessary

Bibo
Piazza S Felicita 6-7r
Tel 298554   GS L-7
Ristorante   DC Tue
Res: Desirable

Boboli
Via Romana 45
Tel 226401   GS F-9
Trattoria   DC Wed
Res; Not Necessary

Boccale, Il
Borgo SS Apostoli 33
Tel 283384   GS H-7
Birreria   DC Mon
Res: Not Necessary

Bordino
Via Stracciatella 9
(Nr Pontevecchio between
Via de Bardi & Costa
S.Giorgio)
Tel 213048   GS H-8
Trattoria   DC Sun/Mon
Res: Not Necessary

Borghesi
Via de'Calzaiuoli 107
Tel 211431   GS I-6
Ristorante   DC Wed
Res: Not Necessary

Borgo Antico
Piazza S Spirito 6
Tel 210437   GS G-8
Trattoria   DC Sun
Spec: Pizzeria
Res: Not Necessary

Bronzino
Via delle Ruote 25
Tel 495220   GS I-3
Ristorante   DC Sun
Res: Not Necessary

Bruno, Da
Via L. Alamanni 29
Tel 215413   GS F-4
Ristorante   DC Mon
Res: Not Necessary

Buca Lapi
Via Trebbio 3/r
Tel 213768   GS G-6
Ristorante   DC Sun
Spec: Tuscan
Res: Not Necessary

Buca Mario
Piazza degli Ottaviani 16/r
Tel 214179   GS G-6
Ristorante   DC Wed
    & Thu Lunch
Res: Not Necessary

Buca Dell' Orafo
Volta dei Girolami 28
Tel 213619   GS H-7
Trattoria   DC Sun/Mon
Res: Desirable

Buca Poldo
Chiasso degli Armagnati 2/r
Tel 296578   GS I-7
Ristorante   DC Thu
Spec: Tuscan
Res: Not Necessary

Buca San Firenz
Via Condotta 9r
Tel 296804   GS L-7
Ristorante   DC Wed
Res: Not Necessary

Buca S Giovanni 8
Tel 287612   GS I-5
Ristorante   DC Tue
Spec: Tuscan
Res: Not Necessary

Bussola, La
Via Porte Rossa 58
Tel 293376   GS H-6
Ristorante   DC Mon
Res: Desirable

Buzzino
Via dei Leoni 8r
Tel 298013   GS I-7
Trattoria   DC mon
Res: Not Necessary

Cafaggi Ciancarlo
Via Guelfa 35r
Tel 294989   GS I-4
Trattoria   DC Sun
   eve/Mon
Res: Not Necessary

Caffe Concerto
Lungarno C.Colombo 7
Tel 677377   GS Q-8
Ristorante   DC Sun
Res: Not Necessary

Caminetto, Il
Via Studio 34
Tel 296274   GS I-6
Trattoria   DC
              Tue/Wed
Res: Not Necessary

Cammillo
Borgo San Jacopo 57/r
Tel 212427   GS H-7
Ristorante   DC
              Wed/Thu
Spec: Truffles
Res: Essential

Campane, Le
Borgo la Groce 87
Tel 678218   GS L-7
Trattoria   DC Mon
Res: Not Necessary

Campidoglio, Al
Via Campidoglio 8r
Tel 287770   GS I-6
Ristorante   DC Thu
Res: Not Necessary

Cantine, Le
Via de'Pucci 4
Tel 298879   GS I-5
Ristorante   DC Sun
Res: Not Necessary

Cantinetta Antinori
Piazza Antinori 3
Tel 292234   GS H-6
Ristorante   DC Sat/Sun
Spec: Tuscan
Res: Desirable

Cantinone Del Gallo Nero
Via S Spirito 6r
Tel 218898   GS G-8
Trattoria   DC Mon
Res: Not Necessary

Capanna, La
˙Via Cavour 112
Tel 210095   GS I-4
Pizzeria   DC Sun
Res: Not Necessary

Capannina Di Sante, La
Ponte Da Verrazzano
Cnr Piazza Ravenna
Tel 688345   GS R-9
Ristorante   DC Sun
Spec: Scrve only fish
Res: Desirable

Carabaccia, La
Via Palazzuolo 190
Tel 214782   GS G-5
Trattoria   DC Sun
  & Mon Lunch
Res: Desirable

Carlo
Via Isola delle Stinche 1
Tel 214410   GS L-7
Trattoria   DC
              Mon/Tue
Res: Not Necessary

Carmine, Del
Boprgo del Carmine 18
Tel 218601   GS F-7
Trattoria   DC Sun
Res: Desirable

Carretto, Il
Piazza del Mercato
  Centrale 17
Tel 283906   GS H-4
Trattoria   DC Tue
Res: Not Necessary

Casa Del Vin Santo
Via Porta Rossa 15/17r
Tel 216995   GS H-7
Ristorante   DC Wed
Spec: Tuscan
Res: Not Necessary

Cavallino
Piazza della Signoria 28
Tel 215818   GS I-7

Ristorante   DC Tue
  eve/Wed
Res: Not Necessary

Cave Di Maiano, Le
Via delle Cave 16, Fiesole
Tel 59133   GS Off Map
Trattoria   DC Thu/Sun
  evening
Res: Desirable

Celestino
Piazza Santa Felicita 4
Tel 296574   GS I-7
Ristorante   DC Sun/Mon
Spec: Tuscan
Res: Desirable

Ceserino
Via Pepi 12
Tel 241756   GS M-7
Trattoria   DC Wed EVE/Thu
Res: Not Necessary

Cibreo
Via De'Macci 118
Tel 2341100 GS N-6
Ristorante   DC Sun
Closed from 20.07-10.09
Spec: Inventive Cuisine
Res: Essential

Cinghiale Bianco Osteria
Borgo San Jocopo 43
Tel 215706   GS H-7
Osteria   DC Wed
Spec: Tuscan
Res: Desirable

Cinque Amici
Via dei Cimatori 30
Tel 296672   GS I-6
Trattoria   DC Sun/Mon
Res: Not Necessary

Clara
Borgo Santa Croce 59
Tel 2480783   GS L-7
Pizzeria   DC Changes
   Seasonally
Res: Not Necessary

Club Pippo-Poppo
Borgo Pinti 10/r
Tel 2480470 GS M-6
Trattoria   DC None
Res: Desirable

Coco Lezzone
Via Parioncino 26
Tel 287178   GS G-6
Ristorante   DC Sun/
   Tue eve
Res: Desirable

Coccodrillo, Il
Via della Scala 5
Tel 283622   GS G-5
Ristorante   DC Sun
Res: Desirable

Conca D'Oro, La
Piazza della Indipendenza 3
Tel 486752   GS H-3
Trattoria   DC Wed
Res: Not Necessary

Corona
Via Nazionale 90
Tel 294256   GS H-4
Ristorante   DC Sun
Spec: Tuscan
Res: Not Necessary

Corsini
Lugarno Corsini 4
Tel 217706   GS G-6
Ristorante   DC Mon
Spec: International
Res: Essential

Cosimo, Da
Via dell'Oriuolo 16
Tel 2480410 GS L-6
Trattoria   DC Sun
Res: Not Necessary

Cotton Club
Via de'Castellani 22
Tel 215759   GS I-7
Pizzeria   DC Mon
Res: Not Necessary

Croce al Trebbio
Via delle Belle Donne 49
Tel 287089   GS H-5
Trattoria   DC Mon
Res: Not Necessary

Cusscussú, Il
Via L.C. Farini 2/r
Tel 241890   GS N-5
Ristorante   DC Sun eve
Spec: Kosher
Res: Essential

Danny Rock
Via Pandolfini 13
Tel 2340307 GS L-6
Ristorante   DC Mon
Res: Desirable

Da Noi
Via Fiesolana 46
Tel 242917   GS M-5
Ristorante   DC
              Sun/Mon
Spec: Tuscan and Inventions
Res: Essential

David, Il
Piazza della Signoria
Tel 292188   GS I-7
Pizzeria   DC Sun
Res: Not Necessary

71

Dino
Via Ghibellina 51/r
Tel 241378   GS L-8
Trattoria   DC Sun
  eve/Mon
Res: Desirable

Dino
Via Finiguerra 8
Tel 287088   GS F-5
Ristorante   DC Sat
  & Sun alternately
Res: Not Necessary

Don Burger
Piazza Santa Croce 12r
Tel 242672   GS M-7
Self-Service   DC Mon
Spec: Chicken/Pizza
Res: Not Necessary

Don Chisciotte
Via Ridolfi 4
Tel 475430   GS H-3
Ristorante   DC Sun/
  Mon morning
Res: Not Necessary

Drago Verde
Via del Leone 50
Tel 224002   GS F-7
Ristorante   DC Sun
Res: Not Necessary

Due "G", I
Via Gennini 6
Tel 218623   GS G-3
Trattoria   DC Sun
Res: Desirable

Edo La Gratella
Via Guelfa 81
Tel 218865   GS I-4
Trattoria   DC Sun
Res: Not Necessary

Edy. Da
Piazza Savonarola 9
Tel 588886   GS N-2
Trattoria   DC Sat eve/Sun
Spec: Tuscan
Res: Not Necessary

Eito
Via dei Neri 72
Tel 210940   GS L-7
Ristorante   DC Mon
Spec: Japanese
Res: Desirable

Enoteca Pinchiorri
Via Ghibellina 87
Tel 242777   GS L-7
Ristorante   DC Sun
Res: Desirable

Enzo & Piero
Via Faenza 105
Tel 214901   GS H-4
Trattoria   DC Sat eve/Sun
Res: Not Necessary

Fagiano, Il
Via dei Neri 57/r
Tel 287876   GS I-7
Ristorante   DC Mon
Spec: Tuscan
Res: Essential

Fagioli, Del
Corso dei Tintori 47
Tel 244285   GS L-8
Ristorante   DC Sat/Sun
Spec: Tuscan
Res: Not Necessary

Falterona
Via Zannoni 10
Tel 216112   GS H-4
Trattoria   DC Tue eve/Wed

Res: Not Necessary

Federigo
Piazza dell'Olio 10/r
Tel 212090 GS I-6
Ristorante DC Tue
Spec: Tuscan/International
Res: Desirable

Fior de Loto
Via Servi 35/r
Tel 298235 GS L-4
Ristorante DC Mon
Spec: Chinese
Res: Not Necessary

Firenze
Piazza della Liberta 32/a
Tel 583596 GS L-1
Trattoria DC Mon
Res: Not Necessary

Follie, Le
Lungarno Tempio 52
Tel 677693 GS 08
Pizzeria DC Thu
Res: Not Necessary

Fonticine Con Girarrosto, Le
Via Nazionale 79
Tel 282106 GS H-4
Ristorante DC Sat
Res: Desirable

Fortunato
Via Palazzuolo 31
Tel 218846 GS G-5
Trattoria DC Tue
Res: Not Necessary

Francescano, I'
Via S. Giuseppe 26
Tel 241605 GS M-7
Trattoria DC Wed

Open only evenings
Spec: Casalingo
Res: DesirableTel

Gabriello
Via Condotta 54
Tel 212098 GS I-7
Trattoria DC Sat/Sun
Res: Not Necessary

Galleria, La
Via de'Guicciardini 48
Tel 218545 GS H-8
Ristorante DC Changes
    Seasonally
Res: Not Necessary

Ganino Osteria
Piazza Cimatori 4
100m north of Piazza della
Signoria along Via Cerchi
Tel 214125 GS I-6
Osteria DC Sun
Spec: Tuscan
Res: Essential

Garga
Via Moro 9
Tel 298898 GS G-6
Trattoria DC Sun
Res: Desirable

Gatto e La Volpe, Il
Via Ghibellina 151
Tel 2632634 GS L-6
Osteria DC Tue
Res: Not Necessary

Gennaro, Di
Via de'Castellani 4
Tel 218822 GS I-7
Trattoria DC Wed
Res: Not Necessary

Ghibellini, I
Piazza S. Pier Maggiore 8
Tel 214424   GS L-6
Ristorante   DC Wed
Rès: Not Necessary

Giannino In San Lorenzo
Borgo San Lorenzo 35
Tel 212206   GS I-5
Rosticceria   DC Tue
Res: Not Necessary

Giardino
Via della Scala 61
Tel 213141   GS G-5
Trattoria   DC Tue
Res: Not Necessary

Gigi, Da
Via Giglio 14r
Tel 218563   GS H-5
Ristorante   DC Sun
Spec: Tuscan
Res: Desirable

Giglio Rosso
Via de'Panzani 35/r
Tel 211795   GS H-5
Ristorante   DC Sun
Spec: Toscana
Res: Not Necessary

Giovacchino
Via de'Tosinghi 34/r
Tel 313276   GS H-6
Self-Service   DC Sun
Res: Not Necessary

Golosi, I
Via Pandolfini 13
Tel 2340307   GS L-6
Ristorante   DC Mon
Res: Not Necessary

Gourmet, Il
Via Il Patro 68
Tel 294766   GS E-4
Ristorante   DC Changes
    Seasonally
Res: Not Necessary

Greppia, La
Lungarno Ferrucci 4
Tel 6812341   GS P-9
Ristorante   DC Mon
Res: Desirable

Griglia, La
Piazza della Stazione 42
Tel 298141   GS G-4
Ristorante   DC Thu
Res: Desirable

Grotta Guelfa, La
Via Pellicceria 5
Tel 210042   GS H-6
Ristorante   DC Sun
Spec: Tuscan
Res: Desirable

Guido, Da
Via Faenza 34
Tel 263746   GS H-4
Trattoria   DC Wed/
    Thu morn
Res: Not Necessary

Harry's Bar
Lungarno Vespucci 22
Tel 296700   GS F-6
Ristorante   DC Sun
Spec: American Grill
Res: Essential

I Che C'e C'e
Via de' Magalotti ll
Tel 262867   GS L-7
Trattoria   DC Mon
Res: Desirable

Italy Italy
Piazza della Stazione 2
Tel 217270   GS G-4
Fast Food   DC Tue
Spec: Italian fast food/
    Hamburgers
Res: Not Necessary

Lampada, La
Via dell'Agnolo 93
Tel 245764   GS N-7
Ristorante   DC Mon
Res: Desirable

Lampara, La
Via Nazionale 36
Tel 215164   GS H-4
Ristorante   DC
              Mon/Tue
Res: Desirable

Latini
Via Palchetti 6
Tel 210916   GS G-6
Ristorante   DC Mon/
    Tue mornings
Spec: Tuscan
Res: Desirable

Leo in Santa Croce
Via Torta 7
Tel 210829   GS L-7
Ristorante   DC Mon
Res: Not Necessary

Loggia, La
Piazzale Michelangelo 1
Tel 287032   GS M-9
Ristorante   DC Wed
Spec: International
Res: Essential

Lorenzaccio
Via B Rucellai 1

Tel 217100   GS F-4
Ristorante   DC Sun
Res: Desirable

Lume di Candela, Al
Via Terme 23/r
Tel 294566   GS H-7
Ristorante   DC Sun
Spec: Fish

Luna, La
Via V. Gioberti 93
Tel 675944   GS P-6
Trattoria   DC Mon
Spec: Pizza
Res: Not Necessary

Macellaria, La
Via San Zanobi 97
Tel 486244   GS I-3
Ristorante   DC Sat
    morning/Sun
Spec: Tuscan
Res: Not Necessary

Mamma Gina
Borgo San Jacopo 37
Tel 296009   GS H-7
Ristorante   DC Sun
Res: Desirable

Mandarino, Il
Via Condotta 17
Tel 296130   GS I-7
Ristorante   DC Mon
Spec: Chinese
Res: Not Necessary

Marchigiana, Alla
Via Corso 60
Tel 214961   GS I-6
Tavola Calda DC Tue
Spec: Pizza
Res: Not Necessary

Maremma, La
Via G.Verdi 16
Tel 244615 GS L-7
Ristorante DC
          Wed/Thu
Res: Desirable

Marino, Da
Via Della Canonica 1
Tel 210285 GS I-6
Trattoria DC Mon
Res: Not Necessary

Mario
Via Rosina 2
Tel 2184550 GS H-4
Trattoria DC Sun/
  every day for lunch
Res: Not Necessary

Mario, Da
Via Guelfa 103
Tel 218827 GS I-4
Trattoria DC Sun
Res: Not Necessary
       .

Mario, Da
Borgo Ognissanti 141
Tel 298704 GS F-6
Ristorante DC Mon
Spec: Casalingo (country
home cooking)
Res: Not Necessary

Marione
Via della Spada 27r
Tel 214756 GS H-6
Trattoria DC Wed
Spec: Tuscan
Res: Not Necessary

Martinicca, La
Via Del Sole 27
Tel 218928 GS G-6
Ristorante DC Tue

Spec: Tuscan
Res: Desirable

Maximilian
Via degli Alfani 10
Tel 2478080 GS M-5
Ristorante DC Sun
Spec: Toscana-classica
Res: Desirable

Mister Hang
Via Ghibellina 134
Tel 283811 GS L-6
Ristorante DC Mon
Spec: Chinese
Res: Desirable

Money Money
Via Cavour 61r
Tel 294105 GS I-4
Fast food DC Sun
Res: Not Necessary

Monnalisa
Via Faenza 4
Tel 210298 GS H-4
Ristorante DC Mon
Res: Desirable

Montecatini
Via dei Leoni 6
Tel 284863 GS I-7
Ristorante DC Wed
Res: Not Necessary

Mossacce
Via del Proconsolo 55
Tel 294361 GS I-6
Trattoria DC Sun
Res: Not Necessary

Murate, Alle
Via Ghibellina 52/r
Tel 240618 GS L-6
Ristorante DC Mon
Res: Desirable

Nanchino
Via dei Cerchi 40
Tel 213142   GS I-6
Ristorante   DC Mon
Spec: Chinese ·
Res: Desirable

Nandina, La
Borgo SS Apostoli 64
Tel 213024   GS H-7
Ristorante   DC Sun
Res. Desirable

Nannoni
Piazza del Duomo 27
Tel: 216678   GS I-5
Ristorante   DC Sun
Res: Not Necessary

Narciso
Viale G.Amendola 24
Tel 244207   GS O-7
Ristorante   DC Sat
Spec: Mushrooms
Res: Desirable

Natale
Lungarno Acciaiuoli 80
Tel 213968   GS H-7
Ristorante   DC Tue
Res: Not Necessary

Natalino
Borgo Albizi 17
Tel 263404   GS L-7
Trattoria   DC Sun
Res: Desirable

Nella
Via Terme 19
Tel 218925   GS H-7
Trattoria   DC Sun
Res: Not Necessary

Nello
Borgo Pinti 56/b
Tel 2478410   GS M-5
Trattoria   DC Sun
Res: Not Necessary

Nello
Borgo Tegolaio 21
Tel 218511   GS F-7
Trattoria   DC
Mon/Tue mornings
Res: Not Necessary

Nuova Campana, La
Borgo San Lorenzo 24
Tel 211326   GS H-5
Ristorante   DC Wed
Spec: Tuscan
Res: Desirable

Nuova Cina
Piazza Santa Maria Novella
9
Tel 215837   GS G-5
Ristorante   DC Wed
Spec: Chinese
Res: Not Necessary

Nuti
Borgo San Lorenzo 24
Tel 210145   GS H-5
Pizzeria   DC Mon
Res: Not Necessary

Oliviero
Via delle Terme 51
Tel 287643   GS H-7
Ristorante   DC None
Res: Essential

Omero
Via del Pian Dei Giullari 11
Tel 220053   GS N10
Ristorante   DC Tue
Res: Essential

Orcagna
Piazza della Signoria 1
Tel 292188   GS I-7
Ristorante   DC Sun
Res: Not Necessary

Oreste
Piazza Santo Spirito 16
Tel 262383   GS G-7
Trattoria   DC
            Tue/Wed
Res: Not Necessary

Osteria Della Bistecca
Viale Gori 3
Tel 372657   GS I-5
Osteria   DC Sun
Res: Not Necessary

Osteria "1" Rosso
Via del Moro 22 and
1 Borgo Ognissanti
Tel 284897   GS G-6
Ristorante   DC Sun
Res: Desirable

Otello
Via degli Orti Oricellari 28
Tel 215819   GS F-4
Ristorante   DC Tue
Res: Desirable

Ottorino
Via delle Oche 20
Tel 218747   GS I-6
Ristorante   DC Sun
Res: Desirable

Pacini
Via dei Neri 74
Tel 262723   GS I-7
Rosticceria   DC Mon
Res: Not Necessary

Paiolo, Il
Via del Corso 42/r
Tel 215019   GS I-6
Ristorante   DC
            Sun/Mon
    morning
Res: Desirable

Pala D'Oro, La
Via XXVII Aprile 12-14
Tel 483435   GS I-3
Pizzeria   DC Wed
Res: Not Necessary

Paoli
Via dei Tavolini 12
Tel 216215   GS I-6
Ristorante   DC Tue
Res: Not Necessary

Pasquini
Val di Lamona 2
(Between P.del Mercato Nuovo
& Via Pellicceria)
Tel 218995   GS H-6
Trattoria   DC Sat eve/ Sun
Res: Not Necessary

Peking
Via del Melarancio 21
Tel 282922   GS H-4
Ristorante   DC Tue
Spec: Chinese
Res: Desirable

Pennello, Da
Via D.Alighieri 4
Tel 294848   GS L-6
Ristorante   DC Sun eve/Mon
Spec: Tuscan
Res: Desirable

Pepe Verde
Piazza d. Mercato Centrale 17

Tel 283906   GS H-4
Ristorante   DC Tue
Res: Not Necessary

Pentola d'Oro
Via de Mezzo 26
Tel 2451808   GS M-7
Ristorante   DC   Mon/Tue
Res: Not Necessary

Pepolini
Via Ferrucci 16
Tel 608905   GS O-9
Osteria   DC Sun
Res: Not Necessary

Perseus
Viale Don Minzoni 10
Tel 588226   GS M-1
Ristorante   DC Thu
Spec: Grill
Res: Essential

Piezzo
Via dei Neri 40
Tel 217718   GS I-7
Pizzeria   DC None
Res: Not Necessary

Pino & Bambu
Lungarno Corsini 12
Tel 212281   GS G-7
Ristorante   DC Wed
Chinese
Res: Desirable

Pinocchio
Via della Scala 28
Tel 218418   GS G-5
Ristorante   DC Sat/Sun
Spec: Tuscan
Res: Not Necessary

Pit-Stop Pizza
Via F. Corridoni 30
Tel 472089   GS Off Map
  -north
Ristorante   DC Tue
Spec: 128 kinds of Pasta/
  90 kinds of Pizza
Res: Not Necessary

Pizzeus
Viale Gramsci 9111
Tel 672980   GS O-6
Ristorante   DC Thu
Res: Not Necessary

Porta Gialla, La
Via dell'Oriuolo 26
Tel 2340371   GS L-6
Pizzeria   DC Wed
Res: Not Necessary

Posta, La
Via de'Lamberti 20
Tel 212701   GS I-6
Ristorante   DC Tue
Spec: Seafood
Res: Desirable

Profeta, Il
Borgo Ognissanti 93
Tel 212265   GS F-5
Ristorante   DC Sun/
  Mon
Res: Desirable

Pro-Polis 80
Borgo Pinti 10
Tel 2480470   GS M-4
Ristorante   DC None
Spec: Country Kitchen
Res: Not Necessary

Quattro Leoni
Via dei Vellutini 1
Tel 218562   GS G-8

Trattoria   DC Sun
Res: Not Necessary

Quattro Stagioni, Le
Via Maggio 61
Tel 218906   GS G-8
Trattoria   DC Sun
Res: Desirable

Queen Victoria
Via Por Santa Maria 32
Tel 296152   GS H-7
Self-Service   DC Mon
Res: Not Necessary

Quinto
Piazza dei Peruzzi 5
Tel 213323   GS L-7
Osteria   DC Mon
Res: Desirable

Rampe, Le
Viale G. Poggi 1
Tel 6811891   GS M10
Ristorante   DC Sun
Res: Desirable

Renard, Le
Borgo Ognissanti 45
Tel 283714   GS F-6
Ristorante   DC Sun
Spec: Tuscan
Res: Desirable

Rinaldo
Via San Agostino 23
Tel 210208   GS F-8
Trattoria   DC Mon
Res: Not Necessary

Robertino
Via V.Malenchini 8/r
Tel 219176   GS L-7
Trattoria   DC Tue
Res: Not Necessary

Rose's Café
Via del Parione 26
Tel 287090   GS G-6
Ristorante   DC Sun
Spec: American Bar
Res: Not Necessary

Rosy, La
Viale Flli. Rosselli 45
Tel 475991   GS E-3
Pizzeria   DC Mon
Spec: Hamburgers/Hotdogs

Sabatini
Via Panzani 41
Tel 282862   GS H-5
Ristorante   DC Mon
Spec: Tuscan/Classic
Res: Essential

Sacrestia, La
Via de'Guicciardini 27
Tel 210003   GS H-8
Ristorante   DC Mon
Res: Desirable

San Agostino
Via San Agostino 23
Tel 210208   GS F-8
Trattoria   DC Sun eve/Mon
Res: Not Necessary

San Gallo
Pizza della Liberta 10
Tel 499293   GS L-1
Pizzeria   DC Wed
Res: Not Necessary

Santa Croce
Via San Giuseppe 26
Tel 241605   GS L-7
Trattoria   DC Wed
Res: Not Necessary

Santosuosso Giovanni
Via Guelfa 94
Tel 475269   GS I-4
Trattoria   DC Thu
Res: Not Necessary

San Zanobi
Via San Zanobi 33
Tel 475286   GS I-3
Trattoria   DC Sun
Res: Not Necessary

Sasso Di Dante
Piazza delle Pallottole 6
(Within Piazza del Duomo)
Tel 282113   GS I-6
Ristorante   DC Thu/Fri
Res: Desirable

Scala, La
Via della Scala 41
Tel 219265   GS G-5
Trattoria   DC Wed
Res: Not Necessary

Scala Pizzeria, La
Borgo La Croce 59
Tel 2480783 GS N-6
Pizzeria   DC Wed
Res: Not Necessary

Self-Service in San Lorenzo
Borgo San Lorenzo 31
Tel 218219   GS I-5
Self Service DC Sun
Res: Not Necessary

Sel-Service Leonardo
Via de'Pecori 5
Tel 284446   GS H-6
Self Service DC None
Res: Not Necessary

Self-Service Nazionale
Via Nazionale 17

Tel 287703   GS H-4
Self-Service DC Sun
Res: Not Necessary

Self-Service Old Bridge
Via dei Bardi 64
Tel 212915   GS H-8
Self-Service DC Sun
Res: Not Necessary

Self-Service Pizzeria Jolly
Via del Canto de'Nelli 38
Tel 218922   GS I-5
Pizzeria   DC Sun
Res: Not Necessary

Serragli, I
Via de'Serragli 108
Tel 225001   GS F-9
Trattoria   DC Sun
Res: Not Necessary

Shangai
Piazza Liberta 32
Tel 583596   GS M-1
Ristorante   DC Mon
Spec: Chinese
Res: Not Necessary

Silio, Da
Via Guelfa 90
Tel 475291   GS I-4
Trattoria   DC Wed
Res: Not Necessary

Silvio
Via del Parione 74
Tel 214005   GS G-6
Ristorante   DC Sat/Sun
Res: Desirable

Sorelle, Le
Via di San Niccolo 30
Tel 284422   GS O-9

Ristorante   DC Tue
Res: Not Necessary

Sostanza
Via del Porcellana 25
Tel 212691   GS F-5
Trattoria   Dc Sat/Sun
Res: Not Necessary

Spada, La
Via della Spada 62
Tel 218757   GS G-6
Rosticceria   DC Tue
Res: Not Necessary

Spada, La
Via della Spada 62
Tel 218757   GS G-6
Ristorante   DC Tue
Res: Desirable

Spuntino, Lo
Via del Canto de'Nelli 14
Tel 210920   GS I-5
Pizzeria   DC Wed
Res: Not Necessary

Strettoio, Lo
Via Serpiolle 7
About 5km north of
Florence near Careggi
Tel 403044   GS Off Map
Ristorante   DC Sun/ Mon
Spec: Tuscan
Res: Essential

Tally-Ho
Via Condotta 7
Tel 296804   GS I-7
Birreria   DC Wed
Res: Not Necessary

Tarocchi, I
Via de'Renai 12
Tel 217850   GS L-9

Pizzeria   DC Mon
Res: Not Necessary

Teatro, Il
Via degli Alfani 47
Tel 2479327   GS L-5
Trattoria   DC Sun
Res: Not Necessary

Tirabuscio, Il
Via dei Benci 34
Tel 2476225   GS L-7
Ristorante   DC Thu/Fri
Res: Not Necessary

Tito
Via San Gallo 112
Tel 472475   GS L-3
Trattoria   DC Sun
Res: Not Necessary

Tittup
Via dei Benci 13
Tel 214162   GS L-7
Trattoria   DC Tue
Res: Not Necessary

Toto
Borgo SS Apostoli 6
Tel 212096   GS H-7
Ristorante   DC Wed
Res: Not Necessary

Tredici Gobbi
Via del Porcellana 9
Tel 298769   GS F-5
Trattoria   DC
                Sun/Mon
Res: Not Necessary

Tre Jolly
Piazza San Felicita 617
Tel 298554   GS H-8
Ristorante   DC Tue
Res: Not Necessary

Vargas
Via de'Macci 113
Tel 241171   GS M-7
Rosticceria   DC Mon
Res: Not Necessary

Vecchia Bettola
Viale L.Ariosto 34
Tel 224158   GS E-7
Ristorante   DC Sun/Mon
Res: Not Necessary

Vecchio Carlino
Via Flli Rosselli 15
Tel 353678   GS F-3
Ristorante   DC Tue
Res: Desirable

Vecchia Firenze
Borgo degli Albizi 18
Tel 294163   GS L-6
Ristorante   DC Mon
Res: Not Necessary

Verandina, La
Via Cavalieri 2
Tel 293048   GS H-6
Trattoria   DC Changes
  Seasonally
Res: Not Necessary

Vien
Volta dei Peruzzi 3
(Between Via de Benci &
Pza. de Peruzzi)
Tel 284021   GS L-7
Ristorante   DC Tue
Res: Essential

Yellow Bar
Via del Proconsola 39
Tel 211766   GS I-6
Pizzeria   DC Tue
Res: Not Necessary

York
Borgo San Jacopo 43
Tel 215706   GS H-7
Ristorante   DC Wed
Res: Desirable

Zi Rosa, Da
Via de'Fossi 12r
Tel 287062   GS G-6
Ristorante   DC Thu
Res: Desirable

Zodiaco, Lo
Via delle Casine 2
Tel 2340984 GS N-7
Ristorante   DC Sun
Spec: Seafood
Res: Desirable

Reading the Menu

There is a vast armoury of words describing dishes and variations on dishes, because of the great richness and variety of Italian cuisine together with its local specialities. Some general phrases are worth noting e.g. *'alla casalinga'* which simply implies something done in the style of 'home-cooking' (usually to be recommended). *'Bollito'* means 'boiled', *'Fritto'* fried and *'stufato'* casseroled. Stewed dishes may also be described as cooked *'al umido'*. *'Pasta ascuitta'* is the generic term for all the hard wheat variations of spaghetti, macaroni, tagliatelle etc. The sauces it comes with are too various to mention but the commonest are *'al sugo'* or *'bolognese'* both of which mean with a meat sauce, and *al pomodoro* with a tomato sauce. The phrase *'alla Milanese'* applied to veal will mean fried in breadcrumbs and *alla cacciatora* applied to chicken means cooked in the oven with stock and chopped vegetables such as tomatoes. onions, etc.

Specific Dishes:
Minestre (*soups*)
Minestrone: clear soup with vegetables, sometimes with slices of bread in it.
Stracciatella: a broth with raw eggs broken into it. Originally a Roman speciality.

Pasta
The most common are:
Spaghetti or *spaghettini:* with dozens of different sauces or just with butter and oil.
Tagliatelle/Taglierini: ribbon strands of egg noodles.
Rigatoni/Penne/Maccheroni: tubular pastas of different sizes and design.
Ravioli/Tortellini: two different types of stuffed pasta. Tortellini with cream (*alla panna*) is especially good.
Pappardelle alla lepre: Tuscan speciality of pasta with hare sauce.

Carne (Meat)

Bistecca alla Fiorentina is the special Florentine T-bone steak.

Maiale: pork; (sometimes *'carne suina'*). *Arista* is roast pork.

Fegato: liver, lamb's or pig's; *fegatini* are chicken livers from which the excellent moist paté or croûtons, *'crostini'*, are made.

Manzo: beef (sometimes *'bue'*); *Arrosto di manzo* is roast beef.

Pesce: fish. *Baccalà* is salt cod, a Genoese speciality but found elsewhere. *Dentice* and *orata* are small bream-like Mediterranean fish (the *orata* is larger) which can be grilled with herbs or cooked in white wine (usually the *orata*). *Spigola* is bass, *trota* is trout and *calamari,* squid. Mussels are *cozze* and clams, which make an excellent spaghetti sauce with garlic, are *vongole.* You will find the word *'scampi',* but more commonly *'gamberi'* for prawns. A Livornese speciality is *'cacciucco',* a fish stew with hot sauce.

Pollo: chicken; (*Petti di pollo* — chicken breasts)

Rognoncini: kidneys

Stracotto is beef cooked very slowly in red wine — local speciality.

Vitello: veal. *Piccate* or *scaloppine* are small fillets fried in various ways with Marsala, lemon etc. *Saltimbocca* is made of fillets of veal wrapped in ham with sage and marsala. *Arrosto di vitello* is roast veal. *Ossobuco* is a stew of shin of veal. *Polpettoni* are meat balls, made with veal or beef. *Lombatina* is a large cutlet or chop.

Verdura: vegetables. *Insalata verde* is green salad, *Insalata mista* is mixed salad. *Pomodori* are tomatoes, *cetrioli* cucumbers, *piselli* peas, *melanzane,* aubergine, *fagioli* kidney beans, *fagiolini,* green string beans, *zucchini,* courgettes and *patate,* potatoes. A Tuscan dish is *'Tortino di carciofi',* a baked artichoke omelette.

Olio e aceto: oil and vinegar

Burro: butter

Sale e pepe: salt and pepper

Formaggio: cheese, is plentiful. The best are *Gorgonzola* in both soft and harder varieties and *Pecorino,* a delicious local cheese made from ewe's milk.

Pane: bread. *Fettunta* is a toasted garlic bread which can be found in some *rosticcerie* and the like. The little Pizzeria off the main square in Fiesole serves it.

Drinking

Vino: wine. *Vino Rosso* (sometimes *'vino nero'*) is red wine and *'vino bianco'* is white. There aren't many decent *'rosés'* but if you must have one, the word is *Vino rosato*. *Abboccato* or *amabile* mean sweet and *secco* dry.

Good wines also come from *Montepulciano, San Gimignano* (*Vernaccia* — Michelangelo's favourite), *Orvieto* (the dry white is excellent), the Etruscan region south of *Grosseto,* and *Elba.*
Some reliable brands: *Badia a Coltibuono, Antinori, Frescobaldi,* and the expensive *Brunello di Montalcino* (Colombini). Recently there has been an attempt to establish the equivalent of a Beaujolais Nouveau with the *Vino Novello di Chianti* available November/December. It is not as good.

Good Chianti
Chianti is made from the native *Sangiovese* red grape and produces a fresh fruity wine mostly drunk young; but a few prestigious vinyards age their wine and can produce something exceptional. Perhaps the most famous is the *Colombini* family's *Brunello di Montalcino* (very expensive) produced near Siena, but other marks that are usually guarantees of quality are *Frescobaldi, Antinori and Brolio.* The story behind Brolio (possibly apocryphal) is entertaining. An ancestor of the present Baron Ricasoli, married in middle age a younger beauty and in order to remove her from the temptations of city life retired to his castle and devoted himself to viticulture; the happy result was an improved version of the ancient *Brolio.*
True Chianti is administered under the D.C.L. system — that is, the wine is denominated ɑѕ coming from a region of controlled viticulture and certified as to quality. It is analogous to the French *Appellation Contrôllée.* You will recognise it not only by the D.O.C. appellation but by the 'Black Rooster' (*Chianti gallo*) labelling on the neck of the bottle. You will also see the description *Chianti Classico.* Slightly less prestigious but also good is the *Chianti putto* with a cherub on the neck of he bottle.

Acqua: water. *'Acqua potabile'* is drinking water and *'acqua minerale'* is mineral water. If you definitely want the fizzy variety, specify *gasata.*

Beer:
Italian Peroni beer is refreshing if uninteresting. *Nastro Azzurro* is probably the best. German beer can be had - at a price.

Coffee:
One of the joys of Italy is the coffee with its distinctive slightly over-roast flavour. If you want it with frothy milk, ask for a *Cappuccino* (a morning drink); or strong short and black, ask for *Espresso*. *Caffellatte* is like French *café au lait* and there are other variations about which locals are inordinately fussy e.g. *Latte macchiato* which means hot milk with just a spot of coffee in it, or conversely *caffé macchiato*.

Liqueurs and Vermouths:
There are various appetisers and vermouths, interesting or appalling according to taste. *Martini* and *Cinzano* produce aperitifs and in a bar you can buy the refreshing ready-made bottles of *Campari Soda*. A good summer drink is *Americano*, a mixture of vermouths, perhaps with a squirt of soda. Add gin and it becomes a *Negroni*.

After a meal, *Grappa* - real fire-water - is on offer, or the aniseed flavoured *Sambuca* served in a glass with coffee beans floating in it and lit like a Christmas pudding. The brandies are *Stock* and *Vecchia Romagna*, the latter rather smoother than all but the highest grade *Stock*.

Galleries, Museums & Gardens
With Opening Times

STATE MUSEUMS   **Closed on**
Entrance Free on 1st and 3rd Saturdays and second
last Sundays of each month

North of the Duomo

Cappelle Medicee   Working Days   9-19   Mondays
(Tombs by Michelangelo)   Holidays   9-13
Piazza Madonna
degli Aldobrandini

Galleria degli Uffizi   Working days   9-19   Mondays
Loggiato degli Uffizi, 6   Holidays   9-13

Galleria dell'Accademia   Working days   9-14   Mondays
Via Ricasoli 60   Holidays   9-13

Museo Archeologico   Working days   9-14   Mondays
Via della Colonna 36   Holidays   9-13

Museo di San Marco   Working days   9-14   Mondays
Piazzo San Marco 1   Holidays   9-13

Opificio delle Pietre Dure   Mondays 09.30-13.30   Holidays
Via degli Alfani, 78   Wednesday
                   Friday

South of the Duomo

**Museo della Casa
Fiorentina**   Working days   9-14   Mondays
Antica - Palazzo
Davanzati   Holidays   9-13
via Porto Rossa 13

**Museo Nazionale del
Bargello**   Working days   9-14   Mondays
Via del Proconsolo 4   Holidays   9-13

Faces, Faces. Little wonder that Florentine pageants attract so many tourists. The authenticity of garb, and the elan with which the participants conduct themselves provides countless opportunities for the camera enthusiasts.

South of the Arno

Palazzo Pitti, Piazza Pitti			
Apartamenti Monumentali	Working days	9-14	Mondays
	Holidays	9-13	
Galleria d'Arte Moderna	Working days	9-14	Mondays
Galleria Palatina	Working days	9-14	Mondays
	Holidays	9-13	
Museo degli Argenti	Working days	9-14	Mondays
	Holidays	9-13	
Giardino de Boboli	Mar-Apr/		
(Boboli Gardens)	Sep-Oct	9-17.30	
	May-Aug	9-19.00	
	Nov-Feb	9-16.30	
Museo delle Porcellane	Tu Thu Sat	9-14	Mondays
(Boboli Gardens)	Holidays	9-13	
Collezione Contini	By application	9-12	
Bonacossi (Boboli Gardens)	Temp -Closed		

MUNICIPAL MUSEUMS AND GALLERIES
Entrance Free on Sundays

North of the Arno			
Chiostri Monumentali	Working days	9-14	Friday
di Santa Maria Novella	Holidays	8-13	
Museo Storico Topografico			
Firenze comera	Working days	9-14	Thursday
Via dell'Oriuolo, 4	Holidays	8-13	
Quartieri Monumentali	Working days	9-19	Wednesday
di Palazzo Vecchio	Holidays	8-13	
Piazza della Signoria			
Raccolta di Arte Moderna	Working days	9-14	Tuesday
A. della Ragione	Holidays	8-13	
Piazza della Signoria, 5			

South of the Arno ('Oltrarno')

Cenacolo di S. Spirito e	Working days	9-14 Monday
Fondazione Romano	Holidays	8-13
Piazza S. Spirito 29		

Museo Bardini e Galleria	Working days	9-14
Corsi	Holidays	8-13 Wednesday
Piazza de Mozzi 1		

SCIENCE MUSEUMS
North of the Duomo

Museo e Orto Botanico - Via La Pira, 4 - Tel: 248.411. Mondays, Wednesdays, Fridays 9-13. First Sunday of month except Jul, Aug, Sep 9.30-12.30. Entrance free.

Museo di Geologia e Paleontologia dell'Università - Via La Pira, 4 - Tel: 262.711. Mondays 14-18 - Thursdays and Saturdays 9-13. Closed on Holidays and from the 15th July - 31st August. Entrance free.

Museo di Mineralogia e Litologia dell'Università - Via La Pira, 4 - Tel: 296.876. Weekdays 9-13, Wednesday also 15-18. Entrance free.

South of the Duomo

Museo di Antropologia ed Etnologia - Via del Proconsola, 12 - Tel: 296.449. Wednesdays & Fridays 9-13. First and third Sundays of month 9-13. Guided tours by appointment for school groups: Entrance free.

Museo di Prestoria - Via S. Egidio, 21 - Tel: 215.788. Open 9.30-12.30. Closed on Sundays. Entrance free.

Instituto e Museo do Storia della Scienza - Piazza dei Giudici, 1 - Tel: 293.493. Weekdays 10-13; 14-16 - Closed Saturday afternoons and Sunday.

South of the Arno

Museo Zoologico 'La Specola' - Via Romana, 17 - Tel: 222.451. Visits to the Zoological Section Tuesday and Sunday 9-12 (free). Visits to the Anatomical Section: Saturdays, Summer opening 15-18 - Winter opening 14-17.

OTHER MUSEUMS

North of the Duomo

Museo Stibbert - Via Stibbert, 26 - Tel: 475.731. Weekdays 9-14. Holidays 9-13. Closed on Thursdays. Entrance free on Sundays.

Galleria dello Spedale degli Innocenti - Piazza della SS. Annunziata, 12 - Tel: 298.997 - Summer 1/6-31/10 9-19. Winter 9-13. Holidays 9-13.   Closed on Mondays.

South of the Duomo

Casa Buonarroti - Via Ghibellina, 70 - Tel: 241.752. Open 9-14. Holidays 9-13. Closed on Tuesday.

Casa di Dante, Via Santa Margherita 1 - Tel: 283.343. Weekdays 9.30-12.30; 15.30-18.30 - Summer. 9-12.30, 15.30-18.30 Winter. Holidays 9.30-12.30. Closed Wednesdays

Scavi di S. Reparata (Cathedral's interior) Tel: 213.229. 9.30-12.30; 15.30-18.30. Holidays 9.30-12.30.

Cupola del Brunelleschi e Campanile de Giotto - 8.30-12.30; 14.30-17.30.

Forte di Belvedere - Free entrance to terraces and bastion.

Museo del Bigallo - Piazza S. Giovanni, 1 - Tel: 215.440. Weekdays 14-19. Closed on Sundays. Entrance free.

Museo della Fondazione Horne - Via dei Benci, 6; 9-13. Closed on Saturdays and 2nd and 4th Sundays each month.

Museo dell'Opera di Santa Croce - Piazza S. Croce, 16 - Tel: 244.619. Summer 9-12.30; 15-18.30. Winter 9-12.30; 15-17. Closed Wednesdays.

Museo dell'Opera di Santa Maria del Fiore - Piazza Duomo, 9 - Tel: 213.229. Summer 9.30.-13; 14.30-17.30; Sundays 10-13; 14-17. Holidays 10-13. Entrance free on Sundays.

Orsanmichele (Entrance Palazzo dell Arte della Lana) - Via Arte della Lana, 1. Tel: 294.580. Weekdays 9-14. Closed on Sundays. Entrance free.

Palazzo Medici Riccardi - Via Cavour, 1 - Tel: 217-601. Weekdays 9-12.30; 15-17. Holidays 9-12. Closed on Wednesdays. Entrance free.

Villa Medicea dei Poggio Imperiale - Tel: 220.151. Open on Wednesdays 10.30-12.30. Entrance free.

MUSEUMS, VILLAS AND MONUMENTS
IN THE VICINITY OF FLORENCE

Castello - Villa Medicea di Castello - Closed to the public
- Entrance to the garden: Summer 9-18.30 - Winter 9-16.30.
Holidays: 9-13. Closed on Sundays. Entrance Free.

Castello - Villa Medicea La Petraia - Visit to the villa 9-14 - Tel:
451.208. Entrance to the gardens: Summer 9-19 - Winter
9-16.30. Holidays 9-13. Closed on Mondays. Entrance free.

Fiesole - Museo Bandini - Tel: 59.061. Summer 9-12; 16-19 -
Winter 10-12; 15-17. Closed holidays and Sunday afternoons.

Fiesole Museo Archeologico e Teatro Romano - Tel: 59.477.
Open March, April and October 10-12.30; 14.30-18 - from
November to February 9.30-12.30; 14-17 - from May to
September 10-12; 15-19. Closed on Mondays.

Galluzzo - Certosa - Tel: 2.049.226. Summer 9-12; 16-19 - Winter
9-12; 15-17.

Poggio a Caiano - Villa Medicea - Temporarily closed - Tel:
877.012. Entrance to the gardens: Winter 9-16.30; Spring 9-17.30;
Summer 9-18.30. Closed on Mondays. Entrance free.

Sesto Fiorentino - Museo di Doccia - At the Richard-Ginori
Chinaware factory - Via Pratese - Tel: 4.410.453. Open 9.30-13;
15.30-18.30. Closed on Sundays and Mondays.

DAYS WHEN ALL STATE MUSEUMS ARE CLOSED

* January 1st
* Easter
  April 25th
* May 1st
  June 2nd (only if it falls on a Sunday, otherwise the first Sunday
  of June)
* August 15th
* Christmas

---

* Municipal Museums Close On These Days.

Florence: A—Z

Florence has a double street numbering system for private and commercial addresses. The latter are numbered in red. Where this applies the word 'red' appears in brackets after the number.

N.B. A useful current listing of events in Florence may always be obtained from the *Azienda Autonoma di Turismo;* it is called *Florence Today.* Also the *Diary of Events* from the *Ente Provinciale per il Turismo.*

Airline Offices

British Airways, *Piazza Antinori 2* (*red*) Tel: 218 655.
Alitalia, *Lungarno Acciaiuoli 10/12* (*red*) Tel: 27 88.
British Caledonian Airways, *V. Palestro 4* Tel: 26 08 78.

Art

Università Internazionale dell'Arte, Via Incontri 3

Banks and Exchange

Universalturismo, Via Speziali 7 (*red*).   Foreign currency exchanged at competitive rates. Also (less competitively) at the station.

Banca d'America e d'Italia, Via Strozzi 4, Credito Italiano, Via Vecchietti 11 and many others will attend to more complicated needs.

American Express,
Office: Via Tornabuoni 2 (red) (Card Division)
Bank: Via della Vigna Nuova 2 (red)

Bookshops

B.M. Bookshop, Borgognissanti 2 (*red*), on the edge of *Piazza Goldoni*, run by an American proprietress, has a good selection of books on history and the arts relating to Florence, both American and English. Members of the American Booksellers Association. Largest selection of English Books in Florence.

Paperback Exchange, Via Fiesolana, 31 (red) Tel: 2478154. Large stock (20,000 titles) of used, English-language paperbacks. New titles also stocked and subjects include English and American literature, Italian Art and History, and travel guides. The shop is easy to find: 'east of the Duomo and north of Santa Croce'.

Libreria Caldini, Via Tornabuoni. Large selection of antiquarian books including art, local history etc.

Libreria Seeber, Via Tornabuoni, 70 (red) has an international selection of books, including plenty of English paperbacks.

Libreria del Porcellino, Piazza Del Mercato Nuovo. Good selection of paperbacks in English, guides etc. They take credit cards.

Libreria Feltrinelli on *Via Cavour* also carries plenty of paperbacks. The emphasis is on books that appeal to the younger generation, the flavour generally radical.

'Centro Di', Piazza dei Mozzi No. 1 Particularly hard to find; useful for students of art as they sell works on the fine arts, exhibition and sale catalogues etc.

Camping

There are sites below the *Piazzale Michelangelo* (*Viale Michelangelo 80*), at *Fiesole* (*Via Peramonda, Fiesole,* Tel: 599-069) and elsewhere. Main roads are normally well supplied with signs to camp sites.

Car Concessionaires in Florence

British Leyland — *Garage Zaniratti, Viale Fratelli Rosselli 55.*
   Tel: 471465
Citroen — *Garage Excelsior S.a.S, Via Palazzuolo 94,*
   Tel: 296137.

General Motors — *Autoscana s.r.l., Viale Cialdini 6/12,* Tel: 600229

Peugeot — *Aglietti, Via Lanzi 10,* Tel: 483323

Renault — *Renault Italia S.P.A., Viale Corsica 15/23,* Tel: 351082.

Talbot — *Automobil, Viale Lavagnini 44,* Tel: 480981

Toyota — *Menegatto, Via Rusciano 4,* Tel: 672512

Volkswagen/Audi/NSU — *M. Ignesti & Figli, Via Pratese 166,* Tel: 373741

Volvo — *Zaniratti & C. s.r.l., Viale Talenti,* Tel: 703150

Churches

Catholic Churches offering Confession in English

Duomo *Piazza del Duomo*

S.S. Annunziata *Piazza S.S. Annunziata*

S. Marco *Piazza S. Marco*

Non-Catholic Churches

Anglican Church of St. Mark *Via Maggio 16*

Baptist *Borgo Ognissanti 6*

Methodist (Wesleyan) *Via de Benci 9*

American Episcopal *Via B. Rucellai 15*

Lutheran *Lungarno Torrigiani*

Christian Science *Via della Spada 1*

Synagogue *Via Farini 4*

Cinema

Cinema Astro, Piazza S. Simone shows films in English. Otherwise all films are dubbed into Italian.

Consulates

The British Consulate is in *Lungarno Corsini 2,* Tel: 212 594 Open 9.30-12.30 Mon-Fri, 2.30-4.30 Mon & Fri.

The American Consulate is in *Lungarno A. Vespucci 38,* Tel: 298 276. Open 9-12 and 2-4 Monday through Friday.

Golf:

Ugolino Golf Club — *Via Chiantigiana, near Impruneta,) Guest* rates). 12 km/7 miles from Florence at *Grassini.* Tel: 20-11-963.

Languages and Cultural Courses

University of Florence, Via San Gallo 25
Centro di Cultura per Stranieri, Via Bolognese 52
Centro Linguistico Dante Alighieri, Via dei Bardi 12
Eurocentro, Piazza Santo Spirito 9
The British Institute of Florence, Palazzo Ferroni, Via Tornabuoni (courses in Italian Language, Literature and Art)

Libraries:

The British Consulate, *Lungarno Corsini 2.* Reading room with English periodicals.

The British Institute, *Palazzo Lanfredini, Lungarno Guiccardini 9.* Open to members (Subscription payable). Substantial library of English literature, together with the Francis Toye music library.

The Kunsthistorisches Institut is the most well-equipped library for serious art history students. *Via Giusti 44.*

Biblioteca Nazionale Centrale - Piazza Cavalleggeri, 1.

Motoring Organisation:
A.C.I. (Automobile Club d'Italia) — Viale Amendola 36, Tel: 27-841 (See also Emergency Telephone Numbers)

Music Festivals and Events:
Maggio Musicale Fiorentino: (opera ballets concerts) May, June and July.
   Saturday afternoon concerts organised by *Amici della Musica* (Friends of Music) take place in the charming 19th century *Teatro della Pergola (Via della Pergola No. 18).* Tel: 210-097. *Abbonamenti* (subscribers' season tickets) can be applied for. The series runs on Saturday afternoons from October through April. The *Amici della Musica* office is in *Via Rondinelli, 10. Tel: 296 233.*

Teatro Comunale seasons: Stagione lirica (opera season: December-February)(*Corso Italia 12-16. Tel: 263-041*).
Stagione sinfonica (symphony season) in the winter, November through March.

Summer series of concerts in the *Cortile* (open air) of the *Palazzo Pitti.* And in winter there are concerts in the *Pitti's Sala*

97

The Mediaeval Pageants which draw so many tourists to Florence are supported by Florentines from all walks of life. This rider who could have stepped out of a rather earlier age, is none other than Emilio Pucci a present day Florentine whose creations are sold across the world.

(Photo by Courtesy of EPT Firenze)

Bianca. Always book well in advance. The cheaper tickets at the Teatro Comunale represent good value compared with other European opera houses, since the theatre is of such modern design,and acoustics and visibility are good. In the *Teatro della Pergola* the *Loggione* cheap tickets entitle you to a stone step to sit on!

A useful diary of forthcoming events is issued by the *Ente Provinciale per Il Turismo.* Copies are available in English.

Night Life: The booklet *Florence Today* gives a good listing of clubs and discothêques, of which there are now many. Tastes are very individual in such matters, but if you like a beery communal atmosphere and unlimited noise *The Red Garter* in *Via dei Benci 33,* near *Santa Croce* offers a rock band, or sometimes an American banjo band, mugs of foaming beer, and generally extravagant bonhomie. It is cheap as night spots go. The *Mach Due* in *Via Torta 4,* the same area, near *Santa Croce,* is a strobe light discotheque of the swinging sixties, still swinging a bit. The latest English and American discs are played as well as the local material. Entrance and *consumazione* (1 drink) costs Lire 5,000. There are many others, some very expensive indeed, so check carefully before committing yourself.

Pharmacies:
Farmacia Comunale No. 13 di S. Maria Novella (in the station).
Roberts Farmacia Inglese, Via Tornabuoni 97 (red).
Farmacia Molteni, Via Calzaioli 7 (red).
Comunale, Via de Serragli 4 (red). Open at night. (Oltrarno)
See also local newspapers for list of pharmacies opening at night in rota.

Petrol:
There are late night filling stations in certain areas, e.g. *Agip* : *Via Rocoa Tedalda,* Self-service *Via A del Pollaiuolo. Amoco: Via Senese. Esso: Viale Europa. I.P. Via Baccio da Montelupo. Texaco:* Self-service, *Viale Guidoni.*

Post and Telecommunications:
The central Post Office (*Ufficio Postale*) is off the *Piazza della Repubblica* (*Via Pellicceria*). Parcels will be rejected if, in the opinion of the overworked and often brusque clerks, they are insufficiently wrapped. Happily there is a wrapping service to the right of the main entrance. Packages weighing more than 2 kilos (4.4 lbs) must be sent *pacco postale* (parcel post). Forms

to be filled out for sending them overseas may be obtained in the room on the right as you go in. Then take the package and form round the corner to *Piazza Davanzati 4.*

Money Orders are taken on the first floor of the Post Office.

Telegrams are sent on the ground floor. Undelivered telegrams may be collected at *Via Anselmi 1* (north side of Post Office).

Letters may be sent *'raccomandata'*, registered, or *'espresso'*, express. Take these to windows 21-2 in the Post Office. Stamps may be bought on the ground floor and there is a window for philatelists.

Telephones on the ground floor are both local and long distance *(interurbani)*. You need to purchase *gettoni* for 200 lire to use them. For overseas calls (and trunk calls) apply to the reception desk in the telephone room on the ground floor and wait until a cabin has been designated free for you to use. They will monitor the length of the call and you pay as you go out.

Stamps, cigarettes and matches are on sale at bars which are also licensed tobacconists; they are recognised by the big T sign outside and the word *tabacchi*. Tobacco is still a state monopoly. Foreign cigarettes are also available.

Seaside:
In summer the *Freccia del Tirreno* express goes from Florence to Viareggio in an hour. LAZZI buses from the *Piazza della Stazione*, go there too and on to *Forte dei Marmi, Marina di Pietrasanta* and *Ronchi.*

Shopping:
Florence contains a lot of fashionable and expensive shops but leather goods are perhaps its most famous commodity. The outdoor markets in *San Lorenzo*, the *Mercato Nuovo*, the *Loggia of the Uffizi*, and the leather school of *Santa Croce*, at least provide an opportunity to haggle. You won't get far haggling in *Gucci, Via Tornabuoni* however, or in the shoe shop *Ferragamo, Via Tornabuoni 16 (red)*. Outside the tourist season some of the shops clear stocks in sales (say Jan. - Feb.) when the prices are reduced from the very overpriced to the slightly less overpriced.

Fashion: Old England, in *Via Vecchietti; Neuber* and *Principe, in Via Strozzi; Zanobetti and Ugolini, in Via Calimala: Pucci*, in *Via Ricasoli.*

Clothes off the peg (often very attractive) can be found in the supermarkets *Upim (Piazza della Repubblica)* and *Standa (Via de'Panzani 31 (red))*. Otherwise a lot of clothes are made to order.

Children's clothes: Anichini, in *Via del Parione; Cirri,* in *Por Santa Maria.*

Reproductions of works of art can be purchased at *Alinari,* (*Via Nazionale 6;* branches in the *Via Strozzi* and on the *Lungarno Corsini*). The range is extensive and quality of reproduction high. For the serious inquirer who wants good black and white prints the *Gabinetto Fotografico della Soprintendenza alle Gallerie, Piazzale degli Uffizi 2* will assist. (Hours 11.00—13.00 Tuesdays through Fridays).

Straw markets are the *Mercato Nuovo* (off *Via Porta Rossa*) and in *Piazza San Lorenzo.*

Ski-ing:

There is ski-ing in the Apennines at *Abetone* (above Pistoia). Buses leave *Piazza S. Maria Novella* (CO.PI.T. Line) and *Piazza della Stazione* (LAZZI line) between 6 and 7.30 a.m. in the season and seats must be reserved at least a day in advance.

Swimming Pools:

Bellariva, Lungarno Colombo, 6 (with children's playpark). Tel: 677.521
Costoli - Viale Paoli - Tel: 675744.
Le Pavoniere - Viale degli Olmi (*cascine*) - Tel: 367506.

Tourist Offices:

Azienda Autonoma di Turismo — Via Tornabuoni 15: Tel: 215 544, 263 607, 263 290. 9-13 daily.
Ente Provinciale per il Turismo di Firenze 8.30—13.30 daily — *Via Manzoni 16* - Tel: 678 841.

Town Plans:

L.A.C. (Litographia Artistica Cartographica) a Florence publisher produces two excellent plans of the city which are available from kiosks and bookshops. They are worth asking for specifically. 'Firenze' 5,500 lire and the smaller 'Firenze Centrale' 3,000 lire. They are both at 1:9,000 scale.

The same firm also produces an excellent single sheet road map of the Region of Tuscany 'Toscana' at 1:250,000 scale (4 miles to the inch) which sells at 5,500 lire. Excellent for general touring by car.

For readers wanting maps at a larger scale — perhaps for walking or with an eye to property purchasing — LAC have maps of each of the nine provinces of Toscana. Arezzo, Firenze, Crosseto and Siena at 1:150,000 scale and Livorno, Lucca, Massa, Carrara, Pisa and Pistoia at 1:100,000 scale. These are sold in 'self covers'.

One of the 'Straw' Markets in Florence. A view of the Loggia of the Mercato Nuovo as one approaches it from the Ponte Vecchio along the Via Por S. Maria. Another, even larger is by the Church of San Lorenzo north west of the Duomo.

Transport in the City:

Buses: Orario is the word for timetable.

(1) *In the city:* The city bus service (A.T.A.F.) is efficient and goes everywhere. You enter by the rear door and insert your ticket in the machine at the back to validate it. Exit is only by the middle doors so move up a crowded bus once you have your ticket. The front door is supposed to be reserved for season ticket holders. You yourself may buy a 3,300 lire ticket (*tessera*) from tobacconists which is good for 11 town journeys or 5 suburban and 1 town. This ticket is punched in the red machine in the buses. The bus to Fiesole leaves from Piazza della Stazione (no. 7).

(2) *Country Buses:* The lines LAZZI (*Piazza Adua, Tel:* 215 154), SITA (*Via S. Caterina da Siena, 15,* Tel: 278-611) and CO.PI.T. are all services to places outside Florence. They all end up in or near the *Piazza della Stazione.* Many start early in the morning and return in the evening from outlying villages. You will usually have to buy a ticket a day or two in advance to be sure of a seat.
  The bus to Pisa airport goes from the Lazzi terminal.

(3) *Intercity Buses:* SITA, Via S. Caterina da Siena 15.
Taxis: There are taxi ranks at the station, in *Piazza San Maria Novella,* in *Piazza San Marco, Piazza della Repubblica, Piazza Santa Croce* and the main square at Fiesole. In Florence dial: 47-98 or 27-55 for a radio cab. The cabs are painted yellow and metered. Tipping is customary.

Horse Carriages:
Not recommended; they exist solely for tourists. If you take one, fix a price for a round trip *before* you get in. They are quite expensive.

Car Hire:
Avis-Europa Garage, Borgo Ognissanti 96. Tel: 23.629
Hertz, Via Maso Finiguerra 23a. Tel: 282 260.
Maggiore - Via Maso Finiguerra 11R - Tel: 294 578.

Feet:
Really the best method, but make sure you invest in a pair of strong well-cushioned shoes. The pavements are not only hard but irregular.

Travel Agents:

Thomas Cook Limited, Piazza Strozzi 14-15 (*red*). Tel: 325 744.
C.I.T. (Italy's answer to Thomas Cook) - *Via Cerretani 57/59* (*red*). Tel: 294 306. *Piazza Stazione 51* (*red*), Tel: 284 145.
Universalturismo, Via Speziali (red). Tel: 217 241 (Associated with American Express)

A Camera Tip

Many tourists carry cameras. 35mm cameras often have shoulder straps, but the smaller and quite popular 110 cameras seldom do. It may interest visitors to Florence to know that there is an artisan in leather — Paolo Casalini, Via del Moro 44 rosso, 50123 Firenze, who is able to make belt holsters for such cameras, to order.

He measures your camera, cuts a wooden block 1mm larger in each dimension and fashions a Florentine style leather case around it, open at the top end. You can chose your own leather colour and he will even apply decoration if you are so inclined. It fully protects the camera and will probably outlast it.

He also makes jewellery and trinket boxes in various shapes, colours and sizes.

Straw Market (Mercato Nuovo) One of the irressistible attractions of Florence for the majority of tourists. Leatherware, silks, sun hats and an endless variety of attractively priced merchandise assures the stall holders of a steady turnover.

A Tour of Florence

Firstly a tip for those who have not booked accommodation in advance and find themselves at a loss in a strange city: the *Tourist Information Office* at the main station (the staff is friendly and English is spoken) provides information about available accommodation in all price categories and will make reservations. Usually they will find some sort of accommodation for you, though you will find there is limited choice in the high season. *See Hotels and Pensioni and Locande* pages 44-53.

Piazzale Michelangelo

Since one needs at least five days for even a brief insight into the art and architecture of Florence and at least three weeks for some degree of understanding, an overall view of the city may help to orientate the newcomer. Take the bus up to *Piazzale Michelangelo*. (Bus No. 13 from the station; by car follow the signs across the Arno).

From this vantage point you will get a marvellous view of the city. Follow the wide *Viale Michelangelo* in the shade of the pine and cypress trees up to the square. In the centre stands a bronze copy of *Michelangelo's David* surrounded by copies of the sculptures on the Medici tombs in *San Lorenzo*. Standing at the balustrade, (be careful, it's crumbling) you will see Florence's red-tiled rooftops, high towers and the brown Arno laid out at your feet. At the centre of the curve of hills opposite is Fiesole and behind that, in the distance, the hazy outline of the Appenines, one of the finest stretches of unspoilt countryside in Tuscany.

As you look down into the gardens of some of the more opulent villas you will begin to see why this was known as the *Città dei fiori,* the city of flowers. The coat of arms of Florence, a red lily on a white background (unlike the Bourbon lily this one has a stem), is said to come from the white lilies which grew wild in the Arno valley; nowadays, they are grown under glass and exhibited at the annual Iris Show in May on the Piazzale.

The flowers also have allegorical significance, since the whole city once "flourished" and even the towers grew like flowers above the rooftops. The tower of the *Palazzo Vecchio* resembles a stylised lily and the dome of the cathedral (*Duomo*) dedicated to *Santa Maria del Fiore* looks like a gigantic bud.

Tuscany is remarkably endowed with wild flowers clinging to the crevices of long cultivated terraces. D.H. Lawrence has described the spring flowers movingly in his essay *Flowery Tuscany* and especially the half wild irises in May when the fields are "lit up with their mauve light and so much scent in the air …"

San Miniato al Monte

Behind the Piazzale Michelangelo (5 minutes walk along the Viale Galileo) is the green and white marble mediaeval façade of romanesque *San Miniato,* one of the oldest churches in Florence; the current structure, on the site of an even earlier church, was built between 1018 and the end of the 11th century. It is a little jewel of a building. In addition to the rather insensitively restored Byzantine mosaics in the chancel (19th century restorers generally caused more damage than the ravages of time), there are frescoes by *Aretino,* a pupil of *Giotto,* in the sacristy, and several other important works of art by *Luca della Robbia, Rossellino* and *Baldovinetti;* and a beautiful crypt which contains reliquaries. In front of the crypt is a fine tabernacle by Michelozzo. 'The Three Saints' by the Pollaiuolo brothers in the chapel on the left is a copy of the well-known picture which may be seen in the Uffizi

The cloisters have frescoes by *Paolo Uccello* and a synopia by *Andrea del Castagno.*

The view of Florence and the surrounding district from *San Miniato* is even more impressive than from the *Piazzale Michelangelo.*

If you continue along Viale Galileo for some way, or take the bus (13) for three stops, you reach *Via di S. Leonardo.* Proceed down the hill as if on your way to the *Forte di Belvedere* and you will arrive at the mediaeval city gate, *San Giorgio.* The walk is delightful. Behind the grey walls are gardens and villas. In spring the violet blooms of wisteria and the silver-grey branches of the olive trees hang over into the street. The *Via di San Leonardo* was the favourite street of the *Macchiaioli,* a neglected group of Florentine painters who were contemporaries of the Impressionists. Here, in the mid-day heat, alone with slumbering cats and lizards, you can discover something which is rare in Florence; peace and quiet and a chance to reflect. Turn left at the *Porta di S. Giorgio* for the Forte di Belvedere.

Forte di Belvedere

It was built by Giovanni de Medici and designed by Buontalenti. It never had to resist an enemy and indeed seems to have been more a symbol of power over the Florentine people than over their enemies. There is a secret passage connecting the Forte with the Boboli Gardens.

A fine view across Florence may be had from the top and it is a particularly pleasing spot for an outing on a warm summer's evening.

The fortifications of Florence, built by the Republic's greatest military architect, Michelangelo, run laterally from Forte di Belvedere to Porta Romana on one side and Porta S. Niccolò on the other. During the siege by the Emperor Charles V's forces, which put an end to the Republic, Michelangelo left here for the city to complete his final work in Florence, the figures for the Medici tombs in the New Sacristy in San Lorenzo. The sadness of the figures shows vividly how the Republican Michelangelo must have felt during these last days of freedom in the city.

The Fort di Belvedere is now used for exhibitions.

Ponte Vecchio

Built in 1345, it is the city's oldest bridge. The Via Cassia, the historic trade route from the east through Italy to France, crossed this bridge. When it celebrated its 600th anniversary in 1945 it was the only bridge in Florence undamaged by the ravages of the war. We owe its continued existence to an officer of the Wehrmacht who refused to destroy it. An older bridge on this site, destroyed over and over again by fire or by floods, was built in the 12th century.

In the 13th century the statue of the pagan protector of the city, Mars, God of War, stood here at the entrance to the city centre; appropriately enough, for, when the years of strife between the Guelphs and the Ghibellines began with the murder of Buondelmonte in 1216, the assassins used the statue as a rendezvous.

The Arno swept away Mars and time eventually healed the worst family feuds. Bakers and butchers moved out of the tiny shops on the bridge (it is said because Cosimo was bothered by the stench of meat as he passed along the corridor above it) to make way for the goldsmiths and jewellers who are still there today.

Typical Street scene. Looking south along the Via Por S.Maria in the direction of the Ponte Vecchio.

The Ponte Vecchio (Old Bridge). One of the major sights and focal points of Florence and spanning the River Arno, it lies on the direct route between the Piazza della Repubblica on the North bank and the Uffizzi Palace in Oltrarno (The South Bank).

Tourists wandering at will on the Ponte Vecchio. Saved by the refusal of a German Wehrmacht Officer to blow it up during World War II this ranks with the Rialto Bridge in Venice as one of the best known bridges in the world. Most of the bridge is lined with jewellery shops, but the central portion is open, yielding a view of the buildings lining the river frontage with their characteristically wide eaves for protection from the sun.

Since the 16th century, the bridge has joined the later residence of the Medicis, the *Palazzo Pitti,* and the *Palazzo Vecchio,*
in which the history of Florence was decided. In 1550 Cosimo I,
his wife, Eleanora of Toledo and their eight children moved
from the old mediaeval building which had become too small for
them, into the huge palace on the other side of the Arno, which
had become too costly for its owner, a rich burgher of the city
named Pitti. Cosimo had *Vasari* build a passageway to connect
the *Palazzo Vecchio* with the *Uffizi,* the *Ponte Vecchio* and the
new residence. If you look out of the window of the *Uffizi* on the
river side you will get a view of this passageway, which contains
a gallery of artists' self-portraits. It is however usually closed
because parts of it are becoming unsafe, but can be seen by
special permission. (*Inquire at the ticket office of the Uffizi*).
After Eleanora's death, the lonely Grand Duke fell in love with a
beautiful commoner, Camilla Martelli, who lived in one of the
houses on the bridge.

Now that traffic has been banned from the bridge it is like an
oriental bazaar. There is always a colourful and cosmopolitan
crowd lingering by the tiny shopwindows which are filled with
stylish, and sometimes valuable, pieces of jewellery. Young
people camp on the ground, playing their guitars, selling their
costume jewellery or just gazing through the archways in the
centre of the bridge at the river.

The Flood

On November 5th, 1966, the Arno burst its banks after weeks of
rain had swollen its tributaries to raging torrents, the flood-
water mingling with oil from burst heating tanks and filth from
overflowing sewage plants. It was the worst flood in Florence's
history. The oily water reached a depth of nineteen feet in
churches, homes and palaces, destroyed frescoes and paintings,
stuck to sculptures and threatened to drown the city completely.
An army of volunteers, including many foreigners, joined forces
with the soldiers who were brought in to assist in the state of
emergency, and helped to dig irreplaceable treasures out of
mud. They formed chains with the soldiers, passing along it
dripping lumps of mud from the cellar of the National Library on
the Arno which contained manuscripts and thousands of priceless books. Like most of the works of art, many books were
saved. But it was years before Florence recovered from the
disaster.

Lungarno Archibusieri. At the North east corner of the Pontevecchio, this arched walk lines the river bank.

Restoration work still continues in the *Fortezza da Basso* near the main railway station, where in 1966 the best restorers in the world came to offer their assistance and expertise. Unfortunately, despite higher walls along parts of the *Lungarni,* (the streets that run along the river banks) another disaster cannot be ruled out. The Arno is comparatively shallow bedded and the rise of flood waters, aggravated by factors such as melting snow in the Apennines, can be rapid and lethal.

In a number of shops and restaurants may be seen little plaques twelve to fifteen feet up on the walls which mark the highest point of the 1966 floodwaters.

The Pitti Palace and the Boboli Gardens

The amusing fat gnome on the back of a tortoise (the post-card of the statue is a popular greetings card for friends with a sense of humour) is one of the most bizarre statues in the Boboli gardens. Pietro Barbino, Cosimo I's court dwarf, was the model for the statue. The expressive, petulant face is said to be a portrait of Cosimo, whom the sculptor (*Valerio Cioli*) disliked. The gardens (which are behind the Pitti), are well worth a quiet stroll before going into the Palace. Eleanora of Toledo, one of the Spanish Medicis, had them laid out in 1550, when she moved into the palace with her children. What a sigh of relief she must have given when she saw her brood of little princelings amidst so much greenery and space! The gardens are so large that one can always find a quiet corner to be alone with the thrushes, the marble deities and the tinkling fountains.

On a May or June evening, during the *"Maggio Musicale"* (Florence's annual May musical festival) you might have the pleasure of seeing an opera performed here. Opera, of course, was a Florentine invention. Count Bardi founded his '*camerata*' in the 16th century and this group of poets and composers produced the first recognizable opera, *Dafne* by Iacopo Peri (1957).

One of the garden's many delights is the *Buontalenti grotto,* an artificial niche of stalactites, built so that courtiers could quench their thirst on hot days; it has three rooms, each one smaller that the one before. On the stalactites are copies of Michelangelo's *Prisoners,* between the shells, moss, tiles and shepherds. The originals from the unfinished tomb of Pope Julius II stood here before they were moved to the Accademia. In the last grotto, a *Giambologna Venus* rises, naked and virginal, from her shell, leered at by four satyrs.

114

Oltrarno The southern end of the Ponte Vecchio. The road ahead, bearing right, leads to the Pitti Palace, some 300 yards further on, on the left.

The ever dominant Duomo and Campanile from the hilly ground behind the Pitti Palace across the Arno.
(Photo by Courtesy of EPT Frenze)

A corner of the Boboli Gardens behind the Pitti Palace. A sequestered zone giving respite from the bustle of the city.

117

A Pavilion in the Boboli Gardens affording an excellent vista of the city.

The Pitti Palace

This, the largest palace in Florence, was begun by *Brunelleschi* in 1458 and extended by *Ammannati:* further additions were made as late as the 19th century, when it reached its present size. The Palace has three important galleries, not to mention the paintings and art treasures stored in its basement because of lack of hanging space. *The Galleria Palatina* contains masterpieces by *Raphael, Titian, Tintoretto, Rubens, Van Dyck, Velasquez, Murillo* and numerous others, in a setting which has not changed since the days of the Grand Duke's private collection. It covers mainly the 16th and 17th centuries. On the 2nd floor is the *Galleria d'Arte Moderna* and the *Museo degli Argenti*, 16 rooms of goldsmith's and silversmith's work, precious stones, ivory, porcelain, furniture and other treasures. Across the courtyard of the palace a doorway directs you towards the *Museo delle Porcellane*, in the Boboli gardens, a fine collection of Italian, French and German porcelain.

Piazza della Signoria, Palazzo Vecchio and Loggia dei Lanzi

After crossing the Ponte Vecchio, we reach, on óur right, the *Piazza della Signoria* built by *Arnolfo di Cambio*, which is still a centre of the city's commercial life, as it was in the days of the Commune. It is the seat of the Municipal Government. In front and to the right of the *Palazzo Vecchio* is the *Loggia dei Lanzi* which contains original Renaissance sculptures including *Benvenuto Cellini's Perseus*. The name of the Loggia derives from Cosimo I's private guard, which was stationed here. The marble *David* at the entrance to the Palazzo Vecchio is another copy of Michelangelo's original. The *Fountain of Neptune* by *Ammannati* and *Giambologna*, though genuine, is not particularly attractive: the locals call it the *biancone*, the fat white man.

The Piazza, the Palace, the Loggia and the surrounding buildings are best contemplated from a seat in Rivoire, the cafe on the corner (you can get home-made hot chocolate there) and are a perfect example of the severe elegance of the city. Of the many works of art in the *Palazzo Vecchio* special mention should be made of *Verrocchio's Fountain* with a boy (or 'putto') holding a fish, which is on the second floor in what was once Machiavelli's office, the *cancelleria*. (A copy is in the entrance hall).

The fine crests of the Hapsburg cities painted around the entrance hall are in honour of Joan of Austria, the wife of Francesco I de Medici, and were done by Vasari.

In the *Cinquecento hall* (also called the *Sala del Maggior Consiglio*) there are remnants of an unfinished battle scene by

Leonardo da Vinci beneath *Vasari's* frescoes. He had painted it using the new tempera technique which he also employed for his later work *The Last Supper* in Milan. The colours ran from the walls when he tried to dry them with burning faggots. Facing you as you enter is *Michelangelo's* statue of *Victory.*

When Savonarola reformed the republic along Venetian lines the Grand Council of 500 members met here to deliberate. Elsewhere in the *Palazzo Vecchio* there are important works by *Bronzino,* the *Ghirlandaio, Pietro Lorenzetti, Giambologna* and others. You should also visit the tower and enjoy the superb view.

The Flag Throwers in the Piazza della Signoria overlooked by the Palazza della Signoria the seat of ancient government and the Loggia dei Lanzi (on the right) which houses between its columns the bronze statue of 'Perseus' by Benvenuto Cellini (1545-54), and the marble group 'Rape of the Sabines' (1583) by Giambologna. Other statutary is housed within the loggia.

(Photo by Courtesy of EPT Firenze)

Piazza della Signoria. In the foreground the statue of Neptune.
(Photo by Courtesy of EPT Firenze)

The Uffizi

The entrance to the Uffizi is to the right of the *Palazzo Vecchio*. It is generally considered to contain the most important collection of paintings in Italy, but it is so extensive that an attempt to see it all in one visit will be doomed to failure. It would be more sensible to make several visits either to look at particular periods *e.g. Duccio, Giotto, Cimabue* and the early Tuscan painters of the 13th and 14th century; then the pictures of *Botticelli* and the 15th century; then the later Mannerist paintings of *Pontormo* and others. There are also rooms devoted to foreign artists (i.e. non Italian) and the Venetian school. Alternatively it is often worth going to see a few pictures that you are interested in, or the work of a particular artist who attracts you. In any case find time to see the superb Madonnas by *Giotto* and *Duccio* and *Cimabue* in Room 2, *Paolo Uccello's Battle of San Romano* (Room 7) with its magnificently ferocious cart-horse and *Piero della Francesca's Portrait of Federigo da Montefeltro* and *Battista Sforza* in the same room. Most of Room 8 is devoted to the work of *Filippo Lippi*. And few people will need urging to see the superb *La Nascita di Venere* (Birth of Venus) and *Primavera* (Spring) of *Sandro Botticelli* in Room 10. Off this room is the *Sala di Leonardo*. Other rooms contain work by *Michelangelo* (25), *Raphael* and *Andrea del Sarto* (26) an´ *Titian* (28). The sensual *Bacchus* of *Caravaggio* is in Room 44

Orsanmichele

After traversing the *Piazza della Signoria*, we encounter the *Via de Calzaiuoli* leading to the spiritual centre of the city, the Cathedral, *(Duomo)* the *Baptistery* and *Giotto's Campanile*.

The *Via de Calzaiuoli* is one of the smartest shopping streets in the city: the others are the *Via Tornabuoni* and one of its side streets, the *Via della Vigna Nuova*.

Off *Via de Calzaiuoli* is the former granary of the Republic, *Orsanmichele*, half way along on the left as you walk towards the square of the Cathedral *(Piazza del Duomo)*. In the ground floor church, a haven of quiet after the busy street outside, stands a magnificent *Orcagna* altar with a *Madonna* by *Bernardo Daddi*. Upstairs the spacious chamber with its Gothic windows is now used for exhibitions.

On the walls of the building are its most intriguing features, the sculptures of the patron saints of the guilds fitted into niches, by *Ghiberti, Verrocchio, Nanni di Banco, Donatello* and others, with roundels from the *Della Robbia* workshops. The Florentine guilds commissioned the leading artists of the day to depict their patron saints. And so, amidst the hum-

122

The Clock Tower of the Palazzo della Signoria. Photographed from a nearby cafe, the construction of buildings has not been allowed to interfere with this memorable view. Town planning of a better kind!

drum of everyday life, stand *Donatello's Saint George* and *Verrocchio's Christ with Doubting Thomas*, one of the most moving heads of Christ in religious sculpture. Too many visitors pass the granary as they dash along, heads down and bags crammed with straw hats, gloves and souvenirs from the famous *Straw Market* (*Mercato della Paglia* or *Mercata Nuovo,*) in the next street.

A short walk down the rest of *Via de' Calzaiuoli* brings you out into *Piazza del Duomo.*

Piazza del Duomo - the Baptistery, Campanile and Duomo

In front of the Duomo stands the octagonal Romanesque *Baptistery*, the baptismal church of *Dante* and many Florentines even today. The poet called it *"il mio bel San Giovanni"*, (St. John is the patron saint of Florence).

The cluster of people by the portal of the Baptistery, will lead you to the most famous of the three doors, decorated with gilded reliefs by *Ghiberti: Michelangelo* called it the "Gate to Paradise". *Ghiberti* worked for over twenty five years on the ten scenes from the Old Testament, which are as expressive and lively as a painting. The fourth head from the top in the left central section is a self-portrait.

The Gothic quatrefoils, showing scenes from the life of Christ, the Apostles and the Holy Fathers, on the north portal, are also by *Ghiberti.* It was not until after the last war that someone noticed that Ghiberti's reliefs were covered in real gold.

Andrea Pisano is the sculptor of the beautiful, pure Gothic figures from the *Life of John the Baptist,* to whom the *Baptistery* is dedicated, on the south portal. The work was done in 1330.

In the interior of the baptismal church are 13th century mosaics. *Donatello's "Magdalene"* in wood was rescued from the oily mud during the flood and restored to its former beauty (it is now in the Museo dell' Opera del Duomo No. 9, Piazza del Duomo, east end of the cathedral). His tomb for the anti-Pope, John XXII, whose name was cleared and vested with new honours by Roncalli, the modern Pope John XXIII, is to the right of the apse.

Giotto's Campanile next to the Cathedral, begun in 1334 and completed by *Andrea Pisano* between 1343 and finally Fr. Talenti, 1359, is the finest in Italy. The architecture with reliefs based on designs by *Giotto,* by *Pisano* and *Luca della Robbia* fuses Gothic and Classical into a surprisingly harmonious whole. You may ascend the 414 steps to the top of the tower. The view from the top is certainly worth it.

The Campanile of the Duomo in Florence. Sadly, Giotto di Bondone who designed this magnificent tower and who supervised the early stages of construction did not live to see it completed.

(Photo by Courtesy of EPT Firenze)

The Baptistery of the Cathedral. The cluster of people at the doors nearest to the Cathedral itself marks the doors decorated with gilded reliefs by Ghiberti. "These are the gates of Paradise" said the great Michelangelo when he first saw them.

(Photo by Courtesy of EPT Frenze)

A detail from the 'Doors of Paradise' by Ghiberti, at the main portal of the Cathedral Baptistery. The head and shoulders leaning out of the circular opening on the right, are said to be of Ghiberti himself. In the great flood of 1966 the waters beat at these priceless doors up to a height of 14 feet. One wonders if they should not be covered in gold once again.

127

Giotto di Bondone, designer of the great Campanile in Florence, captured in stone outside the Uffizzi Gallery, a mecca for students of art from the four corners of the world.

The façade of *Santa Maria del Fiore* (*Duomo*) was not enhanced by 19th century alterations. It is surmounted, however, by a miracle: a dome of 132 ft diameter consisting of two shells, grafted on to two drums linked together. It is the work of *Brunelleschi*, who had spent many years studying the Pantheon in Rome. It was built between 1420 and 1434. The cracks are blamed on the traffic which has not yet been banned from the city centre.

Brunelleschi built the dome without scaffolding a generation before the dome of *St. Peter's* (by *Michelangelo*) which copied its design, though *St. Peter's* is smaller. After losing the commission for the doors of the *Baptistery*, (to *Ghiberti*), Brunelleschi left his native city in disgust to learn a craft at which no one, least of all *Ghiberti*, could surpass him. When he returned to Florence he went to the Signoria and asked for the commission to erect the dome. Even in his lifetime, it was regarded, justifiably, as one of the new wonders of the world. Its diameter is still the greatest in the world.

The Florentines erected a monument in his honour as a token their gratitude. In a niche in the wall on the right as you enter the Cathedral sits Brunelleschi in stone, above his tomb, looking alert and critical just as if he were still supervising the stonemasons. The next niche along contains a bust of Giotto with a eulogistic Latin inscription beneath it.

The vast echoing interior of the cathedral may seem cold at first. Find a moment when Michelangelo's uncompleted *Pietà* in the left apse (first chapel, but temporarily in the centre of the church during restoration work) is not surrounded by crowds. This and his *Pietà Rondanini* (in the Castello Sforzesco in Milan) are probably his most moving pieces of sculpture, studies of pain and suffering fixed in stone. The head of Nicodemus is said (by Vasari) to be the sculptor's self-portrait.

The huge clock over the door, restored in 1973 uses the '*hora italica*' method of counting time which was current in Italy until the 18th century. The last hour of the day (XXIlll) ends at sunset, or Ave Maria. It is decorated by Paolo Uccello, who also did the frescoed memorial to the English mercenary (*condottiere*) Sir John Hawkwood in the North Aisle.

The Medici Palace

Take the *Via de'Martelli* leading into the *Via Cavour* from *Piazza del Duomo;* about 300m./270 yards along on the left, is the oldest Renaissance palace in Florence: *Palazzo Medici-Riccardi*. This building witnessed the great era of the Medicis and its owners provided hospitality for the most illustrious artists and humanists of their day; much of the thought and discussion that brought forth the spirit which was to transform the Western world was generated beneath its roof. Today the rooms in which *Lorenzo il Magnifico* grew up and where his humanist friends came and went, are the offices of the prefecture. Its treasures were either plundered, (Napoleon was the last to do so), or put into museums; the first free-standing statue since Classical times, *Donatello's San Giovanni* is now in the *Bargello*. The *Medici Museum* on the ground floor is chiefly of interest to scholars. But a visit to the *Medici family chapel* on the first floor, with its gloriously colourful frescoes by *Benozzo Gozzoli*, the pupil of *Fra Angelico* is essential: the frescoes, which have never been restored, tell the story of the journey of the Three Wise Men to Bethlehem. The kings and their entourage are journeying through the Tuscan countryside; their faces are those of the princes, scholars and artists of the period. Paleologos, the Emperor of Constantinople, rides with Lorenzo and his sisters; the humanists stride through this scene of flowers and animals to the Madonna and her child. The central section, the *Madonna*, is a contemporary copy of a *Filippo Lippi*. The original hangs in Berlin.

There are a number of *Lippi's Madonnas* in Florence; their features are remarkably similar for the following reason: *Filippo Lippi* was an orphan who had been put into the Carmelite monastery by a strict aunt, though he felt more drawn to painting than to the priesthood. One day he went before the abbot to ask for freedom for himself and the young nun whom the Carmelites had fetched from a nearby convent to sit as his model. They both moved to Prato nearby and *Filippo* continued to paint Madonnas, all with the features of his beloved wife. *Filippo's* son, *Filippino*, returned in later years to the Carmelite monastery and completed *Masaccio's* work in the Basilica del Carmine. (See page 133).

Also on the first floor is the brilliant baroque *Sala* frescoed by *Luca Giordano*, a striking example of the Florentine sumptuous grandiloquence depicting the Apotheosis of the second Medici dynasty.

San Marco
At the North end of the *Via Cavour* on the *Piazza San Marco* stands the monastery of the same name, with frescoes by *Beato Angelico* in the Great Refectory. These are some of the finest and most characteristic evocations of the Tuscan landscape and buildings, softly poetic and colourful. Had *Fra Angelico*

guessed that his painting would draw crowds of people into the cells centuries after his death, he would probably have laid down his brushes. Unlike his contemporaries, he did not paint for the world at large: whereas they portrayed the scriptures in such a way that Florence and its citizens could recognise themselves in the paintings, *Fra Angelico's* painting was symbolic and doctrinal. One of his frescoes, *The Scourging of Christ,* is particularly powerful. Poised around the head of Christ are the hand of one of his tormentors, the instruments of torture and the head of a bold and brutal soldier puckering his mouth to spit into the defenceless face before him.

The cells of *Cosimo il Vecchio* (the Elder) (Rooms 38,39), who came here in search of a retreat, and the rooms occupied by *Savonarola* (Rooms 12-14), who was dragged on his funeral pyre from *San Marco* to the *Piazza della Signoria,* complete the two wings of the monastery.

Between Cells 42 and 43, a corridor leads into the large *library* (Europe's oldest public library), designed by *Michelozzo,* to which Cosimo The Elder bequeathed his writings.

In the small refectory as you go down the stairs to the ground floor will be found *Ghirlandaio's The Last Supper.*

Galleria dell'Accademia
Situated one hundred metres south of the Piazza San Marco along the Via Ricasoli, this gallery houses important examples of Florentine painting between the thirteenth century and the Rennaissance. It also contains several of Michelangelo's most famous works including the original statue of *David.*

Piazza Santissima Annunziata
A few steps along the *Via Battisti* from the *Piazza San Marco* will take you to the *Piazza Santissima Annunziata,* perhaps the most harmonious square in Florence and dominated by the cupola of the *Duomo.*

Florentine brides carry their bouquets of orange blossom into the church of *Santissima Annunziata.* On summer evenings, the chapel of the miraculous *Madonna of the Annunciation,* (W. end of the church) a treasure trove of baroque splendours and votive offerings, smells of the sweet perfume of orange groves. There is a story behind this beautifully austere *trecento* (14th century) Madonna with her head held forward expect- antly. It is said that the unknown artist, having finished the angel and the figure of the Virgin, fainted as he started to paint the face. When he revived, an angel had completed the painting.

Ospedale degli Innocenti
To the left of the entrance to S.S. Annunziata, *Brunelleschi* erected his first pure Renaissance building in 1420, the earliest orphanage in Europe. Each arcade - the pillars are Greek in style, the width of the arches is Roman - has on the central section a bluish-white roundel of babes in swaddling clothes by *Andrea della Robbia* in glazed *terracotta*. From a distance they look like ornaments; from close up, like the real-life foundlings, whom sympathetic hands lifted from the steps of the church in days gone by and passed through a revolving window into the orphanage. The horseman in the centre of the square, Ferdinand I de' Medici, is trying hard to look warlike. But there are always pigeons sitting on his head, hand and sword, and the effect is warm and friendly as befits this centre of charity and good works.

A few steps further on is the *Museum of Archaeology (Piazza SS. Annunziata No. 9),* of considerable interest to the layman.

From the Piazza San Firenze to the Church of Santa Croce
The *Bargello* (off *Piazza San Firenze*) looks like a mediaeval castle and houses the most important collection of Renaissance sculpture in Florence. The building was started in 1255 and served as a criminal court and prison during the Republic. There are works by Michelangelo including his famous *Drunken Bacchus,* an early work which dates from the same period as his *Pietà* in St. Peter's. *Giambologna's Mercury, Donatello's David* (it is interesting to compare this with the same subject by *Michelangelo*) and another *David* by *Verrocchio*; works by *Desiderio da Settignano, Brunelleschi, Ghiberti.* A special visit to the *Della Robbia* room is recommended where the highly coloured *terra cotta* glaze work by this family (father, Luca, nephew Andrea and his son, Giovanni) is on show. So successful was the glazing process discovered by Luca, that the family founded a business which made works only of this kind. Though their output became increasingly stylised and sentimental, much of their work remains a delight to the eye.

Benedictine Badia Church
The church was built in the 10th century and rebuilt in the 17th century. In addition to the *Mino da Fiesole* tombstones, the *Badia Church* opposite the *Bargello* has one of the finest and best preserved paintings by *Filippino Lippi* of the *madonna* appearing to Saint Bernard in a romantic rocky landscape.

From the church there are cloisters leading to the *Via Dante Alighieri,* where Dante's birthplace has been reconstructed.

Passing some impressive palaces, we move east along the *Via Ghibellina* to the *Casa Buonarroti,* which *Michelangelo* bought for a nephew. In addition to the original drawings by Michelangelo, it contains his earliest work, completed when he was 17, the *Madonna of the Stairs.* The house also contains the vivid frieze, *The Battle of the Centaurs,* and the only surviving sketch for a sculpture by *Michelangelo.*

Santa Croce
Opposite the Casa Buonarroti is the *Via delle Pinzochere,* so-called after the widows and maidens who assumed the grey gowns of the Franciscan tertiaries and lived in this area in the 13th and 14th century. If *Boccaccio* is to be believed the reputation they had was hardly one for religious devotion however, and to this day the area has a slightly equivocal ambience. At the end of the street is the *Basilica di Santa Croce,* the largest *Franciscan* church in Italy. After the 1966 floods the monks were to be seen rowing through the huge Gothic interior searching for their lost treasures in the mud. Thick muddy oil had to be cleared from the tombs of the great: *Dante* and *Michelangelo, Machiavelli* and *Galileo,* the dramatist *Alfieri,* and the humanist *Leonardo Bruni, Rossini* and *Ugo Foscolo,* to name but a few. (The tomb of *Alfieri* is by the great 18th century sculptor *Antonio Canova*).

All that survived of the great *Cimabue Crucifixion* were the pieces that escaped the flood water and a few coloured fragments. It was carried through the devastated streets of Florence, and people knelt before it on the pavements, bareheaded and with tears in their eyes.

The sandstone frieze of the *Annunziata* in the south aisle, is one of *Donatello's* finest works. There is also his celebrated Crucifix in wood in the Bardi chapel. There are works by *Giotto* and his shop (the altarpiece of the Baroncelli chapel), frescoes by *Agnolo Gaddi* (*The Legend and the Finding of the True Cross* cycle), *Bernardo Daddi* and others.

Some of the most pleasing works in *Santa Croce* are the *chapels* next to the sanctuary some of which were painted by Giotto and his pupils. In the *Peruzzi* and *Bardi chapels* to the left of the sacristy, are frescoes from *Giotto's* most mature period: scenes from the life of John the Baptist, John the Apostle and from the life of Saint Francis.

In the *Museo dell'Opera di S. Croce* will be found *Cimabue's* great *Crucifix* and fragments of *Orcagna's Triumph of Death.* The Cimabue has been restored as much as possible after being virtually destroyed in the 1966 flood.

The Porta San Frediano. In Oltrarno (South Bank) between the Ponte A. Vespucci and Ponte Alle Carraia.

Nearby is *Brunelleschi's* magnificent Pazzi chapel.

Vasari, painter, court architect and the editor of the first art history, did not admire mediaeval art; unfortunately, he succeeded in destroying what he saw as "the bunglings of an earlier age" in *Santa Croce.* He painted over whole walls of Gothic frescoes or concealed them behind Renaissance altars. It is quite a shock to read his confession that only lack of funds prevented him from painting over the *Capella dei Bardi __ Giotto's* frescoes — or "improving" on them in the style of the times.

Santa Croce can be spoiled by noisy tourists, some of whom only use the church as a short-cut to the Leather School housed in the old cells of the cloisters. Nevertheless, it is fascinating to watch apprentices working at all conceivable forms of leather-ware in the tradition of the great Florentine craftsmen. Their wares can be found all over the city, for example in the *Loggia* of the *Uffizi* and in *S. Lorenzo.*

Oltrarno ('Beyond the Arno'), Santo Spirito and Santa Maria del Carmine

Cross the river by the *Ponte Santa Trinita* and you will be in *Oltrarno.* On the way to *Santa Maria del Carmine* time may interestingly be spent in the *Via Maggio,* formerly the finest street in the city; the palaces of Florence's aristocratic families lined the street from the 14th to the 17th century and it is now the home of the antique dealers and furniture makers who have ancient and famous traditions. They will not object to being watched at their craft.

At the end of the *Via Maggio* is the *Piazza San Felice:* from here turn right into the *Via Mazzetta* which leads to the *Piazza Santo Spirito.* The church of the same name conceals behind a plain, understated façade, one of the purest Renaissance creations planned by *Brunelleschi* between 1428 and 1434.

The alterpiece of the Nerli Family contains a fine *Madonna and Child* by Filippino Lippi which also features members of the Nerli family. The church contains a large number of pictures and sculptures from various periods. The former Refectory of *Santo Spirito* now the *Fondazione Salvatore Romano* contains a *Crucifixion* and *Last Supper* by followers of Andrea Orcagna. (*Entrance to the left of the church*).

The Convent Church of Santa Maria del Carmine is in San Frediano, the poor quarter of Florence, and a place of pilgrimage for painters. Its finest treasure, the *Brancacci Chapel* with *Masaccio's* frescoes, was miraculously saved in the

18th century when almost the whole church was destroyed by fire. *Masaccio's* real name was Tommaso Guidi, though he has gone down in history under his nickname - Masaccio, the clumsy one. He was never to know of the acclaim his frescoes were to receive from the greatest painters of the day and all later generations of artists. *Raphael* was to copy the Peter cycle seven times. Of the many anecdotes about the frescoes, the oddest is told by *Benvenuto Cellini* in his autobiography. He relates how *Pietro Torrigiani* became involved in a very heated exchange with *Michelangelo* as they looked at the frescoes, an exchange which finally ended in a fist fight. Michelangelo came out of it with a broken nose and Torrigiani was banned from Florence. Exact attribution of some of the frescoes on which Masaccio collaborated remains doubtful, but it is generally agreed that he did the marvellous *Expulsion from the Garden of Eden, The Tribute Money*, and began *The Raising of the Prince of Antioch's Son*, and did part of the *Life of St. Peter. Masolino* worked on the frescoes, and, much later *Filippino Lippi.*

Botticelli, Leonardo da Vinci, and many other great painters have been influenced by the revolutionary new power of expression in Masaccio's work and his advance in the technique of perspective. He is regarded as one of the founders of modern painting.

The Dominican Church of Santa Maria Novella
Only a short walk southwards from the impressive, if soulless, main railway station is one of the finer churches in the city, that of the Dominicans' *Basilica di Santa Maria Novella;* this will introduce you to the characteristic two-toned mellow green and white marble façades of Florentine churches; others are a black and white. Part of this façade was the work of *Leon Battista Alberti* — one of the greatest architects of the Renaissance. Inside the church may be seen major works by *Orcagna,* and his brother *Nardo di Cione* (in the *Cappella Maggiore* and *Strozzi* chapels) and *Masaccio's The Trinity with Two Donors* (beyond 2nd altar, North Aisle).

At the end of the ·south aisle on the right are dramatic frescoes by *Filippino Lippi* which show a monster killing the son of a heathen king with its stench, and in the Sanctuary behind the main altar is one of *Ghirlandaio's* most famous works, the cycle of frescoes on the life of Mary.

In the chapel immediately to the left (Capella Gondi) is the only surviving sculpture (1568) in wood by *Brunelleschi. Vasari,* whose *Lives of the Artists* contained much contemporary information that has proved invaluable to art historians,

136

explains that the crucifix was carved to prove to *Donatello* that it was possible to represent the Saviour in a dignified manner. That was after his acid comment on Donatello's crucifix that hangs in S. Croce, which he said was 'a mere peasant on a cross'.

In the *Strozzi Chapel* in the left transept is one of the earliest and most impressive representations of the next world in Tuscan art. *Nardo di Cione's* portrayal of *Paradise, Inferno* and *The Last Judgement* are clearly inspired by Dante's *Divine Comedy.* The faces of the chosen are bathed in the pinkish-gold and blue glow of Heaven; *Dante* is represented among the blessed in the *Last Judgement.* Nardo was the brother of the more famous *Andrea di Cione* known as *Orcagna,* who did the altarpiece of this chapel.

Come out of *Santa Maria Novella* and turn right along its façade to the door of the cloisters inside which are some of *Paolo Uccello's* marvellous greenish blue frescoes of *The Flood.* These are located in the refectory. The others are still being restored after the damage sustained in the 1966 flood. In the former Chapter House of the cloisters the Spanish Chapel's interesting 14th century frescoes tell the story of the Dominican order, the *"Domini canes:"* on one of the paintings, the black and white "Dogs of the Lord" put their captors to flight.

San Lorenzo and the Medici tombs

At least one whole morning is needed to visit *Piazza San Lorenzo* (a five minute walk from the main railway station and from the *Piazza del Duomo*). Apart from the picturesque market crammed with leather goods, chunky white knitwear, clothes and tempting bric-a-brac, and colourful alabaster eggs from Volterra, there is the church of *San Lorenzo,* (works by *Donatello* and *Desiderio da Settignano*), and nearby the *Prince's Chapel, (Capella dei Principi),* (entrance from Piazza Madonna degli Aldobrandini at rear of church) and *Michelangelo's* new sacristy (*Sagrestia Nuova*) also known as the Medici chapel. It is reached by a corridor from the *Capella dei Principi.* Here are Michelangelo's tombstones for Lorenzo II, the grandson of Lorenzo the Magnificent, and his nephew, Giuliano, Duke of Nemours.

These are the most mature of Michelangelo's Florentine sculptures. Allegories of *Day* and *Night* recline at the foot of the allegorical portrait of Duke Giuliano. On the sarcophagus of figures of *Dawn and Dusk* (this is to the left of the entrance) Michelangelo created the most moving of all these figures, *Night,* after the fall of Florence to the forces of the Emperor led by the Prince of Orange in 1530. He summarised the anguish he felt at the time in the following lines:

> *"I long to sleep, but more, to be of stone*
> *Amidst such infamy and shame."*

So much of what Michelangelo held dear seemed to be at risk. During the siege he had not only attended to the fortifications, but also, in a pathetic gesture, hung the walls of *S. Miniato* with mattresses to try and protect its beautiful belfry from the attackers' gunfire.

A few years ago huge drawings were found on the walls of the rooms in the cellar beneath the New Sacristy; these were thought at first to be synopia (the rough drawings for a fresco). But art historians have established that they are drawings by Michelangelo and his pupils, who rested here during their work on the sacristy. If the cellars are still not officially open to the public, you should persuade one of the custodians to take you round.

To the left of the bare façade of *San Lorenzo,* (access also from the left aisle of the church) are the cloisters, a harmonious and elegant building in the manner of *Brunelleschi*. From the loggia there is a fine view of the Cathedral. From here you have access up some steps to the *Biblioteca Laurenziana. Michelangelo* was commissioned by the Medici Pope Clement VII and started building in 1523. His bold design for the staircase, which was completed by *Ammannati*, was far ahead of its time, the High Renaissance, and already heralds the Baroque.

The contents of the library are as fine as the building itself. Started by Cosimo the Elder and extended by Lorenzo the Magnificent, who gave it its name, the Medici family library contains one of the most important collections of hand-written manuscripts in the world. They include early Mss. of Virgil, Petrarch's copy of Horace and illuminated books. Displayed in the main hall are some of the 180 Dante manuscripts and the records of the final session of the Council of Florence in 1439. The Council met to discuss the reunification of the Orthodox and Catholic Churches and was originally to be held in Ferrara; but it was moved to Florence because of an outbreak of the plague and brought in its train the most learned representatives of Greek scholarship: they were members of the temporal and spiritual entourage which accompanied the Emperor of Byzantium, John VIII Palaeologus, and the Patriarch. (They feature in *Benozzo Gozzoli's* painting in the *Palazzo Medici-Riccardi,* see p. 104).

A Tour of the Florentine Villas

Boccaccio's *Decameron* reads thus at the start of the third day:

> *"The sight of this beautifully tended garden, the trees, the fountains and the little streams, pleased the ladies and the three young men so much that they agreed that if they could create a paradise on earth, they could think of no more beautiful form than this garden. They could not conceive of anything of beauty that was lacking."*

The Florentines needed respite from their busy lives and so they built their summer homes outside in the hills amidst vines, figs and olives. The spirit of that magnificent era has remained more alive in these villas than in the venerable palaces on the Arno.

'Villa', in the Italian sense, has little in common with our notion of middle class suburban splendour or the holiday homes of the rich on the coast. The Florentine villas were more like stately homes. With their gardens and parks, and often with farms and fields also, (the word 'villa' covers all of this), they bring to mind the verses of Horace: moderation, grace, and idyllic pastoral refinements. Unhappily some of the Florentine villas have suffered the dilapidation of age and occasionally the depredation of 19th century bad taste. But many still stand and may be visited.

The house associated with Boccaccio's *Decameron* is one. The fountains still play in the garden of the *Villa Palmieri* below Fiesole as in the days when a group of young aristocrats in retreat from the plague recounted their tales. The Medici villas remain monuments to munificence and good taste and are mostly state monuments that can be visited. And in addition, each spring the owners of some of the most beautiful villas open their gates to the public. A Villa Tour by coach may be joined to take advantage of this. (see p.21)

One of the finest villas is *Villa La Petraia* with its magnificent garden containing Giambologna's famous fountain of *Venus Wringing out her Hair*. Previous owners included Brunelleschi and the Strozzi family. Later it passed to King Victor Emmanuel II of Savoy who entertained his beautiful Florentine, the delightful Contessa Mirafiori there. Other Medici villas worth visiting are *Careggi* (partly designed by *Giuliano da Sangallo*), *Poggio a Caiano* with works by *Allori, Andrea del Sarto* and a particularly interesting set of frescoes by the Mannerist *Iacopo Pontormo;* and *Artimino* with its fine views of the Tuscan landscape.

The most famous 'Italian garden' in Florence, (the Baroque garden became known all over Europe under this name), is at *Villa La Pietra:* it was laid out under the patronage of Arthur Acton, whose descendant, the distinguished historian and aesthete Sir Harold Acton, lives there today.

Those who are interested in art history will be intrigued by Bernard Berenson's *Villa i Tatti,* the great collector's home near Settignano, now owned by Harvard University. There is a substantial library.

Agriturist (Via del Proconsolo 10, Firenze. Tel: 055/28 78 38) organise coach excursions to the most beautiful villas and gardens outside Florence.

Football Florentine Style

The *Calcio* ("football"), is an officially permitted and financed opportunity for the Florentines to give full rein to their natural contentiousness. The event takes place on *May 1st, June 24th,* and in *mid-August.* The Florentines claim to have invented football and that their teams demonstrated the game to the English colony in Livorno in the 17th century: the game gained international popularity only much later. But as early as the Middle Ages, the citizens were running after a ball. Then as now, it was not a spectacle for the nervous. The rules seemed to be elastic, to say the least, and opportunities for families to settle personal scores were not to be missed.

The tradition of *Calcio* was not abandoned even in the direst emergency, when Florence was under siege by the Emperor Charles V's troops in 1530. The city was starving and on the brink of despair. The cannon balls whistled around the ancient towers. To raise citizens' morale, the Signoria decided to hold a football match. They played the most solemn match in their history on *Piazza Santa Croce* which was still being talked about long after the city was conquered and freedom extinguished. The modern games are in commemoration of this famous match; four teams from the city's four historic districts take part (Santa Croce, Santo Spirito, San Giovanni and Santa Maria Novella). You should watch the final match, which is the most exciting, as a white ox is the prize for the winner. Teams are selected from former prize-fighters and wrestlers, and the whole affair is preceded by a procession through the streets with drums and pipes. Each time a goal is scored the occasion is marked by a cannon-shot.

Football which, it is claimed, was first played in Tuscany. Rivalry between teams from the four quarters of Siena is intense and the game ferocious. (Photo by Courtesy of EPT Firenze)

The Scoppio del Carro

The *Scoppio del Carro* on Easter Sunday is a church festival, an amalgam of the sacred and the worldly, of High Mass and fireworks. The origin of the custom is as follows: A Florentine crusader brought a splinter of the Cross back from the Holy Land. This precious relic is kept in the main altar of the Cathedral. On Easter Sunday, a spark is symbolically struck from it; the spark is carried by a "dove" to *"bel San Giovanni"*, the Baptistery. The *Carro*, or cart, however, stands between the Cathedral and the Baptistery and is the focus of the popular festival.

All through Easter Saturday, people work feverishly to erect the stands in front of the *Duomo*, *Giotto's Campanile* and the *Loggia del Bigallo.* The next morning, all Florence gathers in the square. A pair of white oxen pull the *"Carro"* — a high wooden fabrication covered in flowers and pictures with fireworks stuck all over it — into the square between the Campanile and the Baptistery. Across the silent square, the bell rings for High Mass which the Archbishop celebrates in the Cathedral.

At the moment when the "Gloria" resounds from the altar, there is a flash from the door (a mechanical substitute for the dove), which strikes the top of the *"Carro"* and sets it alight. As it disappears in clouds of smoke, clattering, rattling and banging, all the bells in the city slowly start to ring. Suddenly you realise what has been missing for the previous two days: the sound of church bells. From the eve of Good Friday onwards, the bells have been silent to commemorate the agony of Golgotha. It is said that "The bells have gone to Rome"; now they have come back to rejoice for the resurrection of Christ. The tradition is that if the *Carro* goes with a tremendous bang, it will be a good year with fruit, grain and olives in plenty.

As the smoke from the explosion disperses, the pair of oxen disappear down the street, and the crowds go home, your eye wanders to the monumental creation in green and white marble, *Santa Maria del Fiore.* Above the portal is a medallion with a lamb. The symbol of Christ perhaps? Not at all. The symbol of the Guild of Wool who appointed Giotto to restart work on the Cathedral in 1334. At that time the Wool Guild was the most powerful and the richest of the Florentine Guilds and they wanted everyone, including God, to see it; and so their instructions were to build the largest and most magnificent church that man had ever seen, to honour God, the Madonna — and the Guild of Wool.

Faces, Faces. A study at a mediaeval pageant in Florence. (Photo by Courtesy of EPT Firenze)

Fiesole

Motorists will find the road to Fiesole well sign-posted from *Piazza della Libertà*, which is reached via the *Via Cavour* from the *Duomo*. Those without a car can take the bus No. 7 from the *Piazza San Marco*.

The main square of Fiesole presents a charming spectacle in Summer with the village's inhabitants dotted around it selling straw hats, little baskets, slippers and a variety of more or less attractive souvenirs which in many cases they have spent the winter making.

In winter Fiesole is the haven of peace of which tourists dream. Souvenir sellers, tour guides and waiters rest after the toils of the summer; only the basket weavers know no rest. They must prepare for the next campaign.

At any time of year, other than the high season, it is rewarding to walk along the narrow roads that run between Fiesole and neighbouring villages, past the silent gardens of handsome villas, and let your imagination fill them with people from a golden age reading the verses that were written here among the laurel hedges and marble deities. The first of the great *quattrocento* villas, the *Villa Medici*, stands on this hill; it was built by *Michelozzo* for *Cosimo the Elder*. The villa became one of the favourite meeting places of the Platonic Academy founded by his grandson, *Lorenzo*.

The inhabitants of the ancient *Faesulae*, the rich Etruscan fortification built in the 7th century *B.C.*, probably looked down into the Arno valley with quite different feelings. Swamps, malaria and enemies lurked below and it was prudent to take shelter behind the Cyclopean walls on the hill. But on the day the Romans set up their camp by the river, even the stoutest walls could not hold out much longer. As everywhere else in Ancient Etruria, the Etruscan craftsmen had to make way for the young barbarians from Rome. Temples to new Gods rose up next to their shrines; a flourishing city grew at the foot of the hill spreading out from the fortress which guarded the ford. A thousand years later, the fully grown offspring of Fiesole had not forgotten its displeasure at its little parent on the hill. One day in 1125 the Florentines marched solemnly up to their neighbours in Fiesole, ostensibly to celebrate their Saint's Day, that of Saint Romulus. But when they reached Fiesole they turned on the people and razed the village to the ground, plundering the marble from the old pagan temples to build the church of San Miniato. Since then Fiesole has been under the hegemony of her powerful and rich neighbour.

While in Fiesole visit the Romanesque cathedral and the Roman amphitheatre (open in the summer 9 a.m.—12.00, 15.00—20.00). Then walk up the hill on the west of the square to the tiny Franciscan monastery at the top, visiting the attractive *Basilica of S. Alessandro* on the way.

The Franciscan Monastery

Few places in Italy give such a feeling of mystical tranquillity as this little monastery. Everything is small-scale. The cloisters are charmingly miniature, and there is an empty wing of tiny cells with narrow windows. Missals lie open on bare wooden desks. But the marvellous views of the peaceful cloisters on one side and the Settignano hills shimmering in a heat haze on the other, must have been some consolation for the solitary life. Here, as in the Roman theatre, the restorers have tried a little too hard. The spirit of the former occupants has been driven out by over-zealous attention to historical detail.

A flight of steps leads down between the walls to the monastery's *Oriental Museum* on the ground floor. Twenty years ago, the donor and guardian of these treasures, a soft-spoken old monk, used to tell the story of each piece. He lived as a young missionary in China during the wars, forgot his Franciscan vows of tolerance in those desperate times, climbed on to a horse and saved a province. Since he had no need for worldly possessions, he sent all the gifts he had received in gratitude back to the monastery in Fiesole.

A good place to eat in Fiesole is the little Tavola Calda *'da Il Lordo'* just off the main square, where you can sample the excellent *'fettunta'* ot garlic bread which they offer.

San Domenico di Fiesole and the Badia

If you descend from Fiesole, preferably on foot on the Via Vecchia Fiesolana, you can turn off right at San Domenico for the *Badia Fiesolana*, formerly the cathedral for the town, now the home of the European University. It remained the cathedral till 1018, and the interior shows one of the finest examples of Florentine 15th century architecture in the style of Brunelleschi. The church in San Domenico is also worth visiting.

The Carthusian Monastery at Galluzzo

If you take the motorway from the Florence South junction, you will see the Carthusian monastery of Galluzzo (*Certosa del Galluzzo*) quite clearly on a hill in the distance: the last Carthusian monks left in 1957, partly, it must be said, victims of tourism. Of the 245 monasteries owned by the Carthusian Order in its heyday, only a few remain: there are four in Italy, including the second oldest (after the Grande Chartreuse near Grenoble), the monastery of Sierra San Bruno in Calabria, dedicated to himself by the founder of the order.

Nowadays a few energetic Cistercian priests live within the beautifully restored walls at Galluzzo, showing the tourists round and dispensing their Benedictine (not Chartreuse). You can also buy their honey and lavender.

The founder of the monastery was Nicola Acciaiuoli, warrior and friend of Boccaccio, who had the Certosa built around the middle of the 14th century as a 'balm to his soul and for the forgiveness of his sins'. In the cloisters of the church there are 62 terracotta heads by *Andrea della Robbia* and paintings by *Lucas Cranach* and *Bronzino*.

The monks' quarters can also be visited, consisting of a sleeping cell, a study and a little garden with a fountain. In the field between the cloisters are rows of anonymous crosses: the Carthusians buried their dead brothers without names, explaining that 'God will know them anyhow'.

PART FOUR

The Provinces of Tuscany

Arrezo and Province

Arrezo

Arezzo is 67km (42 miles) and roughly half an hour on the *Autostrada del Sole* from Florence. Information on the town is available from the *Ente Provinciale per il Turismo, Piazza Risorgimento,* close to the station.

Arretium was one of the most flourishing city states of the Etruscan period. The Roman conquerors filled the town with temples and buildings, of which only the ruins of the amphitheatre have survived, together with the famous *"Aretini vases"* or *"corallini"*, which are decorated with relief work made to look like chased metal. These, plus all the Etruscan and prehistoric finds from the area, can be seen in the *Mecenate Museum of Archaeology, Via Margaritone 10.* Arezzo's most famous sons are Maecenas, friend of the Emperor Augustus and patron of poets and artists; Petrarch, who left as a child with his father for exile in Avignon; Guido Monaco, the inventor of the modern system of musical notation; Vasari, the architect, painter and biographer of artists; Pietro Aretino, the most mordant writer of the Renaissance period, and the 17th century poet, Frencesco Redi. From the villages of Arezzo Province came Michelangelo, Piero della Francesca, Luca Signorelli and Sansovino, the architect.

In addition, Arezzo claims to have the best cuisine in Tuscany! You should try it out either in the modern *"Spiedo D'Oro, Via Crispi 11,* or in the typical *"Buca di San Francesco"*, *Via San Francesco 1* — or in the dull modern surroundings of the *"Hotel Restaurant Cecco", Corso Italia 215,* which has excellent cuisine. In the surrounding district : the *"Antica Trattoria al Principe* in *Giovi,* 8km (5 miles) from Arezzo on Road 71 towards *Cesena,* and the *"Torrini"* at *Madonna del Torrini* 8km (5 miles) from Arezzo on Road 73 towards *Sansepolcro.*

As for shopping in Arezzo, gold plate work, costume jewellery , handicrafts in metal, wood or straw are available. Wine and oil are excellent here.

Exploring Arezzo

Arezzo suffered badly in the last war. The *'centro storico'* remained intact however, or has been well restored, so that it retains its attractive medieval appearance, and can be explored on foot in a few hours.

One of the greatest miracles of European painting, *Piero della Francesca's "Story of the True Cross* is to be found in the chancel of the Gothic church of *San Francesco,* off the *Via Guido Monaco.* The painting which was done gradually between 1452 and 1466, tells the story of the True Cross as it is set out in the *Legend Aurea* by *Iacopo da Voragine.* On the two side panels are vividly dramatic battle scenes. The lunettes above them relate the dramatic sequences of the legend. The story runs from left to right. The archangel Michael instructs Seth, Adam's son, to lay a twig from the tree of knowledge in the mouth of his dead father (sadly this section is almost ruined). The twig grew into a tree from which the Saviour's cross was eventually to be cut. On the orders of Solomon, the tree was felled and used to build a bridge over which the Queen of Sheba journeyed to Jerusalem. The true destiny of the wood in the bridge is revealed to her in a vision, whereupon Solomon has the wood buried in a swamp. The face of the servant who is carrying the wood away looks like the face of the Saviour. Piero does not recount how the Jews found the wood again to build the cross. He does tell however, that, following the battle between Constantine and Maxentius at the Milvian bridge which the Emperor had foreseen in a vision (*"in hoc signo vinces"* said the angel) Constantine sent his mother, Helena, to find the true cross. She found it, together with the crosses for the thieves, in Jerusalem.

This brief outline of the story says nothing of the classical greatness which emanates from these dramatic paintings. The strong colours have a glint of silver about them which make them truly Tuscan.

Piero della Francesca was little understood by his contemporaries and given scarcely any commissions. He died unknown and almost blind: it was not until this century that his genius was widely recognised. Other works by him may be seen in the *chancel chapel* in *San Francesco,* where he painted two saints and an angel's head; and at the end of the left aisle of the cathedral (*Duomo*) where there is a *Mary Magdalene.*

S. Maria delle Pieve

To the right of San Francesco the *Via Cavour* leads past 14th and 15th century palaces to the architectural heart of the town. Halfway along on the right, you reach the *S. Maria della Pieve,* one of Tuscany's most beautiful Romanesque buildings with its lively façade beneath the forty arched windows of the *Campanile.* The most splendid work in the triple - naved interior is a *polyptych* by *Pietro Lorenzetti.*

Giostra del Saracino

To the right of the church the elegant fan-shaped Piazza Grande opens out, bordered by the Palazzo della Fraternita dei Laici (the lay brothers) and Vasari's Palazzo delle Logge. On first Sunday of September, the Giostra del Saracino, an historic tournament, is held on the steep square. Each of the four districts of the town provides two knights on horseback, who use their fixed lances to try and hit the Saracen's shield, the 'Saracen' being a revolving wooden doll. If they are slow moving out of the way after impact, they may be shot from their saddles by the balls which the blackamoor swings on an iron chain in his other hand.

In the nearby *Via del Orte 28* stood the birthplace of Petrarch (1304). The library here is well worth a visit.

The Renaissance *Fortezza* is on the steep *Via del Pileati,* and there is an excellent view of the surrounding countryside from it to *Pratomagno* and the *Apennines.* To the left is the huge Gothic *cathedral.* It contains many interesting frescoes, vivid tales of knightly deeds on the relief tableaux below the sarcophagus of *Bishop Guido Tarlati* (said to have been designed by *Giotto*); and in the left aisle, next to it — before the transept— the powerful gaze of *Piero della Francesca's* Mary Magdalene. Next to the chancel are some rather beautiful works by *Andrea della Robbia* in the *Chapel of Our Lady of Comfort.*

From the *Palazzo Comunale* opposite the *Duomo* go along the *Via Ricasoli* and turn right into the *Via di Sasso Verde,* which leads to the Romanesque church of *San Domenico.* This church contains important frescoes, in particular, *Spinello Aretino's "Stories of Saint Philip and Saint Jacob".* The *"Crucifixion"* on the high altar is an early work attributed to *Cimabue* and is one of the first portrayals of Christ in which the abstraction and rigidity of the Byzantine models is replaced by a more human approach. Since the severe damage in the Florentine flood disaster of 1966 to Cimabue's huge masterpiece in Santa Croce, the *Crucifixion* in Arezzo has become a place of pilgrimage for Cimabue scholars.

From the *Via San Domenico* opposite the church, turn left into the *Via XX Settembre*. *Giorgio Vasari* lived at Number 55 from 1540 till 1548: he decorated the house himself with frescoes in the Tuscan Mannerist style. There is an interesting museum and archives on Vasari, the painter, architect and the first biographer of his fellow artists.

Cortona *(Prov. Arezzo)*

Road 71 leads south from Arezzo to Cortona, an Etruscan town on a hill above Lake Trasimene. A pine and olive tree lined road leads down to the old town and the *"Tomb of Pythagoras"*, an Etruscan vault from the 4th century *B.C.*, at the side of the road, half way down.

You come next to the church of *San domenico,* which has a fresco attributed to *Fra Angelico,* who spent a few years of exile in the town as a young man. There are also works by *Luca Signorelli*. Signorelli was a native of Cortona and died here in 1523, when he fell from a scaffolding he was erecting for the tower of the Palazzo Passerini. His finest work, *The Last Judgement,* can be seen in Orvieto Cathedral.

The 13th century *Palazzo Comunale* is the finest of the many beautiful palazzi: close to it, on the *Piazza Signorelli,* is the Palazzo Pretorio which dates from the same period and houses the Etruscan Museum. Its finest exhibit is the 16-burner bronze lamp from the 5th century *B.C.;* it was discovered in a nearby field in 1840.

You should also visit the 10th century Cathedral, which was altered to Renaissance style by followers of Sangallo: the Chiesa del Gesù which has an extraordinarily beautiful *"Annunciation"* by *Fra Angelico* and paintings by *Pietro Lorenzetti:* the *church of San Francesco,* which guards a splinter from the Cross in a Byzantine reliquary, and the church of *Santa Margherita,* which has one of the finest Gothic tombs in Tuscany built for the patron saint of the town who died in 1297.

From the *Fortezza* above the town there is a fine view across *Lake Trasimere* and to *Monte Amiata.*

Coming down from the *Fortezza* there is a sign on the left to the *Franciscan monastery* which is still occupied by a few Capuchin monks. The road is a firm clay track through beautiful countryside. Crickets chirp and birds sing in the silence surrounding the monastery — birdsong being sadly too rare in Italy. A plaque tells how St. Francis was carried from here to Assisi to "meet Brother Death".

You can have an excellent meal and a rest in the *"La Loggetta"* restaurant, and the *"Logge di Pescheria"*. Almost as good are the *"Cacciatore", Via Roma 11,* or the *"Miravalle"* in *Torreone* 2.5km (1.5 miles) along the road to *Città di Castello.*

Monte Savino (Prov. Arezzo)
Leave Cortona and take the *Autostrada del Sole* towards Florence and you will come to Monte Savino (15km, 9 miles south of Arezzo). Here you will encounter the delle Vertighe Byzantine Madonna, the patron saint of the motorway, a popular place of pilgrimage.

In the distance, in the midst of olive groves and cypresses can be seen the Castello di Gragonza, which was Dante's first exile.

Monte San Savino is full of old palazzi and churches. It was the birthplace of the sculptor, Andrea Contucci, called Sansovino. The most beautiful and starkly elegant Renaissance buildings were designed by *Antonio da Sangallo.* The town is famous for its pottery, furniture and antiques. A secret recipe for *"porchetta"* (roast suckling pig) and beef makes the town a favourite destination for local gourmets.

Sansepolcro (Prov. Arezzo)
Follow road 73 from Arrezo east to *Sansepolcro* through deserted woods and hills till the road divides shortly after Le Ville: from there take Road 221 to *Città di Castello (Umbria).* 3.5km (2.1 miles) beyond the junction you come to Monterchi where Piero's mother was born and buried. There is a castle on the hilltop. Pass the village on the left and turn off to the cemetery at the signpost for the *"Stadio Comunale".*

In the cemetery chapel, you will see Piero della Francesca's *'Madonna del Parto"* watched over by two angels in red and green boots. The painting, which had been considered lost for centuries, was found again in 1888, cleaned and brought here to the chapel. It is the most beautiful of all the majestic, austere Madonnas painted by della Francesca and it is far removed from the delicate daintiness of his contemporaries.

The battle painted by da Vinci, which hangs in the Palazzo Vecchio in Florence (see p.119), was fought and lost at the little mediaeval walled town of *Anghiari* (13km, 8 miles from Le Ville on the road to Sansepolcro). In addition to the winding streets, palaces and churches, Anghiari has a popular antiques market every Sunday, where you can find everything from junk to real treasures at fairly reasonable prices.

From Anghiari it is 8km (5 miles) to Piero della Francesca's birthplace, correctly *'Borgo Sansepolcro'.* The little art gallery houses della Francesca's most famous paintings: the *"Madonna"* and the *"Resurrection"*.

From Sansepolcro head north towards Bibbiena in the area known as the *Casentino,* stopping first at *Pieve Santo Stefano* on the Tiber. In the *Palazzo Pubblico,* there is a large *terracotta* figure by *Luca della Robbia, "The Samaritan Woman at the Well".* In the *Collegiata,* there are more fine ceramics from the *della Robbia* School.

Every year since 1589, a torchlight procession has left the *"Tempietto delle Ninfe del Tevere"* ("The little temple of the Tiber nymphs") near Pieve on September 8th, for the miraculous *Madonna delle Lumi.* In days gone by it was said that brightly shining angels visited the picture of the Madonna each night and bestowed on it powers of healing. Gourmets claim that the game and fish specialities (from the Tiber), in the simple inns in Pieve Santo Stefano are also worth a pilgrimage.

8km (5 miles), in *Caprese,* Michelangelo was born on March 6th, 1475, the son of Ludovic Buonarotti, who was the local Mayor. In his birthplace and in the Castello at the top of the hill, you can see plaster casts of his works.

La Verna (prov. Arezzo)

You must negotiate the tortuous bends through the wild and magnificent Apennines to reach the Franciscan monastery of *La Verna,* which stands on the mountain of the same name. Here Saint Francis is said to have received the stigmata, the sacred wounds of Christ. It is a huge, grey complex of buildings with a magnificent church filled with beautiful works by *della Robbia.* Even the view around the tranquil landscape seems to breathe the Franciscan spirit. Men can spend the night here: women must go to the convent at the bottom of *La Verna.*

If you enjoy the solitude of a monastery, an even more beautiful and atmospheric place to stay is the Camaldolese monastery, which is the headquarters of the order (22km, 14 miles from Bibbiena on Road 71). It stands in one of Italy's most beautiful mountain forests and, faithful to the spirit of Saint Benedict, it offers the hospitality of a comfortable *"foresteria".* A few kilometres away is the *"Eremo",* the secluded monastery of the white monks; women are not allowed into the cloisters which surround their tiny cells.

Pieve di Socana (Prov. Arezzo)

Before returning to Florence via Bibbiena, it is worth visiting the village of *Pieve di Socana* (7km, 4.3 miles to the south heading towards Arezzo). In addition to the pure Romanesque church, the village boasts a unique piece of Etruscan archaeology which was uncovered in 1975. This is a huge altar from which steps, which are clearly visible in a break in the church wall, lead down to the largest Etruscan temple yet to be discovered. In the 6th century, an early Christian church was built on the foundations of the temple: the Romanesque church was built in the 11th century. The foundations of the temple, however, extend beyond those of the church.

In order to see the *"ara"* (altar) and the Etruscan foundations, and the round Roman watchtower beneath the hexagonal Campanile, you have to go into the rectory garden, and through the wooden gate (no nameplate), immediately next to the rectory by the church. Passing under the vines and through the vegetables and chickens, you come to the spot which has been used for religious worship for two and a half thousand years without interruption.

The priest, Don Alfio, is a walking encyclopedia. He is the editor of a series of beautifully illustrated books on the Romanesque churches in Casentino and topics of local history; he relates how, whilst a vain search for the Etruscan settlement was in progress new burial grounds and Langobard tombs containing huge skeletons were found. Don Alfio can also tell you all about the *"Laghetto degli Idoli"* (the little lake of idols) close to the source of the Arno on Monte Falterona, where they discovered Etruscan statuettes; and about the castles in the area, where Dante first found refuge after he was banished from Florence.

Castello Poppi (Prov. Arezzo)
The largest of these castles, the *Castello Poppi* which belonged to the Counts of Guidi, towers on a rock overlooking the whole valley: it is 10km (6 miles) north of Bibbiena, off to the left of the main Bibbiena-Firenze road. The library, which is opened for visitors on request, has seven hundred early books and four hundred and thirty-two codices and manuscripts, some of which are decorated with priceless miniatures. The collection includes one of the first copies of the *"Divine Comedy"* dated 1319 (Dante died in 1321).

Romena is 7km (4.3 miles) from Poppi: it has the ruins of another Guidi fortress which gave refuge to Dante, when he was in exile and the most impressive of the Romanesque parish churches in the *Casentino*. The primitive but moving capitals on the pillars depict stories from the Bible. In the crypt of the church, which was built during a famine in 1152 — *"tempore famis"* — is a small Etruscan altar and stone tablets with inscriptions.

A detour worth making is to the *Vallombrosa* monastery on the way back along the scenic road No.70 through the Consuma Pass to Florence. It is a grandiose 16th century monastery which also takes in overnight guests. John Milton stayed here in 1638 and there are evocative references to Vallombrosa in *Paradise Lost*.

From here it is a beautifully scenic drive winding through the Tuscan hills back to Florence.

Grosseto Province

Massa Marittima

36km (22.4 miles) further on along Road 441 going towards the sea, you come to Massa Marittima whose magnificent architecture speaks of former glories.

The town, originally an Etruscan settlement, became a bishopric in the early Middle Ages and was a flourishing city state before being taken over, first by Siena, then by Florence.

The old town, which is mainly Romanesque, and the new town, which is Gothic, are the setting each year (May 20th and August 2nd) for an archery tournament in mediaeval costume.

From July 19th till August 20th there is also an interesting exhibition by local craftsmen, where you can buy their work, and, during the same period, the only minerals' market in Italy, which sells ores from the hills in the surrounding district.

The artistic centre of Massa Marittima is the picturesque *Piazza Garibaldi* in the old town, on which stands the huge cathedral, started in the Romanesque style and completed in Gothic. The interior is bright and lofty behind the magnificent façade. The pillars have Corinthian capitals; the walls have 14th century frescoes. The *Madonna delle Grazie* (by *Segna di Bonaventura*) in the left transept brings to mind Duccio's "Maestà" in the Cathedral Museum in Siena. The valuable collection of relics is worth looking at.

Opposite the left side of the Cathedral is the *Bishops' Palace* (excessively restored). Next to it on the left is the Gothic *Palazzo dell' Abbondanza*, which takes its name, "abundance", from the days when it served as a granary for the Republic of Siena.

Above the portal of the Romanesque *Palazzo Pretorio*, to the right of the cathedral façade, you see the coat of arms of Massa Marittima and Siena's she-wolf. Nearby in the *Palazzo Comunale* is the town's greatest treasure, the *Maestà* by *Ambrogio Lorenzetti* (on the right wall of the Mayor's office).

It is delightful to stroll through the streets for a while and wonder at how much has been saved from the past. You will see from the enormous fortress (*Fortezza dei Senesi*) that the rulers in days gone by did not feel too secure.

The *Museum of Minerals* on the left of the *Viale Martiri di Nicioleta* will explain the former wealth of the town: the district had copper, lead, iron, pyrites, zinc and magnetic rock, some of which are still mined.

On the steep road leading down from Massa Marittima, a sign post points to the left to the monastery of *S. Bernardino a Veretra*, from which you have a fine view of the Maremma, the peninsula of Punta Ala, and the desolate prospect of the new buildings around Massa Marittima which have ruined its silhouette.

Punta Ala (Prov. Grosseto)
About 21km (13 miles) further on, you reach the coast at *Follonica*, a loud, busy and unattractive resort. More prepossessing is *Punta Ala*, (22km, 13.7 miles) further — 11km (6.8 miles) southwards on the Aurelia then right at Pian d'Alma. *Punta Ala* is an exclusive resort which has grown in the last decade. There are four or five good hotels (1st and 2nd class), a polo and athletics ground, golf, tennis, excellent beaches and unspoilt woodlands of pine and scrub. But since there are also two camping sites, this last remaining corner of paradise is not the exclusive preserve of the rich.

Driving south on the Aurelia, you come to the most prosperous of the resorts in Grosseto Province, *Castiglione della Pescaia*. Next to the picturesque harbour which is full of fishing boats and motor cruisers, the gently sloping beach stretches down below the *'pineta'* (pine forest). It is difficult to find any space in the holiday village at *Riva del Sole* just to the northeast, because of the hordes of sun-starved Scandinavians. The old town of *Castiglione Castello* stands, sheltered by its high walls, on the hill above the new town. In Roman times, it was the "*Portus Trajanus*": it may even have been the Etruscan "*Hasta*", though that has never been definitely established.

Villages of the Maremma (Prov. Grosseto)
If you take the extremely pretty mountain road inland from *Castiglione*, you come to Vetulonia (approx. 23km, 14.2 miles). About half way along, the road leads to the mediaeval village of *Tirli*, a village of narrow twisting streets. You can have an excellent meal in the "*Cave del Cinghiale*" (Cave of the wild boar). The restaurant specialises in wild boar with apples and

156

roast porpucine. Porcupines are said to be relatively common in the hills around Tirli and Capalbio.

Back on the Aurelia continue south past *Grosseto*, and after 6.5km (4 miles) you will reach the exit for *Alberese-Monte dell'Uccellina.* This stretch of coastal woodland was designated as a nature reserve only a few years ago: its natural beauty makes one regret the havoc which has been wrought elsewhere on the Italian coast. For the whole coast was once like this: scrub and pine forests, the sweet-smelling Mediterranean 'macchia' (scrub), miles of white, deserted beaches.

Since no shooting is permitted, the wild life flourishes. You will see plenty of hare, deer and pheasants. A miracle in Italy! The park is open to the public on three weekdays only, when you may explore the paths through it. If you are lucky, you may meet a herd of wild horses or some of the large-eyed, gentle oxen with their huge horns, or see the "*butteri*", the cowboys of the Maremma riding past on their high saddles.

Close to the sea, there are a few crumbling observation towers, from which, in earlier times, a watch was kept for Saracen invaders. The massive, square *Bella Marsilia Tower* is a reminder of the April night in 1543, when, on this spot, the corsairs of Khair-ed-Din Barbarossa killed all of the Marsili family sparing only the beautiful 16 year old daughter, Margarita, who was to become the favourite wife of Sultan Solimani. The ruins of the *Abazia di San Rabano* stand in a lonely valley close to the tower.

Approximately 17km (10.6 miles) further on, a road leads off to the right to *Talamone,* a fishing village built on a rocky outcrop above the sea and dominated by an old castle. Talamone was a harbour in Etruscan and in Roman times. Siena dreamt of overthrowing the maritime strength of Pisa and Genoa from here, as we saw from the fresco in the City Hall.

The Etruscans in Tuscany:

Vetulonia, Roselle, Sovana, Populonia, Cosa.

From the earliest settlers, the Etruscans, Tuscany inherited both its name and the spirit which distinguishes it as much from the rest of Italy as the number of artists it produced. The Tuscan sense of individuality is also inherited from the Etruscans, which was the name given by the Romans to the people who were their teachers and who ruled over vast stretches of their empire before them. The name they gave to the land of the Etruscans was Tuscia. Tarquinius, the first king of Rome, was an Etruscan. The Roman victory over the Etruscans would not have been so simple but for the fact that they were able to capture each city state individually.

The word Tuscany appears for the first time in the 10th century and is applied to the section of Etruscan territory to the north of the River Fiora (which runs out between Tarquinia and Orbetello), at that time a Langobard kingdom. The southern and larger section in Latium was part of the Eastern Roman Empire, and later became a church state.

The modern approach to archaeology and the move away from collecting treasures in a museum has meant that a start has been made on the excavation of what remains of the Etruscan cities, so that life in ancient times can be studied in context. Previously, only the necropolis, or burial grounds, had given any indication of the lifestyle of this mysterious race.

The Etruscan burial grounds in Tuscany (the most important are at *Vetulonia, Roselle, Populonia, Sovana* and *Chiusi*) are a silent testimony amid a deserted landscape, to the belief of these people in the existence of the hereafter. The most important finds from the tombs, most of which were plundered in Roman times, are in the *Museum of Archaeology in Florence*. But even the smaller museums in Tuscany (Massa Marittima, Grosseto, Siena, Volterra, Orbetello, Chiusi, Arezzo, Cortona) and the collections in Vetulonia and Anciano, are very interesting. By far the most impressive necropolis to visit is *Tarquinia*, with its magnificent painted tombs, together with *Cerveteri* over the border in *Lazio*.

Vetulonia (Prov. Grosseto)

Coming from the coast, it is best to start with *Vetulonia* which you reach from the road Follonica to Grosseto or else by taking a left turn from the Aurelia in Castiglione della Pescaia.

The *necropolis* lies on the left (look for the sign: *Tombe Etrusche)* at the foot of the picturesque, mediaeval village of Vetulonia, which looks across from its hilltop site to the Maremma and the sea. The section of Etruscan wall on the edge of the village, the clean and narrow little streets, the old church, the tiny museum, which has sadly lost most of its treasures, and a village inn where one can eat and drink simple but delicious food and wine, are reason enough for a visit to Vetulonia; the necropolis, the remnants of the Etruscan settlement which have been excavated, and the Roman ruins and mosaics make it a must.

In the tombs of this once powerful city state were found drawings of the *'fasces'* and the *'togu',* the symbols of the power which the Romans had taken from the Etruscans. You can see only a tiny portion of the huge burial ground in which countless tombs have still to be examined. There are clear signs, however, that the tombs have been pillaged in the past by thieves. The *"del Belvedere", "della Pietera"* and "del Diavolo" tombs in the main section, are of architectural interest. What impresses most is the silence and vastness of the countryside in which these people found their final, magnificent resting place.

Roselle (Prov. Grosseto)

Roselle Terme (ancient *Rusellae)*is 16km as the crow flies from Vetulonia and 9km (5.6 miles) north east of Grosseto on the minor road to Siena: it was an Etruscan settlement, a Roman colony as early as 249 B.C. and a bishopric in the Middle Ages. Excavation of the archaeological site on the hill did not begin until 1942.

The earliest section of the *Etruscan wall* (3km, 1.9 miles long and 5 metres, 16 feet high) which surrounded the town, dates from the 6th century B.C., and the latest section from Roman times in the 2nd century B.C. So far only the foundations of the huge Roman buildings have been excavated: the amphitheatre on the north hill, the thermal baths on the slope and the Emperors' Forum at the bottom. On the south hill and in the valley below are the foundations of the Etruscan dwelling houses and the craftsmen's workshops from the 7th to the 6th century B.C. Next to them, we see what has remained from the mediaeval period: the foundations of a tower, the ruins of a fortress and a church.

Malaria and Saracen raiders put an end to the settlements. The vestiges of more than 2500 years of history, the view across the Maremma, the sea in the distance beyond the pine forests, the silence, all make a visit to Roselle worthwhile. *(No admission fee; open all day)*.

Populonia (Prov. Livorno)
Leave the Aurelia at either S. Vincenza and drive south for 11.5km (7 miles) or at Venturina and take the 398 to Piombino. Even ignoring the 3000 years of history, the Gulf of Baratti between *Lido degli Etruschi* and *Piombino* is worth a visit for its scenery, its clear water, the two restaurants on the sea front and the cheap and clean little Albergo Marisa in its idyllic garden setting. Camping is strictly forbidden because of the proximity of the archaeological sites.

The road above the bay takes you up to *Populonia*. All that remains of the once powerful port of *Pupluna,* is a small museum, the remnants of Etruscan and Roman walls, a mediaeval 'rocca' and three houses. As elsewhere, the burial ground is all that survives to remind one of former glories.

Officially you are permitted to visit only one archaeological site which is fenced off across the road, and you must join the guided tour. (The guide expects a tip) It has tombs from the 9th century (Villanova period) to the 3rd century B.C. Beneath the huge burial mound, the four vaults of the *"Tomba dei Flabelli"* (the name comes from the huge bronze fans which were discovered here) contain a number of sarcophagi, apparently scattered at random, and several smaller burial mounds. The important pieces found here at the beginning of the century show the wealth Pupluna had acquired from the working and shipping of ore, are in Florence.

On the slopes of the hill nearby, you will find many other vaulted tombs, including some carved in the rock face, and sarcophagi. The archaeologists and the thieves know that only a tiny part of the necropolis has been uncovered as yet. The state is short of money to excavate and embarrassed by the vast quantity of finds. Modern thieves, who, as descendants of the Etruscans, consider themselves entitled to carry out "genealogical research" after their own fashion, are at their busiest during the shooting season. They scout the woods, disguised as hunters. When a police patrol appears they hastily discard their trowels and hoes, and innocently produce their guns.

At the souvenir stand next to the archaeological site at Populonia, quite well-made reproductions of small heads from the Hellenistic period (5th-4th centuries B.C. can be purchased, along with the usual Etruscan *kitsch*. The heads are made in a factory near Grosseto. They are an inexpensive and attractive souvenir.

Cosa (Ansedonia) (Prov. Grosseto)

Continue south along the coast, for approximately 90 km (56 miles) from Populonia taking the *"strada panoramica"* as far as the turn off to *Ansedonia;* then drive past the two lagoons at Orbetello to the ancient town of *Cosa* which stands on a wooded hillside amidst secluded villas.

Cosa was once a flourishing Etruscan trading centre: in the 3rd century B.C. it became a Roman colony. Little remains from this period except a few gates, walls, wells, mosaics and sections of roadway.

From Cosa take the panoramic route through Ansedonia, turn right at the half-ruined *Chapel of San Biagio,* cross a canal and you come to the ancient harbour of *'Portus Cosanus'* with its square Saracen watch tower. This was the beginning of the so-called *'Tagliata Etrusca',* a magnificent feat of engineering, which made use of the natural break in the cliff to prevent the harbour from silting up. The remains of the Roman harbour wall are visible in the sea, and on the beach next to the tower, where Puccini once lived and wrote part of *Tosca,* stand the remnants of a Roman villa and warehouse buildings.

There are Etruscan so-called 'Cyclopean' stone blocks in many city walls in Tuscany. The most important are in Fiesole, Volterra, which also has an Etruscan city gate, with faded heads (gods, kings, demons?) in relief, and in Cortona. Traces of the Etruscans are found throughout the province and each year new finds are made. The description 'Cyclopean' reminds us of the similarly described Minoan edifices in Greece. Later civilisations tended to describe the architecture whose techniques they had lost, the art of heaving massive stones into position, as emanating from the ancient Gods, the giants or Cyclops.

Sovana, the town of Jeremiah (Prov. Grosseto)

The only well-known burial site on a cliff face in Tuscany is at *Sovana.* If you are interested in the Etruscans, you must include it in your itinerary.

To reach Sovana, take Road 74 east from the Aurelia (at Orbetello-Albinia) via Manciana to *Pitigliano,* which you would look at briefly — especially from a distance. The whole picturesque grey Etruscan settlement, with its twisting streets and the

Orsini Castle , looks as if it is growing out of the rocky outcrop on which it stands. Lots of caves have been dug out at the foot of the rock: nowadays they serve as garages, wine cellars, stabling, and so forth, though they were originally tombs. In front of the Baroque cathedral on the edge of the Piazza, there are several fine Renaissance palaces. You should also sample Pittigliano's famous white wine before venturing up the hill.

The road at the bottom of the hill to the left leads to *Sovana* (8km, 5 miles), the birthplace of Pope Gregory VII (Hildebrand), the powerful Pope who forced Henry IV, the Holy Roman Emperor, to do penance at Canossa. It was probably given the strange name, the "town of Jeremiah", because it so clearly bewails its former glory.

Sovana is a tiny hamlet where visitors fall silent in awe before the decayed and decaying testimonies to the past. By-pass the ruins of a fortress and go through the streets of single-storeyed mediaeval houses till you reach the Piazza. Before us is the strange, narrow *Palazzo dell'Archivio*. Next to it on the left is the little Romanesque church of *Santa Maria* which has interesting frescoes and an 8th century *ciborium* (altar canopy) which stands on pillars. Next to that is the *Loggetta del Capitano,* a Renaissance palace bearing huge Medici crests, and the *Palazzo del Pretorio* which is also decorated with coats of arms.

The battles against Siena and malaria decimated the population of the ancient bishopric. Nowadays the village has only 300 inhabitants who move like shadows amidst the crumbling palaces, stunned by the hordes of visitors.

You will be given a warm welcome in the *'Ristorante Etrusco'* on the right of the square where "original Etruscan" dishes are served on plates with Etruscan designs. Look out for the birthplace of Pope Gregory VII as you go along the street to the field outside the village where the cathedral stands: it has a 10th century octagonal cupola and a simple, early crypt.

Take a sharp left turn as you leave Sovana and a few hundred yards along on the right, you will see the first cliff tombs. The most important of the many tombs is on the cliff face opposite as you come out of the tunnel: the pillars and capitals make it look like a Greek temple buried in the rock. Before you reach the tomb, a yellow sign points off into the bushes: a narrow path leads through thick undergrowth to the *"Siren's Tomb"* which has a carving of a mermaid and an Etruscan inscription.

There are numerous other tombs around Sovana, and in these silent, wooded gulleys, you will come much closer to the secrets of the Etruscans than in the 'municipal' burial grounds.

162

Non-Etruscan sites of the Orbetello region

Go back to Manciano (26km, 16 miles) turn northwards and take the Scansano road for 61km (4 miles) then turn right to Terme di Saturnia. There are also Etruscan and Roman ruins in the vicinity.

As early as Roman times, the sulphuric, radio-active waters of Saturnia were famous for their healing powers: nowadays, Saturnia has a fully-equipped first class spa hotel, a swimming pool with hot sulphurous water (the temperature is constant at 37°C, (98.6F) *fango* (mud) treatments, facilities for the inhalation of fumes, and so forth. People swear by these miraculous cures for every conceivable ailment from rheumatism, and asthma to skin diseases.

The visitors certainly look healthy, and quickly become used to the thick sulphurous fumes, venturing from their comfortable quarters in between their swimming and massage sessions beneath a thundering artificial waterfall.

Return to Road 322 and turn left in Scansano on to Road 323 heading towards Orbetello. The way winds through beautiful, unspoilt countryside to *Magliano in Toscana* (16km, 10 miles) a mediaeval walled village on a hill of olive groves, which is certainly worth a visit: the finest buildings are the three Romanesque churches and the Gothic *Palazzo dei Priori.* The *"Piombo di Magliano"*, a lead plaque bearing a spiral-shaped Etruscan inscription, which is now in Florence, was found in the necropolis in Magliano.

Before going on to Monte Argentario, anyone interested either in the Etruscans, in horses or in nature, should take the road to *Marsiliana* (8km, 5 miles to the south-east), which has an Etruscan burial ground on the so-called *"ager caletranus"* at the foot of the fortress. The many important items which have been found here, including the famous 'fibula corsini', a buckle with its decorated procession of little golden ducklings, are all in the Museum of Archaeology in Florence.

Passing by herds of bullocks and horses grazing on the wide meadows fringed with woodland, you reach the mediaeval town of *Capalbio* (13km, 8 miles) which has a hilltop castle: the town is the main centre of horse breeding in the southern corner of Tuscany. The other centre is *Alberese.*

On the second weekend in October, Capalbio is the setting of the "Riders' Fair", held by the *"butteri"*, as the cowboys of the Maremma are called. They are equal to their North American counterparts in every way.

If your tracker's instinct is acute, you might be fortunate enough to encounter one of the last two surviving herds of wild horses somewhere between Capalbio and the sea. For horse-lovers, it is a wonderful experience to watch these animals which have been born and brought up in the wilds — and also to watch the horsemen who, once every day, have to count the horses as well as the light coloured longhorn cattle, and lasso the two year old foals in the season.

On the way back from Capalbio on the Aurelia (6.4km, 14 miles) you come to the *Lago di Burano* nature reserve, which is separated from the beach by one of the few remaining un-spoilt stretches of macchia scrub. If you are lucky, you will be taken around by Guido, the World Wildlife Fund warden, through myrtle, rosemary and juniper bushes along the nature trail he has laid out around the lake.

Standing on tiptoe and whispering almost inaudibly, he briefs his visitors for the incredible views of the waterfowl through the curtain of reeds. By northern standards, the fauna is nothing spectacular. It consists mainly of coots, occasionaly a few herons, in winter even cormorants and the last *'cavalieri d'Italia'*, the little white ibis.

Monte Argentario (Prov. Grosseto)

Monte Argentario may once have been but is no longer an island. Drive over the causeway from Orbetello and take the road to Porto Santo Stefano. This is a typical fishing village with its tall, yellow houses climbing up the hillside. However it has now been discovered by the international jet-set and the harbour is packed with motor yachts. The locals are incredibly friendly and look like pirates: obviously there were a good few Saracens among their forbears.

A scenic route with panoramic views of the sea, of deep, rocky coves and of the *Isola del Giglio,* runs half way along the coast. To reach the second important port of call on the Argentario, *Porto Ercole,* you must turn back after Porto San Stefano. Here too there are some beautiful villas tucked away in secluded grounds, including the villa belonging to the Dutch royal family.

The islands, the mountains and the harbours are supervised (obviously very well) by Italy's most famous Lady Mayor: Susanna Agnelli, member of parliament and sister of Gianni Agnelli, the Fiat boss, who is known locally as the *"ingegnere"*.

There are good fish restaurants along the waterfront in both *Porto Santo Stefano* and *Porto Ercole* where the *'Gambero Rosso'* is to be recommended.

164

Elba and the Islands

Once you have seen the Monte Argentario peninsula, you will be tempted to visit the real islands. The astonishing thing about Elba is that, despite its popularity, both with Italians and with foreigners, it has managed to retain its beauty and relatively little of the island is built up. Anyone in search of solitude and unspoiled natural surroundings will find both in the interior of Elba, the largest of the islands in the Tuscan archipelago [225 sq.km, 86 sq miles, 29 km long (18 miles) and 18 km wide (11 miles)]. The other islands are *Capraia, Isola del Giglio, Giannutri, Gorgona, Montecristo,* and *Pianosa.*

Pianosa

Pianosa, (Latin: Planasia) lies flat as a flounder only 14 km (9 miles) from Elba. The fossilised remains of bears, horses, and red deer are evidence to support the theory that the island, which has been inhabited since prehistoric times, was once part of the mainland. Since the island is used as a prison it is advisable to give it a miss. There is however a boat that goes there from Piombino, where permission for a visit must be obtained from the judicial authorities. From the sea you can view on the east side the ruins of the Roman villa to which Postumio Agrippa was banished by his uncle, Augustus, who later despatched murderers to have him killed.

Montecristo

From the coast of Elba on clear days you can see quite clearly 40 km (25 miles) away the island of Montecristo, (probably Artemisia in ancient times). It stands like a skittle in the sea. There is no regular service but you could ask at the *Compagnia di Navigazione Toscana* in Piombino to see if any arrangements can be made for a visit. The island is a nature reserve owned by the State, and it is hoped that rare flora and a species of wild goat indigenous to the island, will survive. According to local legend, the goats have gold teeth.

It was neither that it was the hunting lodge of the Italian kings, nor ruins of the mediaeval monastery that were to make Montecristo world famous. but Dumas père with his novel, *"The Count of Monte Cristo".* Montecristo is very popular with divers because of the fantastic rock formations and marine life.

Care needs to be taken when climbing the island rocks. They are said to be overrun with the progeny of a colony of vipers which were bred here on the island for their serum.

Capraia

Capraia (there are regular departures by ship from Livorno (65km, 40 miles) and Portoferraio (55km, 34 miles)) is of volcanic origin and its rugged, indented coastline is much loved by sailing enthusiasts. The interior of the island is mountainous and dry in the summer. Swarms of rabbits and mice welcome the botanist who comes here to revel among the rare species of wild flowers. *The Fortezza San Giorgio* above the island's only village, Capraia (population: 323) was built by the Genoese at the beginning of the 15th century, as protection against Saracen invaders . It is worth taking a walk, even in the heat, to see the water lilies in the lake *(Lo Stagnone)* in the south-east of the island and to enjoy the view from *Monte Arpagna* of the Tuscan islands and nearby Corsica. It is best to go round the island by boat.

Giannutri

Giannutri, the crescent-shaped, southernmost island in the Tuscan archipelago is privately owned but can be visited on the daily scheduled service from Porto Santo Stefano on Monte Argentario.

It is a worthwhile visit since frequent rainshowers and heavy dews (quite a rarity at this latitude) provide a plentiful supply of water for the gardens, vineyards and olive groves and keep the island green and lovely. From the *Cala dello Spalmotoio* in the north-east, where there is a ruined Roman harbour, you come into a modern holiday village. The impressive ruins of a Roman villa stand close to the other jetty.

L'Isola del Giglio

L'Isola del Giglio (Island of the Lily) is a mountainous island, the second largest of the Tuscan archipelago. It can be reached from Ponto Santo Stefano by boat (14km, 8.7 miles approx. 40 mins.). The ferry will also take cars if a reservation is made.

A bus service runs from the picturesque village of *Giglio Porto* to the *"La Ginestra"* holiday village higher up and the fortified village of Giglio Castello 6km (3.7 miles) away. The *rocca* (castle) and old parish church which contains early frescoes and a figure of Christ in ivory by Giambologna, tower above the narrow streets and mediaeval walls of the village. For the imaginative visitor the arcaded labyrinth in Giglio Castello is like a dream fixed in stone. From here, there is a narrow winding tarred road to the sandy beach at *Campese*. Three kilometres (1.9 miles) from the beach is the 'Clary' holiday village: there is also a camping site in the bay by the rock.

Restaurants: "Trattoria da Rosa" in *Giglio Castello, "Da Giovanni" Via Roma.* In *Campese* there are several open air restaurants with a fine view of the sea (some have rooms).

Information: Azienda di Turismo, Via Umberto I Giglio Porto.

Gorgona

Gorgona: the most barren and most northerly island is a rocky outcrop which is virtually uninhabited. It can be reached from Livorno (37km, 23 miles) and from Elba.

The island was occupied both by the Etruscans and by the Romans, and was, for a long period in the Middle Ages, a refuge for monks. Since there is also a prison on the island, in the south-east, access to the *Museum of Archeology* is only possible with prior permission from the Governor *(Direzione della Colonia Penale).*

Elba

Finally we come to Elba (the name is derived from the Greek word for iron). Iron was mined here first by the Greeks and then, from the 6th century B.C., by the Etruscans. The power of the Etruscan empire at its height, (7th-5th centuries B.C.) stretched from Lombardy to Sorrento, from the eastern coast of Corsica to the Adriatic and was largely based on the rich seams of iron ore on the Tuscan coast and on Elba.

To get there it is possible to fly from Pisa. Otherwise a car ferry runs between Piombino and Elba (almost hourly, April— September). The ferry *(traghetto)* takes about an hour, and the hydrofoil *(aliscafo)* about twenty-five minutes. There are also steamers from Livorno which take about three hours direct and five hours with stops at *Gorgona, Capraia* and *Marciana Marina* on Elba itself. Check carefully which Elban port your boat is going to; if you have the car it doesn't much matter, but without it, you should get off at *Portoferraio.* Portoferraio, 'the iron harbour', has little to offer visitors simply in search of sun and sea; but for anyone interested in Napoleon there is the *Palazzino dei Mulini* 6km (4 miles) away, the residence of the exiled emperor, and the *Villa Napoleonica di S. Martino,* his summer residence. (N.B. It is often closed in the afternoon). 5km (3 miles) to the south-east, close to *Terme di S. Giovanni* (therapeutic waters for rheumatism, throat and skin ailments) in the *Le Grotte* district stand the imposing ruins of a Roman villa from the imperial period.

I recommend to the gourmet *"Il Caminetto"* restaurant (near Napoleon's summer villa), the "Zi' Rosa" in Portoferraio and the *"Stella Marina"* also in Portoferraio.

Further information is available from the *Ente per la Valorizz-azione Isola d'Elba, Portoferraio, Calata Italia 26,* (by the harbour).

Elba offers numerous sports facilities (golf, tennis, sailing, riding, scuba diving, and the Tourist Office will provide details of the many camping sites and holiday villages. A guidebook to the island is available at any kiosk.

The fresh breezes and almost total lack of rain in the summer not only guarantee a successful holiday for the sun worshippers from the north but also mean that tropical plants flourish alongside the native vegetation, palms, agaves, Indian figs, and others.

The wealth and variety of minerals on the island make it a paradise for people interested in the subject. They can be given a packed lunch and left for the day in the picturesque mining village of *Capoliveri* to search for glittering stones like the shimmering gold pyrites. If your knowledge of the language is up to it, ask the captain to let you watch the compass as you sail round the eastern end of Elba. When the boat comes level with the Calamita mine, the compass will start to flicker as it is pulled towards the magnetic rock.

The people of Elba gain a living from agriculture (the wines are delicious, especially the heavy *Aleatico,*) fishing and tourism. They have achieved something quite rare on the Italian coast: they have not sold their soul to tourism. They accept it happily and graciously when it comes without making any great effort to organise everything or to change themselves or their island to meet new demand.

The best beaches are at *Procchio* and *Marciana Marina,* which also has a small airport. Otherwise you should bring a boat or hire one to visit the fifty odd tiny bays nestling below steep cliffs, which can otherwise be reached only down precipitous paths, if at all.

In *Porto Azzurro,* formerly called Porto Longone after the star-shaped fortress built in 1603 by Philip III of Spain, sensitive visitors might find it hard to dispel nightmarish thoughts of the prisoners serving life sentences in the fortress, despite their enjoyment of the sea and the excursions. Such thoughts are re-inforced every hour of the day: a procession of old and drably dressed men and women, with parcels and bundles, wheezes its way up the steep path to visit their imprisoned sons.

Livorno

Livorno (Leghorn)

Although Livorno is the most important port on the Tuscan coast it has little appeal for the tourist. At the end of the 16th century, the Medicis commissioned Buontalenti to design the "perfect city" around the remains of a Mediaeval "*borgo*" and the old Porto Pisano. Despite this, Livorno was never to be beautiful.

The English name for the town, Leghorn, derives from the old name Legiorno. The importance of the city was due solely to the harbour. The inhabitants were too busy to find the time or the space for churches, art or noteworthy architecture. There are, however, a few points of interest: the monument known as the *Four Moors* (*Piazza Micheli*), a fine statue of the *Grand Duke Ferdinand I* surrounded by four fettered Moors; and the *Fortezza Vecchia* on the Porto Mediceo, built by *Antonio da Sangallo* in 1534, above which looms the *Countess Matilda Tower.*

Like all ports, Livorno abounds with sailors from all over the world and it has an interesting market. You can eat the local fish specialities (*"Cacciucco"* fish stew, in particular) in any of the cafés around the harbour; but the best and most expensive are served by *"Da Gennarino"*, *Via S. Fortunata 11*, or *"Acquaviva"*, *Viale Italia 60*. If you take the Aurelia towards Rome you have a splendid sea view from *'Torre di Calafuria'* (11 km, 6.8 miles from Livorno) or from *'Il Romito'* (12 km, 7.4 miles).

Of the places worth visiting in the immediate vicinity, the *pilgrims' church in Montenero* (9 km, 15.5 miles is interesting; the ornate baroque interior is like a museum of naive art, for it is filled to overflowing with votive offerings from those saved from shipwreck or drowning, mostly primitive little paintings of ships in storms or the Madonna of Montenero, the patron saint of Tuscany, who is shown pulling dripping sailors from the water.

Lucca and Massa Carrara

Every city and every province in Italy is convinced that it is the most beautiful. In Lucca, the reception I had from the Director of Tourism was cool at first because I had come from Pisa: but his attitude soon changed and, to make amends, he said: "Oh well, Pisa has a few fine buildings and a little art. But in Lucca, everything is beautiful and everything is art."

Lucca's appeal for the visitor — its anachronistic tranquillity, its friendly and phlegmatic citizens who never seem in a hurry, the absence of industry — is also the source of her problems. The population of the city (approximately 90,000) has increased by only 9,000 in this century: it is a city of old people. As a visitor you soon notice this and it is relaxing, but also rather disquieting. There is little to keep young people here.

The countryside around Lucca is varied, fertile, thanks to the waters of the *River Serchio,* and diverse in its geological structure. It has a number of interesting villas, castles and fairytale gardens.

In Lucca itself, you should first walk up to the promenade *(Passeggiata delle Mura),* one of the most beautiful in Europe (you can also go some of the way by car); it was built between 1544 and 1645 all around the city as a rampart and planted with huge plane trees. On summer evenings, like the streets in the centre of Spanish towns, it becomes the *'corso',* half the town strolls up and down here, seeing and being seen, flirting and gossiping: a piece of bourgeois tradition, seldom seen nowadays.

Lucca, a Roman settlement, belonged to the Goths, the Langobards and the Franks, before it developed its own civic culture around 1000, one of the first cities to do so since classical times. It became a free city in 1119 and retained its independence interrupted only by a few tyrants, right up to Napoleon's time. Napoleon made the city a principality and put his sister, Elisa, who was married to a Corsican named Baciocchi, on the throne. *Paganini* gave his first performance in her residence, the classical *Villa Reale* at *Marlia,* 5 km (3 miles) from the city. He is said to have been one of her many lovers. In 1847, Lucca became part of the Grand Duchy of Tuscany.

Lucca owes its wealth of art and architecture, in particular the many Romanesque churches, to its silk trade and its many banks. Though strongly influenced by the Romanesque style of Pisa, Lucca was to develop its own style, which is rich in ornamentation: the *'Maestri Comacini' from Como and* Campione on Lake Lugano, who had travelled in France and Spain and even as far as Russia, contributed much to the architecture of the city.

It also has a great musical tradition, celebrated in May with the *'Sagra Musicale Lucchese'*, and from July till September with the *'Estate Musicale'*. *Luigi Boccherini, Alfredo Catalani* and *Giacomo Puccini,* the most famous of her citizens, were born in Lucca.

Since the new city was able to expand outside the city walls, the centre retained the appearance of a mediaeval city state: narrow streets and high towers, tiny squares in front of the Romanesque churches. The red houses of the tyrannical Guinigi family feature prominently and their tower with the trees on top, has become one of Lucca's landmarks. There are a few palaces from the 16th century though by then the great wealth of the city was beginning to disappear.

Further information is available from the *Ufficio informazioni, Via Vittoria Veneto 40.* It is best to park on the *Piazza Napoleone* where the *Palazzo Ducale* stands. It was started in 1579 by *Ammannati* and completed by the Baroque architect *Juvara.* The *Pinacoteca Nazionale* is now in the Palazzo Mansi, Via Galli Tassi - Lucca. Among many good things in its splendid collection of Renaissance paintings, donated by Leopold II, the Hapsburg Grand-Duke, it has *Tintoretto's* rough drawings for his *'Miracle of Saint Mark'* (which is in the *Academia* in Venice).

The neo-classical *municipal theatre* stands on the *Piazza del Giglio* to the east of the *Piazza Napoleone.*

Continue straight down the *Via Vittorio Veneto* and you will come to the picturesque town centre, the *Piazza San Michele,* the site of the ancient Forum Romanum — hence the name of the church, *'San Michele in Foro'* — on top of which stands a huge archangel killing a dragon. The church is typical of the Luccan-Pisan style. It is richly ornamented and is probably the work of *Guidetto da Como,* one of the Como architects, whom we will encounter again in the Cathedral. The façade of *San Michele* is one of the most exciting examples of Romanesque architecture: the four loggias are piled on top of each other and surmounted by the ungainly dragon-killer, who is flanked by smiling angels.

Go back to the Piazza Napoleone and cross the Piazza del Giglio to the Via del Duomo. On the left of the *Piazza San Giovanni* stands the church of the same name: it has a beautiful 12th century carving above the doorway and Roman pillars in the interior. Like many other churches in Lucca, it was built partially from Roman ruins and altered in the Pisan manner in the 12th century. Next to it is the *Gothic Baptistery* of *San Giovanni* and the *Palazzo Micheletti* which was built by *Ammannati*.

The Romanesque cathedral (*Duomo*) stands on the *Piazza San Martino.* Though founded in the 8th century, alterations continued into the 12th century. Behind the asymetric façade and the richly carved entrance, which is surmounted by three elegant loggias, the main interior of the cathedral is late Gothic.

The finest works in the Cathedral are the group which shows Saint Martin sharing his cloak with the beggar, a motif which is copied on the exterior façade (to the right of the main doorway) and the tomb of *Ilaria del Carretto* in the left transept by *Iacopo della Quercia.* The graceful sleeping woman, the wife of a member of the *Guinigi family* who were despots of Lucca, is one of the most famous works by *della Quercia.* Though it was executed at the beginning of the 15th century, it already displays features typical of Renaissance art.

The much-venerated *'Volto Santo',* the Holy Countenance, which is referred to in *Dante's 'Inferno'* (XXI) is kept in a little octagonal temple of gilded marble. According to legend the crucifix, (it is not in fact a face), was carved by Saint Nicodemus at the command of an angel. It is supposedly of oriental origin, and is the focal point of a candlelight procession through the town on September 13th, starting at the Basilica of San Frediano and ending at the Cathedral.

The most valuable Cathedral treasures are kept in the *Opera del Duomo* on the *Piazza degli Antelminelli* nearby.

Every other weekend in the summer and autumn, an antiques market is held around the Cathedral and in the surrounding side streets. It is great fun to wander through, for the market sells everything you can imagine - even things you could never imagine - furniture and coins, engravings, lace and material, pottery, art and junk.

Take the *Via del' Arcivescovado* behind the Cathedral to the Romanesque church of *Santa Maria Forisportam,* another example of the major influence of Pisa on the local architecture.

A little searching will bring you to the many other Romanesque churches many of which were altered in the Gothic period: *Santa Giulia, San Cristoforo, San Romano, San Frediano, San Pietro Somaldi* and *San Giusto.* Nothing is far away in Lucca ....

Close to *Santa Giulia* stand the red houses of the Guinigi family, the last surviving complex of Romanesque dwelling houses and towers.

Lucca's second National Museum is housed in the *Villa Guinigi* next to the church of *San Francesco* in the east of the city. It contains an archeological collection, mediaeval paintings and sculpture from the 13th to the 19th centuries.

Close to the austere *Basilica di San Frediano* are the foundations of the Roman amphitheatre. The pretty marketplace retains the elliptical form of the arena.

The atmosphere of this charming, very independent town is persuasive and *simpatico.* Sitting in a café in Lucca and watching the locals is like a performance of the *Commedia dell'-Arte* and explains much more clearly than any scholarly treatise where the composers, Puccini, Mascagni, Verdi and Donizetti, found the inspiration for their crowd scenes.

Restaurants
The best restaurants in Lucca are:
  'Buca S.Antonio', Via della Cervia 5;
  'Sergio', Piazza Bernardini 7;
  'Giglio', Piazza del Giglio 3;
  'Antico Caffè delle Mura', Piazza Vittorio Emanuele 4;

In the surrounding districts:
  'Il Settebello' in *Vicopelago,* (3 km - 2 miles along the *Pisa* road);
  'Solferino' in *S.Marcario in Piano* (5 km - 3 miles on the *Viareggio* road);
  'Villa Mansi' in *Segromigno Monte* (11 km - 7 miles);
  'I Cavalieri del Tau' in *Altopascio* (15 km - 9 miles along the Florence motorway) *Via Gavianna 32.*

And in Montecarlo: *'Forassiepi', Via Roma 4;*
  'La Nina', Via San Martino 114.

Forte dei Marmi (Prov. Lucca)
In 1788, Leopold I, the Hapsburg-Lorraine Grand-Duke of Tuscany, built a fortress at the point where the province of Lucca begins. Though the fortress served little purpose, it became famous by giving its name to the resort of *Forte dei Marmi;* which was formerly one of the most exclusive in the area. A hundred years later, when bathing became fashionable, the rich started to build their villas among the pines. Nowadays Forte is only part of the huge complex which stretches virtually from *Marina di Carrara* without a break to *Viareggio.* One bathing establishment follows another, so that you scarcely get a glimpse of the sea from the road because of all the buildings. The cost of admission gives you not only a clean beach but also a sunbed, sun umbrella, showers and changing rooms — and in the smartest establishments — energetic beach attendants who will allow topless bathing for "health reasons" but forbid undressing on the beach.

Three to five kilometres (2-3 miles) beyond *Marina de Pietrasanta* and *Lido di Camaiore,* you reach the inland villages of the same name, both of which have many mediaeval buildings. *Pietrasanta* has a concert season in June and July, with drama and ballet in July and August in the open air theatre 'La Versiliana' at Marina di Pietrasanta. Versilia is the name given to this stretch of coastline at the foot of the Apuan Alps.

In addition to the *Romanesque church* at *Camaiore,* you should also look at the *Benedictine Abbey,* which was founded in the 8th century and refurbished in the 12th century, and the *Pieve of Saint John* and *Saint Stephen,* which has an impressive three-storey Campanile. The word *'pieve'* or parish church comes from *plebs* (people). *'Pieve'* were the central churches of a group, and in the Middle Ages had the sole right to perform baptisms. Nowadays they still retain the privilege of fetching the anointing oil from the diocese and distributing it to the other churches.

There are many interesting villas to see in the immediate vicinity of Lucca. Opera lovers can go on a Puccini pilgrimage. You leave Viareggio along a beautiful avenue of lime trees (Viale dei Tigli) for *Torre del Lago,* where Puccini's villa stands, on the edge of Tuscany's largest lake, the *Lago di Massaciuccoli;* his operas are performed here in the summer in the open theatre.

If your holiday is too precious to waste just sitting on the beach, then a day tour can be recommended. It took us from *Pietrasanta* via *Seravezza,* which has marble quarries and a Medici castle, along winding mountain roads with splendid views, through chestnut forests and down into the *Valle d'Arni* to *Castelnuovo di Garfagnana*. For the passenger, the ride is superb; for the driver it must be a major test of concentration, since you seem to encounter a speeding lorry, loaded with blocks of marble, on every bend.

From *Castelnuovo di Garfagnana*, you look up to the little, grey villages on the slopes of the mountains and imagine how difficult their life must be when the snow comes. They were preparing for a ten day festival when we arrived to celebrate the return of a precious crucifix which had been damaged in a fire and now was being brought back from the restorers.

Pontremoli (Prov. Massa-Carrara)

If your main interest is in the Tuscan coast, then I would recommend the Autostrada A-12 which branches off to the north from the Florence-Pisa road, near Pisa, across the *Cisa Pass* to *Genoa, Sestri Levante* and the *Tuscan coast* (in the province of *Mass Carrara*). This motorway takes you through the wild and lonely mountains of the Apennines in the Lunigiana region where there are castles and ruins in plenty. When you see the women at the road-side brandishing colourful plastic bags at you, stop; they are selling the sparse produce of the mountains. In autumn, these include figs, mushrooms and little round ewe cheeses which make delicious picnic food. At the junction NE of La Spezia turn right onto the A-15. Beyond the Cisa Pass, off to the right, is the little town of *Pontremoli,* the birthplace of most of Italy's "bancarelle", the booksellers who sell their wares from stalls in the open air. In July, the winner of the *'Premio Bancarella'*, the prize for the best-selling book of the year, is elected in democratic fashion in Pontremoli.

The *castello* in Pontremoli, which like most of the fortresses and castles in this area, was built by the Malaspina family, contains in its collection of items from prehistoric times, strange plinths comparable to the menhirs in Northern Europe. The local name for the district is the *"Garfagnana"*.

Luni (Prov. La Spezia — Liguria)

From the winding road down to the coast, you can look across to the snow-white peaks of the Apuan Alps - though it is marble and not snow that you see. Before you reach *Carrara,* you should leave the motorway and take the old Roman road, the Aurelia, which runs parallel, otherwise you will miss the yellow sign for *'Luni Antica'*, situated just north of Toscana in Liguria.

The town of Luni stands on the plains amidst gardens and

meadows: the settlement was originally Etruscan, then Roman: it has an enormous crumbling amphitheatre, a capitol, which was excavated very haphazardly in the 19th century, and a Forum. Recently some Roman mosaics have been uncovered.

Marinella (Prov Massa-Carrara)
A few kilometres further on, you turn right to Marinella, a relatively new resort. It is said to have the cleanest water on the coast and the most reliable weather.

It is not advisable to bathe either in *Marina di Carrara* or in *Marina di Massa*, since the harbour lies between the two and rust from the old hulks which carry the shimmering blocks of marble, does not improve the water. The marble dust from the quarries blows everywhere — it gets on the trees, on the streets and into the lungs. But it is tempting to hunt for pieces of marble on the beach.

If you are visiting *Marinella* or any of the towns further along — *Cinquale, Forte dei Marmi, Marina di Pietrasanta, Lido di Camaiore* or *Viareggio* — all of which still retain some of the charm of their age of glory at the turn of the century, you should also visit the marble quarries.

Carrara
You wind uphill on twisting roads thick with white dust to the largest marble quarries in the world, where white Carrara marble has been mined since Roman times.

Of the three main quarries, *Cave Ravaccione, Colonate* and *Fantiscritti*, the latter is of most interest, since it is said that *Michelangelo* came here to select his marble and in our own day so has Henry Moore. It is an unforgettable experience to look down into the rugged mountain chasms of luminous rock, to think of Michelangelo's monumental plan to build mountains with his own hands, to see his work on hand—breaking, cutting and polishing the blocks. If you are looking for a "weighty" souvenir, you will find plenty here — from kitsch to inlaid chessboards — all in marble.

Lunigiana (Prov. Massa Carrara)
It is not easy to select the most interesting of the many citadels and castles, mighty fortresses and Renaissance palaces, in the *Lunigiana*, the area between the mountains and the coast which derives its name from the Roman town of Luni. I would rate among the best, the *13th century castle* at *Fosdinovo* (15 km - 9 miles north of Carrara) and the *Malaspina Castle in Massa*, which is a fine example of courtly elegance.

176

In the inner courtyard of the *Castello di Carrara,* side by side with other finds from Luni and the surrounding district, stands a small altar dedicated to Jupiter, Hercules and Bacchus, which is known as the *"Fanti Scritti"* (the name was passed on to the quarry where it was found). *Fanti* means children and refers to the tiny Gods on the relief, and *Scritti* means writings, because of the names written on it by famous, if irreverent, visitors. If you enjoy visiting castles, you will love the Lunigiana which has over sixty.

Barga (Prov. Lucca)
Barga is 6 km (3.7 miles) further on situated in the Serchio Valley 35 km from Lucca. The old town rises steeply up the hillside to the Cathedral at the top. Barga is full of churches, monasteries — and Englishmen. How did it happen? Twenty years ago, an English couple fell in love with the picturesque little place and its solemn architecture, superb air and splendid views of the surrounding hills of the Apennines, and moved into an old tower. They then discovered the theatre, which had been dedicated by the poet Leopardi but since forgotten. We should be grateful for the idealism and hard work of this couple, who founded the season of opera and concerts, the *Opera di Barga,* which attracts music lovers here every year in July.

It is an entrancing spot. On our last visit, an eclipse of the moon made it look even more like the setting for a fairytale: the dramatic sky, the silence of the mountains broken only by the chirping of the cicadas, the occasional tolling of a bell or bark from a dog, was as impressive as our visit to the cathedral on top of the hill the next morning. It contains, among other things, a huge archaic wooden *Saint Christopher, a romanesque pulpit* which shows the Three Wise Men on their journey to the Christ Child through a field of shooting stars, and a red *terracotta* (not coloured glaze) *Madonna* by *Luca della Robbia.* The della Robbias had one of their kilns at *Fornaci di Barga* outside the town.

Moving south down the Serchio Valley from Fornaci de Barga, in about six miles the village of Fornoli, where it is worth a short diversion eastwards to Bagni di Lucca, an elegant old spa, where Montaigne and, in the previous century Byron, Shelley, Heine, Carducci and many of the crowned head of Europe sought a cure for their ailments in the hot radio-active waters.

Returning to Fornoli and driving south towards Lucca, one passes through Ponte a Moriano and within a mile is the turning east to Marlia the site of the difficult-to-find Villa Reale, former residence of Napoleon's sister Elisa (no admittance).

Continuing onwards in a southeasterly direction by tertiary roads one reaches in about 6km (3.7 miles) Segromigno where the Villa Mansi is situated. It stands in a magnificent, landscaped park full of marble deities and fountains. Built originally in the 16th century, it was altered in a most adventurous fashion around the mid 18th century by Juvara, a Piedmontese, and is a unique cross between Renaissance and Rococo. The most attractive feature is, however, the park, just as at the *Villa Torrigiani* (crammed with furniture, engravings and paintings) 2 km (1.2 miles) further on. It is almost always empty because of the relatively high admission charge, and provides that rare commodity which is so essential when you have been dashing around for days — tranquility. Legend has it that three hundred years ago in this park, the beautiful Lucinda, mistress of the house, made a pact with the devil: she promised him her soul in return for another thirty years of beauty and youth. And true to his promise, the devil returned to fetch her in a thunderstorm. The ghost of Lucinda is said to haunt the battlements of Lucca on stormy nights, in a golden coach. The water, whose properties were said to have been the source of her beauty, still bubbles from a spring in the bushes to the right of the villa.

Prato to Pistoia and Pisa

The abundance of art in almost all the large towns and many smaller towns in Tuscany dates from the days when many were free city states. For Northern Europeans the wealth of important buildings and works of art even in the smallest, most isolated villages is overwhelming: it was fostered by the feudal lords of the day, by the monasteries or by art-loving prelates, who frequently were members of the great Tuscan families.

In the old centre of the towns, their former glory is still clearly visible. All the important buildings date from about the same period; everything that was built afterwards is generally of little significance. Outside Florence it is not always the Renaissance style that predominates. Prato, Pistoia, Lucca, Pisa or Siena, are noted for their Romanesque (11th and 12th centuries) and Gothic (13th to late 14th centuries architecture.

Prato: riches from rags

After Florence, Prato (13 km, 8 miles along the Viareggio motorway, A11) at first seems like stepping from the Golden Age into the Industrial Age. The busy city has been a famous textile centre since the days of the great Weavers' Guilds in the 12th century, has a population of approximately 150,000 and is one of the richest cities in Italy. Not many people are aware that its riches are based on rags, which are brought here by road, rail and ship from all over the world to be transformed into the most beautiful fabrics in Italy. It was only on a recent visit to one of the central warehouses that I learned that these "rags" which are imported from most of the wealthy nations, including the U.S.A., Switzerland and West Germany, are, in fact, whole shipments of almost new clothes, suits and coats. Now I know too how to recognise a real *"pratese":* by the somewhat deformed right hand, the result of years of ripping out the linings of these expensive cast-offs. The clothes are first sorted out according to colour. Linings and buttons are removed and then they are thrown into the shredder. The present boom in second-hand clothes has meant big business for the dealers in their huts in front of the warehouses, where the clothes are first inspected.

For the art lover, a visit to the centre of the town is worthwhile.

The *Cathedral,* built in the Pisan style, has a green and white diagonally striped marble façade and an outside pulpit by *Donatello* and *Michelozzo* decorated with a garland of cherubs; from here at Easter, on May 1st, August 15th, and September 6th, Prato's most revered relic, the "Sacred Girdle" is displayed to the public. The Cathedral also contains one of *Filippo Lippi's* most mature works: the frescoes depict the dramatic struggle of John the Baptist and the story of Salome, with tremendous grace and energy. The model for Salome was the ex-nun with whom Fr. Lippi eloped after seducing her.

There are other works by *Filippo Lippi* in the magnificent municipal art collection in the massive *Palazzo Pretorio* on the *Piazza del Comune,* which was built in the 13th and 14th centuries. To reach it, take the elegant Via Mazzoni. In the Palazzo Comunale (admission by request, mornings only, the façade of which (14th century) was altered in neo-classical style in the 18th century, you should visit the huge Council Hall *(Salone del Consiglio)* which has interesting frescoes and portraits of the Grand-Dukes of Tuscany.

For me, the most astonishing building in Prato is the *Emperor's Castle* in the centre of the town. This Hohenstaufen castle is the only one of its kind in Northern or Central Italy. The *"Castello dell'Imperatore",* which has recently been very expertly restored, was started in 1237 for Frederick II of Hohenstaufen, the cultured Swabian Emperor who lived in Palermo. The castle is square and has four high rectangular towers and plain walls as far as the crenellated Ghibelline battlements. It is reminiscent of the most beautiful of the the Hohenstaufen castles, the *Castel del Monte* in Apulia and may have been built by Apulian architects. Nowadays it is used for art exhibitions and occasionally for concerts and plays.

Prato has not only the fine *Metastasio Theatre,* but also is the headquarters of Luca Ronconi's theatre workshop, which gained international acclaim for its production of *Ariosto's Orlando Furioso.*

Recommended restaurants are: *"Il Pirana",* Via Velentini 110. *"Da Francesco",* Via Cambioni 27.

"Baghino" in *Via Dell'-Accademia 9* and *"Da Tonio",* Piazza Mercatale 161 are also very good.

Pistoia

Take the Viareggio motorway (A11) from Florence to the first exit beyond *Prato.* It is well signposted.

Pistoia was founded by the Romans and grew rich in the Middle Ages from the fertile land around it and the flourishing craftsmanship of its citizens: it was to become famous for the production of weapons (the word 'pistol' is said to derive from *Pistoia*). All the important buildings date from the 11th to the 14th centuries. The powerful, martial appearance of the secular buildings, the *Palazzo del Podestà* or *Pretorio* and the *Palazzo del Comune*, is explained by the bloody bickering which lasted for centuries, just as in Florence. The family struggle between the white and the black Guelfs started here and was taken to Florence for mediation: the Florentines then inherited it. No building of significance has been erected in Pistoia since the town was taken by Florence in 1530. Its flourishing industries have also declined, since the Bologna — Florence railway line was re-routed away from the town.

It is best to leave your car on the *Piazza San Lorenzo* or one of the side streets, and walk to the Cathedral in the *Piazza del Duomo*, the artistic and historic centre of the town. The Cathedral with its high bell tower, the Baptistery, and, facing each other, the *Palazzi del Comune* and *del Podestà* are all on the square.

The *Cathedral* and the *Campanile*, with its three arcades under the roof, are typical of the Pisan Romanesque style. The octagonal Baptistery, faced with bands of green and white marble, is an example of the earliest manifestations of the Gothic influence. Both Palazzi date from the 14th century. As a group, the buildings lend a unified Medieval appearance to the square.

There are glazed terracottas by *Andrea della Robbia* in and above the lunette above the main doorway of the *Duomo*; the tomb of the poet and lawyer, *Cino da Pistoia*, a friend of Dante, is in the simple and majestic interior of the church in the right aisle. And there is the great *dossale* (silver altar) in the *Capella di San Jacopo*, one of the most important pieces of silverwork in Italy: it took almost two hundred years to complete (1287-1456). In the left aisle there are frescoes by early Sienese painters.

The Gothic Baptistery was built between 1338 and 1359 from a design by *Andrea Pisano*.

In the austere mediaeval inner courtyard of the *Palazzo del Podestà* (nowadays a law court), decorated with coats of arms, you will see the judge's stone bench and table, and, next to it, the bench for the accused.

The Municipal Museum in the *Palazzo Comunale* contains several fine 15th and 16th century paintings.

In the *Ospedale del Ceppo*, which takes its name from the *"ceppo"*, or treestump, in which alms for the hospital were collected is a frieze by the *della Robbia* brothers - six sections of

181

glazed pottery relief work. There are few more moving and vivid representations of the seven acts of charity.

Taking the *Via San Bartolomeo* we reach the *Church of San Bartolomeo in Pantano,* which has a marble pulpit by *Guido da Como.* Two strange lions and a stooping man bear the pulpit on three pillars: eight reliefs show scenes from the Passion of Christ. A comparison with the pulpit by Giovanni Pisano, built only half a century later (*circa* 1300) in the *Sant Andrea* church (*Via S. Andrea*), shows clearly the development towards more animation, which anticipates the Renaissance. Six lions support the pulpit which has reliefs showing the Life of Christ.

It is also worth visiting another church in the Pisan style, *S. Giovanni Fuoricivitas* (take the *Via Roma* from the Cathedral Square, then the *Via Cavour*); its sides are decorated with two rows of pillars and arcades in green and white marble; it also contains inside, *Taddeo Gaddi's* polyptych and *"The Visitation"* by the *della Robbia* workshop.

Recommended restaurants are: the *"Cucciolo della Montagna",* Via Pantiatichi 4, in Pistoia: or *"Il Signorino"* in a village 13 km (8 miles) towards the *Passo della Collina* road.

Pisa: more than just a leaning tower

In Roman times, Pisa was an important naval base. The city was still right on the coast in Dante's time; nowadays it is 12 km (7.5 miles) from the sea in the plains which the Arno has flooded for centuries.

In the 11th century, Pisa — like Genoa, Venice and Amalfi — was a powerful, free maritime republic, ruling over Sardinia and Corsica. The only churches in Sardinia of any architectural importance were built by the people of Pisa in their own native style: pure Romanesque, faced in green and white marble.

The earliest Tuscan art to break with the Byzantine influence came from Pisa, not Florence. First came the Cathedral on the *Campo dei Miracoli* ("Field of Miracles") on the edge of the city. Thereafter came the Baptistery, the Leaning Tower and the Camposanto. The architect of the Cathedral was a Greek, the first man since Antiquity to build in marble. The style is Romanesque and Gothic. The effect produced by the four buildings of luminous Carrara marble is of Antiquity: an Acropolis, the City of God next to the City of Man.

Little else of significance was built in Pisa after the glories of the *Campo dei Miracoli.* In 1248, Pisa was conquered by Genoa, and decadence set in. In 1405, the city fell to Florence and the seal was set on the city's decline.

Pisa was badly damaged by artillery fire during the last war: by some miracle, only the Gothic Camposanto was damaged.

182

Pisa's other claim to fame is the University, the *Scuola Normale*. Its students, like those of the *École Normale Supérieure* in France, are considered to be the best in Italy.

When Buscheto, the Greek who is said to have been sent by the Emperor of Byzantium, started to build the Cathedral (*Duomo*) in 1603, there were few important churches in Italy, except in Rome and Ravenna. If we consider other Romanesque buildings of the period, we realise that here a new style of building, in the Hellenic manner, came into being. The overall impression created by the Cathedral is horizontal, like a temple, emphasised by the diagonal stripes in marble, which are the hallmark of all buildings in the Pisan style. The abundance and the originality of the ornamentation, and the high decorative arches above the pilasters, which cover the huge basilica, produce an almost oriental effect. When we recall the simplicity and clear lines of the Florentine architects, we realise that quite a different spirit was at work here.

The Cathedral was dedicated in 1118: a gallery of pointed Gothic arches was added later around the cupola. The sixty-eight Greek and Roman pillars in the interior date from Roman times: little else remains from that era in Pisa. The flat carved ceiling above the central nave dates from the 16th century. At the end of the central nave stands one of the most important pieces of Gothic sculpture in Italy: *Giovanni Pisano's pulpit*, built between 1302 and 1311. It is mounted on pillars and statues: the dramatic reliefs tell the story of the life of Christ.

Giovanni was the son of *Nicola Pisano*, who came from Apulia to Pisa. As soon as he had acquired full citizenship, he proudly started to call himself "*Pisano*". He was the first to break with the French and Northern Italian influence in sculpture. After studying the classical sarcophagi in the *Camposanto* next door, which had been brought to Pisa by ship much earlier, he introduced into his reliefs and sculpture a dynamism which was hitherto unknown. The art of Tuscany and Italy was enhanced for almost a century by the Pisano dynasty.

Opposite the altar hangs a great bronze lamp known as *Galileo's lamp*. The legend goes that Galileo Galilei, Pisa's most famous citizen, one day noticed the oscillation of the lamp after the sacristan lit it, and from his observation of it worked out his theory of the pendulum. Unfortunately the lamp was cast by *Battista Lorenzi* six years after the discovery.

Other important works are : a huge 13th century mosaic in the apse, "*Our Lord In Glory*" ascribed to *Cimabue;* a crucifix by *Giambologna* on the main altar; and *Tino di Camaiano's* tomb for the Emperor Henry VII in the outermost aisle on the left.

The *Baptistery* next to the main entrance to the Cathedral was started almost a hundred years later by *Diotisalvi* (literally 'May God Save You'). The upper section was completed towards the end of the 13th century with the addition of the figures of the Apostles and the Prophets: the Gothic ornamentation seems almost oriental. Like the Pantheon in Rome the roof was originally open. In the solemn, austere interior, the custodian enjoys surprising visitors by demonstrating the echo.

He will probably have shown you *Nicola Pisano's pulpit* (1260), the first Gothic sculpture in Italy to blend Gothic with the Classical. Black pillars resting on animals and slaves support it; reliefs tell of the Life of Christ.

The *Leaning Tower* leans over far more than you might think. It is an architectural gem, a fact which tends to be overlooked by those more interested in it as a curio. Over 50m (163 ft) high, it leans over approximately 4.30m (14 ft). The cylindrical structure has decorative arcades at the bottom, six open bands of pillars and a narrow tower at the top; it is probably the most elegant Romanesque building in the world.

Its history is almost as exciting as its 'lean'. It was started in 1173, but building had to be stopped, much to the amusement of Pisa's neighbouring rivals in Tuscany, when the sandy soil beneath started to give way. The people of Pisa started work on the building again in 1275 and created, to the annoyance of their neighbours, a new wonder of the world, which, seven hundred years later, still makes Pisa famous.

Many scientists and engineers have tried to make the Leaning Tower safer: a few years ago, cement was injected into the ground underneath. From the top of the tower, Galileo carried out his experiments on free falling objects. If you have a head for heights, you should climb the tower; the view of the sea and the gleaming marble of the Apuan Alps is superb.

In front of the left wing of the Cathedral stands the marble arcaded perimeter wall of the *Camposanto* (*cemetery*), which was started by *Giovanni di Simone* in 1278. Two simple doorways, the right one surmounted by a Gothic tabernacle, lead to the interior, which, by tradition, contains fifty-three cartloads of earth from Golgotha brought back by the Crusaders.

The cemetery was set alight by bombing in 1944. Molten lead dropping from the roof damaged *Benozzo Gozzoli's frescoes* of *Sodom and Gomorrah,* in particular.

The inner courtyard is surrounded by high Gothic alcoves with delicate tracery in the windows. There are *frescoes by Taddeo Gaddi, Spinello Aretino* and other artists in the central section and the remnants of Gozzoli's frescoes in the east wing;

but the most magnificent treasures are the three huge paintings (not frescoes since they are not painted on wet plaster but on a wooden framework set in the plaster): *"Triumph of Death", "The Last Judgement"* and the *"Thebans"*, which portray the life of the hermits in the desert. It has never been established who painted the pictures though they are commonly ascribed to *Francesco Traini*. The theme anticipated *Dante* and is taken up again by *Signorelli* in *Orvieto* and by *Michelangelo* in the *Sistine Chapel*. The paintings bring to mind Nardo di Cione's frescoes of Hell in Santa Maria Novella in Florence and were for many years ascribed to his brother, *Orcagna*. Goethe never saw the paintings but wrote of them in his diaries; the *"Triumph of Death"* inspired the second last scene of his *"Faust"*.

From the *Campo dei Miracoli*, we take the Via Santa Maria and turn left into Via dei Mille, into the ancient centre of the maritime republic, the *Piazza dei Cavalieri*. The Palazzo dei Cavalieri, which dominates the Piazza was designed by *Vasari* in the 16th century. The *Cavalieri*, the Knights of the Order of Saint Stephen, were the vanquishers of the Saracens. Their palazzo is nowadays occupied by the *Scuola Normale Superiore*. Next to it is the church of *S. Stefano dei Cavalieri* designed by Vasari. The beautiful, asymetric *Palazzo Gherardesca* completes the square. It is said to stand on the ruins of the *"hunger tower"*, in which the mad Count Ugolino della Gherardesca (according to Verse *XXXIII* of Dante's *"Inferno"*) ate his own children whom he had starved to death. Ugolino's tomb stands in the church of *San Francesco*, where you should also look at *Taddeo Gaddi's* frescoes and *Tommaso Pisano's* Polyptych.

There are other churches from Pisa's golden age, the 12th and 13th centuries all within walking distance of the Piazza dei Cavalieri. Those with the most impressive façades are perhaps *S. Michele in Borgo* (off the *Borgo Stretto*) and *S. Paolo a Ripa d'Arno*. The *Via delle Belle Torri* has the last surviving Mediaeval turreted patrician houses.

Close to the Arno — which in June 1944 was so full of rubble that it burst its banks and threatened to engulf all that had escaped the bombs — is the *National Museum* in the old monastery of *S. Matteo*. It contains early painted panels, sculptures, including many by the Pisano family and, amongst the Renaissance paintings, an altarpiece (perhaps the only one) by *Masaccio*.

Amongst many other churches and magnificent palaces to discover, the unusual church of *San Sepolcro*, built by the architect of the Baptistery is especially rewarding; and *San Frediano* with the tombs of the Knights of Saint Stephen and of the noble families of Pisa; and the tiny rival of the Leaning Tower, the octagonal leaning *Campanile of San Nicolo:* look at it from the inside too, as it has a remarkable spiral staircase said to be the model for Bramante's staircase in the Vatican.

It is not hard to find *Santa Maria della Spina,* the Romanesque-Gothic church on the banks of the Arno, since it stands like a reliquary next to the river and is visible from a long way off, despite its diminutive size. The thorn from Christ's crown of thorns which gave the church its name, is now kept in the *Santa Chiara* church. The myriad of pointed arches in the roof house gargoyles and miniature towers. In the interior, which is in three sections, four statues by *Tommaso Pisano* stand by the altar.

The *Ponte di Mezzo,* the next bridge, is the traditional setting for the *"Gioco del Ponte,"* a wild knockabout in 12th century costume played between the North bank of the Arno, known as the *Tramontana,* and the South bank, the *Mezzogiorno.* High casualty rates led to the game's abandonment.

The people of Pisa, by tradition, are quarrelsome, and if you understand the language you may hear them abusing their neighbours and rivals — especially the Florentines, the Lucchesi, and the 'unrefined boors from Livorno.'

An illegally parked car from any of these regions seldom escapes a parking ticket.

An unusual hotel, with pleasant historical associations is the *"Albergo Reale Vittoria".* Queen Victoria, Byron, Shelley and many other notables have spent a night there. It has scarcely changed since, and the huge rooms with their slightly shabby but fine furniture speak of former glories.

Marina di Pisa

On the way to the beach at *Marina di Pisa,* where clear water laps the rocks and from where you can see the islands of *Capraia* and *Gorgona,* you should visit the Basilica of *San Piero a Grado,* close to the mouth of the Arno. Legend has it that Saint Peter landed here. In the 11th century, the Romanesque Basilica was built on the ruins of an early Christian church dating from the 6th century. The exterior is as majestic as the three naves in the interior, their pillars surmounted by classical capitals. The cycle of frescoes of the life of Peter appears to have been influenced by Cimabue's frescoes in Assisi. Further information can be obtained at the *Tourist Office on the Piazza del Duomo (Campo dei Miracoli).*

Restaurants

The best restaurants in Pisa are: *"Tre Donzelle"*, Lungarno Pacinotti 2, *"Sergio"*, Via S.Cecilia 32, *"Buzzino"*, Via C.Cammeo 44, *"Emilio"*, Via Roma 26, *"Da Nando"*, Via Contessa Matilde 8.

In the immediate vicinity try *"Ugo"*, 8 km (5 miles) to the North on the *Via Aurelia*, or the excellent *"Rusticiello"*, 12.5 km (8 miles) from Pisa on the same road.

Bookshop

Libreria Feltrinelli, Corso Italia 117. Carries books in English.

The Countryside around Pisa

The three huge pine and scrub forests on the Pisa coast, the *Macchia di Migliarino, San Rossore* and *Tombolo*, are to be turned into a nature reserve. A drive from Pisa through a section of this majestic, almost jungle-like countryside gives some impression of how the coast must once have looked and makes one realise how much has been lost because of clearing and building.

On Sundays, a section of the 5000 hectares (12,355 acres) of the *San Rossore* forest is open to the public. It is worth taking advantage of this, and sitting under the huge pines to enjoy the wide expanse of meadowland at the edge of the forest.

The Carthusian monastery in Calci

A visit to *Calci*, approximately 14 km (8.7 miles) east of Pisa is highly recommended: take a look at the 12th century *Pieve* with its cracked bell-tower and an interesting baptismal font into which candidates for baptism had to climb using the steps. Also the *Carthusian monastery*, the finest in Italy after Pavia, which stands like a fortress behind the village. It was altered in the baroque manner in the 18th century. The last of the silent monks left five years ago and now the monastery slumbers, bereft of its purpose, as a national monument. Only the inscription above the doorway still refers to the paradise of solitude:

Abitantibus oppidum carcer solitudo paradisum est

"For those leaving the hurly-burly of city life, the solitude of a cell is paradise".

The spacious, bare quarters of the monks still tell of lives once devoted in silence to God. If you venture further up the narrow road past the convent to the next village up on the hill, you will find two romantic, abandoned farm-houses with an old coach standing in front of them.

From Calci, you can drive via *Vicopisano* (look at the four gates in the city wall, one of which is said to have been the work of *Brunelleschi,* and the Romanesque *Pieve).* On Road 67 towards *Empoli:* turn off left, shortly beyond *Empoli* to *Cerreto Guidi* and *Vinci.* (Firenze Province)

A Medici Museum

At the end of 1978, the villa of Cosimo I dei Medici, built by Buontalenti, was opened as a museum: it is a building of classical simplicity and beauty, which used to contain portraits of the Medicis and nothing else. But what portraits! The bourgeois Medici family, from the 17th century onwards, married into almost every European aristocratic family, including the Hapsburgs.

In this villa Prince Orsini strangled Isabella of Medici and the morbid may view the rope with which he did it.

Leonardo da Vinci (Prov. Firenze)

Three kilometres to the North-east, huge portraits of Leonardo beside the road announce that you are soon to enter his birth-place, *Vinci.* But pass it by for the time being, and drive through a beautiful olive grove to *Anchiano,* which consists of nothing more or less than one house, the house in which Leonardo was born.

The house of the lawyer, da Vinci, has only three rooms: his maid, Catherina, bore him a son, Leonardo, in 1452. In the last of the three rooms, where young Leonardo gathered leaves, stones, beetles or anything he came across, to study and draw, a slide presentation was set up in the spring of 1978 (it is taste-fully and well done, even if it does spoil the atmosphere a little). The slide-show explains the main works of the versatile genius and includes *"The Baptism of Christ"* (*Uffizi*) by *Verrochio,* da Vinci's teacher, to which da Vinci added the angel on the left. When Verrochio saw it, he broke his brush, recognising that he had found a genius in his pupil.

In the *Mediaeval Castle* in *Vinci.* Leonardo da Vinci's inventions are on display. Reproductions of his drawings (mainly from the *"Codice Atlantico"* collection) and modern models of his incredibly futuristic machines — from the armoured car to the machine gun, to the aeroplane and the mechanical weaving loom. The models are impressive but dull and unexciting compared to the brilliant designs in Leonardo's mirror-writing.

If you want to rejoin the *Autostrada del Sole* in the north near Prato, go via *Poggio a Caiano,* where *Lorenzo the Magnificent* had a villa built by *Giuliano da Sangallo:* it is one of the most magnificent in the Florence area. (It is open until dusk. Ring the custodian's bell).

San Miniato al Tedesco (Prov. Pisa)

If you prefer the old *Emperors' Road,* which led from Pavia to Rome, go back to *Empoli* and then to *San Miniato al Tedesco.* The suffix, 'al Tedesco' means 'of the Germans' and dates from the days when all of Northern Italy had to pay taxes to the Holy Roman Emperors. Many of the Emperors stayed here; Barbarossa was the first).

The old town with its high towers, palaces and churches spread over three hills above the Arno, is worth a visit. And not only in August when religious plays are performed in the impressive open air theatre. Countess Mathilda of Tuscany (1046-1115) came from here, and caused endless dynastic problems by bequeathing her dominions to the church. It also claims to be the original home of the Bonaparte family before they migrated to Corsica.

The finest building — apart from the churches of *San Domenico* and *San Francesco* and the *Cathedral* — is the 12th century *Palazzo dei Vicari dell'Imperatore,* the palace of the Imperial Representatives.

As you leave *San Miniato,* you will pass the excellent *'Carello''* restaurant, on the Piazza in *San Miniato da Basso.*

Certaldo (Prov. Firenze)

Road 429 to *Poggibonsi* takes you into Black Cock country: the Black Cock is the symbol of *Chianti* Classico (See p. 60). Continue up into (approximately 20 km - 12 miles) the old centre of *Certaldo* which is completely built in tile; the warm red glow greets you across the plain. The village consists of only one street, lined with beautifully restored mediaeval buildings. On the left in the middle stands the supposed *birthplace of Boccaccio,* which contains a small library of first and rare editions. The street turns off to the right at the *Palazzo del Vicario,* which is brightly decorated with *terracotta* crests. The palazzo is worth a visit because of the *''cortile''* (inner courtyard), the interesting frescoes and the provocative inscription above the courtroom: "Hate your opponent and have faith in very little".

You can sample the typical game dishes of Tuscany and the chef's speciality, *''Papardelle alla lepre'',* in the garden of the *osteria* next door. If you are lucky, you might find a room in the beautifully peaceful *Albergo Castello* at the beginning of the street.

San Gimignano (Prov. Siena)
Not far from Certaldo is San Gimignano, the most famous of Tuscany's hill settlements (almost all of them date from Etruscan times). From a distance you can see, soaring into the sky, the fifteen family towers which have survived from the original seventy-two. In the Middle Ages, it was the custom among great families to erect a tower above or next to their palazzo as a symbol of their power: if possible it had to be higher than those of their neighbours. Some places, San Gimignano for example, had whole skylines of 'family towers'; they were symbols of pride, envy and the desire for power — a medieval version of Manhattan.

San Gimignano has always had a great impact on its visitors. It so impressed E.M. Forster when he visited it in 1902 that it became the model for the Italian medieval town Monteriano in *Where Angels Fear to Tread.*

The most important building is the cathedral, the *Duomo* or *Collegiata.* It contains frescoes by *Ghirlandaio (Santa Fina Chapel), Benozzo Gozzoli ("St. Sebastian")* and *Taddeo di Bartolo's "The Last Judgement":* the portrayal of Heaven and Hell is clearly influenced by *Dante.* In addition, there are two figures in wood by *Iacopo della Quercia.*

Taddeo di Bartolo from Siena also painted *San Gimignano,* patron saint of the town (he saved the town from Attila) standing in front of the towers which bear his name. The painting hangs in the Palazzo Comunale. The most valuable painting in their collection is *Lippo Memmi's 'Maesta'.*

There are *Gozzoli* frescoes also of the life of Saint Augustine and the death of Monica, his mother, in the chancel of the monastery church of *Sant Agostino.* If there is a vacant cell, you can spend the night in the monastery next door, which is now occupied by only a few old monks. In the morning, you can look from a narrow window across the countryside which was painted by the pious artists of Siena. As you go down into the Cloisters and through the doorway, it comes as no surprise to find the Middle Ages still intact on the outside.

Volterra: ruler of the islands (Prov. Pisa)
To reach Volterra, drive approximately 12.5 km (8 miles) towards Castel S. Gimignano from Gimignano, then take Road 68: Or from Pisa it lies 70 km (44 miles) to the south-east. Take the *Aurelia* and turn inland shortly before *Piombino* (30 km - 19 miles).

The Etruscans name for Volterra was Velathri. It was one of the leading city states of the Tyrrhenian Empire, which ruled over *Elba, Corsica* and the coast from *Livorno* to *Piombino.* The necropolis, probably the largest in Italy, has been swallowed up by the chasms which surround the town. Volterra stands in a lunar landscape of strangely shaped lava hills, which have been eaten away by erosion. All round the *Etruscan city wall,* which was once 7 km (4 miles) long and is still 12 m (39 ft) high in some places, there are gaping chasms or 'balze' coming closer and closer in the slow march of time. Only a few metres separate the ancient deserted abbey of the Camaldolesian monks from a plunge into ruin. The monastery church and its treasures, with frescoes by *Giotto, Ghirlandaio* and *Botticelli,* have long since fallen into a state of irreparable decay.

Volterra's age of greatness ended 500 years ago when the city fell to the Florentines after successfully resisting Romans, invaders from the north and mediaeval tyrants. The massive Medici fortress, nowadays one of Italy's most forbidding prisons, dates from this period. Most of the buildings on the *Piazza dei Priori* date from the period of Volterra's glory, the 13th century: the *Palazzo Pretorio* and the *Palazzo dei Priori* with its five-sided tower, the *Romanesque cathedral* and the *octagonal baptistery.* You should climb up the tower on a fine day and enjoy the magnificent view: the faded hills in the foreground; behind them, the sea and the islands shimmering in the strong light, the Appenines to the east and north — and beyond them, the shining marble peaks of the Apuan Alps.

The Cathedral has a few fine pieces - particularly *Mino da Fiesole's* tabernacle. *The Etruscan Museum (Museo Guarnacci — Via Don Minzoni)* also has an excellent collection, especially of alabaster funeral urns.

The most noticeable feature about Volterra is, however, the atmosphere, which is that of a small town, living on the glories of its past. Rooks caw around the ancient towers, women dressed in black move silently through the streets, where the hum of polishing machines comes from almost every window. Volterra is a town of widows: the men die young here, their lungs eaten away by the alabaster dust which hangs everywhere in white clouds. This is the only place in Europe where alabaster, a rock similar to marble but softer, is found. Since Etruscan times, alabaster has been Volterra's only industry. And if you look at the carving on the Etruscan urns and compare it with the work which is produced today, you will see that the people of Volterra still incline towards *kitsch.*

The Etruscan gate (Porta all 'Arco) in the city wall bears three crumbling heads — emperors, gods, demons? Their significance is not known. Eyeless and silent, they look down on us and on the gaping chasms.

191

Further information is available from the *Associazione Turistica Pro - Volterra: via G. Turazza.* Tel: 86150.

Restaurants
   "Etruria", Piazza dei Priori 8 and *"Il Porcellino". Vicolo della Prigione 18,* can be recommended for good food.

Siena

Siena is one of the most beautiful cities in Italy and certainly the most beautiful of the Gothic cities. Its walls and roofs of tile-reds and russet browns, set on a hill, welcome the visitor with the inscription above the Porta Camollia:

Cor magis tibi Sena pandit: Siena opens her heart wider to you. (i.e. than this gate).

The inhabitants of Siena are said to be the most polite in Italy; they are also said to speak the best Italian. And the heart that beats in these people living in the shelter of the mediaeval walls, is indeed a passionate one. They can also claim a very superior patron. In 1438, the year after the birth of Caterina, the 25th child of a weaver, Benincasa, Siena, was in danger of dying from the plague. Both the city and the child survived. Caterina, who was canonised a century later and declared patron saint of Italy in 1939, became one of the most controversial and learned women in history.

If your visit is only brief, you will have time to see only its art treasures and the architecture of its greatest period (13th—16th centuries). But the essence of the city can be discovered only by wandering through the streets, observing the people and soaking in the beauty of its paintings.

The Ghibelline city of Siena, which supported the Emperors from the North and adopted their northern Gothic spirit, was decimated by the plague; the *Cathedral. (Duomo)* which had been started in the Romanesque style in the 12th century, was continued in the Gothic style. As the plans in the *Opera del Duomo* show, it was to be the largest and most beautiful church in Tuscany, perhaps in Christendom - if only to annoy the Florentines. But when Lando di Pietro, the architect, and his assistants died, the money and courage were lacking, and only the transept and the black and white zebra-striped tower had been completed. The wide arches and pilasters which were to make up the nave show what a magnificent work of art was left unfinished. The interior, with its triple nave, is still splendid beneath the myriad of stars on the lofty, vaulted ceiling which rises above high pillars. Some visitors from Northern Europe may find the black and white horizontal stripes of the marble facing, which also covers the whole interior, too "busy", accustomed as they are to finding tranquillity and seclusion in their Gothic cathedrals, but artistically it is bold and exciting.

The Cathedral

The most important work in the Cathedral is the *octagonal pulpit,* which was started in 1625 by *Nicola Pisano,* assisted by his son *Giovanni* and the Pisan artist, *Arnolfo di Cambio* (the architect of Florence Cathedral). Though it resembles his pulpit in Pisa, the dramatic Gothic spirit is far removed from the style of the Classical sarcophagi which had been his models. Among my favourite works in Siena are the eight little Pinturicchio frescoes in the Chapel of St. John next to the pulpit, and the moving late sculpture (1457) by Donatello, the bronze statue of John the Baptist.

A look at the chapel of the aristocratic Chigi family, which produced one Pope and many leading bankers, will remind music lovers of the Accademia Musicale Chigiana. This foundation is one of the few internationally famous private conservatories of music in Italy and holds advanced courses for young musicians each summer. In the chapel among the statues in the niches of the Piccolomini altar, are four early works by Michelangelo.

From the North Aisle you enter the *'Libreria Piccolomini'* (admission charge), a beautiful Renaissance library with enchanting frescoes by Pinturicchio, who had been commissioned by Pope Pius III to paint scenes from the life of his uncle, Pius II. The frescoes clearly depict the life of a nobleman in the first half of the 15th century, a humanist who became a cardinal and then Pope. The *Libreria* was built to house the library of this famous Piccolomini. In its centre stands the famous *"Three Graces",* a Roman copy of a Greek model which we know from many drawings and encounter again in the work of Botticelli in Florence and also of Raphael and, later, Canova.

From the right side of the Cathedral, you go down to the *Piazza San Giovanni* and enter the *Baptistery* on the left (not the crypt as you might think). The *baptismal font* is one of the principal works of *Iacopo della Quercia.* It was started in 1417 and clearly demonstrates the transition from Gothic to Renaissance.

Returning to the Piazza, we stand in front of the grandiose pillars and arches of the unfinished *'Great Cathedral'.* The first three arches of the left nave have been closed in and now contain the *Cathedral Museum.* (*Museo del'Opera del Duomo or Metropolitana*).

194

Among the many masterpieces from the Tuscan and Sienese School (most came from the Cathedral and are here for safe-keeping) you will find one of the rare, well-preserved works by *Duccio di Buoninsegna,* the *"Maestà"* (painted between 1308-1311). The Madonna and Child, enthroned between angels and saints, represents the beginning of the great Sienese School of painting, which combines the Hellenistic, Byzantine tradition with the delicacy of French Gothic miniatures. The Latin inscription on the step of the throne reads *"Oh, Holy Mother of God, give Siena peace and Duccio eternal life, because he has painted you so beautifully"*. Opposite the *"Maestà"* hang *the predellae,* with scenes from the Passion of Christ. On the right wall is a masterpiece from *Pietro Lorenzetti's* mature period, *"The Birth of the Virgin"* and an early work by *Duccio, "Madonna and Child"*.

There are many other works to admire here, and also the architectural fragments of the *"New Cathedral":* you will see from the plan what a magnificent concept it was.

Opposite the Cathedral is the *hospital (Ospedale di S. Maria della Scala).* You are allowed to go in (ask the porter) and you should. It is not everyday that you see a hospital with frescoes and pillars with Corinthian capitals, and arches.

The Pinacoteca

Of the many fine palaces in Siena perhaps the finest is the late Gothic palazzo of the *Buonsignori:* it houses the *Pinacoteca Nazionale* which is a must for anyone interested in the development of Sienese painting. The collection was started in the 18th century and shows in chronological order, the most important painters in Siena, from the 13th century onwards. The beautiful Renaissance *Piccolomini Palace* contains, among other things, the *National Archives* (open 11-13) which have one main attraction, even for non-historians and non-Italian speakers: the *"Tavolette di Biccherna"*, painted bookcovers dating from between 1285 and 1659, which bound the accounts, tax and customs lists of the city. Some of them were painted by the most distinguished artists of the day, beginning with the *Lorenzetti brothers:* they show symbolic or religious scenes or important historical events.

The *Campo,* the shell-shaped Piazza in front of the City Hall, where the *"Palio"* (see page 198) is held, is one of the most important sights in Siena for a multitude of reasons. The Piazza itself is as beautiful and unique as Saint Mark's or St. Peter's

Square. It is surrounded by Mediaeval buildings of a warm brick red and dominated by the *Torre del Mangia,* the tower of the City Hall (Palazzo Pubblico). It is so-called after its first bell-ringer, a spendthrift whose nickname was *Mangiaguadagni* or 'Eat up one's earnings'.

In the Campo is the great walled fountain, the *"Fonte Gaia"* (the "merry source") which bears (only copies of) Iacopo della Quercia's reliefs. The originals are in the City Hall. It is called *Fonte Gaia* because of the public rejoicing that attended its completion in 1419.

The Palazzo Pubblico

The Palazzo Pubblico, built at the beginning of the 14th century, is probably the most noble and elegant Gothic palace in Tuscany: it was the model for many palaces in Siena. The second floor and the crenellated central section were not added until the 15th century. The frescoes and paintings in the interior turn it into an invaluable museum of early Sienese painting. The most famous paintings from the most important period, the 13th century, hang on the first floor of the Municipal Museum. In the vestibule, a gilded Roman she-wolf suckles the twins, Romulus and Remus. The motif is encountered frequently in Siena. Legend has it that Siena was founded by Senus, the son of Remus.

In the next room the real world takes the upper hand with *Ambrogio Lorenzetti's* allegories, *"Good and Bad Government".* The world is visible on the entrance wall in the portrayal of the theological and the political virtues: Courage, Generosity, Wisdom, Justice, Moderation. Beneath is the army of Siena and the allegories of Justice. Next to it, a scene of the city in Lorenzetti's time (both brothers died of the plague in 1348) and in front of it, almost like a genre painting, the *"Effects of Good Government":* dancing girls, contented farmers, fishermen and hunters. In the background, the harbour at Talamone, from which Siena sought support for its ambition to become a great maritime power.

The frescoes on bad government on the facing wall have, unfortunately, been badly damaged. The horned, snarling figure of Tyranny crouching amidst his followers: Cruelty, Deception, Betrayal, War, the Vices, Envy, Vanity and Pride. The consequences of *"Mal Governo",* all of them vivid horror scenes, have been for the most part been lost. Above the fresco of *"Buon Governo",* smiles a girl, the embodiment of summer: above *"Mal Governo"* there is a frieze of a man shivering in a snowstorm.

196

The small guide book available at the museum, free of charge, provides further details about the many other important frescoes by *Taddeo di Bartolo, Sodoma, Spinello, and others*.

In the last room are more recent frescoes of the life of the first king of united Italy, Victor Emmanuel II. After the glories of Simone Martini and Lorenzetti, this is truly a progress from the sublime to the ridiculous.

The fragments of *Iacopo della Quercia's "Fonte Gaia"* lie in a loggia on the second floor.

In the next room we come to *Simone Martini's "Maestà"*, which is almost as fine as Duccio's. The "Maestà" which captures the regal dignity of the Mother of God, enthroned and surrounded by a whole court of saints, is an invention of the Early Sienese School. Siena was the first city in Italy to choose Mary as their patron saint, so Siena's artists painted her with special feeling. The *"Umiltà"*, another stylised manner of representing the Virgin Mary, is almost as common: Mary is represented, not as a queen, but as a humble, ordinary mother caressing her divine child. Simone Martini is said to have been the originator of this form.

But here we see Mary as Queen: her Child bears a scroll with the inscription *"Your ruler on earth, love justice"*. This was the courtroom of the Republic.

On the facing wall there is a knight in armour, *Guidoriccio Fogliani*, who won two famous victories for Siena and, apart from its colourful dignity, the painting claims two firsts in art history: the figure is surrounded by the first panoramic landscape in European painting (in Duccio's predellae the landscape still resembles a scenario) and it is the first full size painting of a contemporary figure. The painting is one of *Simone Martini's* finest works in the courtly High Gothic style. If you consider the gilded background used by Duccio and the panels by other contemporaries, where the real world has no place, you realise what a bold step this was.

Around the city of Siena

It is important not to overlook the poorly restored Gothic church of *San Francesco*. A cycle of frescoes by *Ambrogio Lorenzetti*, which was thought to have been lost, was discovered beneath the whitewash. What could be saved was taken from the wall and is displayed in the third chapel in the transept. In the chapel of the seminary next door, you can see Lorenzetti's beautiful *"Madonna del Latte"*. In the upstairs room of the *Oratory of Saint Bernardino*, close to the San Francesco church, are important frescoes by *Beccafumi* and *Sodoma*.

197

The infamous *Sodoma* (nick-named thus because of his supposed vice), was a Lombard pupil of da Vinci. He painted his finest frescoes in the church of San Domenico in 1526. His work, *"The Ecstasy of Saint Catherine"*, shows how skilfully even an impious artist could handle pious subjects. San Domenico also has a protrait of the saint painted by her disciple, Andrea Vanni. From San Domenico, follow the Via della Sapienza, then take the Costa Sant Antonio down to the house of Saint Catherine. Further down you come to Siena's most beautiful Gothic fountain, the *Fonte Branda*.

On the way back to the centre, you will see one of the most picturesque mediaeval streets in Siena, *the Via della Galluza*. The *Via Sallustio Bandini*, the *Via del Commune* and the court-yard known as *del Castellare degli Ugurgieri* are also evocative of Siena's magnificent past.

The smartest streets, lined with palazzi and elegant shops, are the *Via di Città* and the *Via Banchi di Sopra*.

If you speak or understand a little Italian, you will notice how the Sienese, tend to aspirate their consonants, saying *"hasa"* for instance, instead of *"casa"* and *"hane"* instead of *"cane"*. This tendency they share with the Florentines, but little else. Indeed they consider themselves on the whole superior to Florence and need little prompting to remind you of the greatest day in their history: the victory of Siena over Florence at the Battle of Montaperti in 1260.

The Palio

By 1555, after a long and bitter siege, Siena was captured by the imperial troops and, four years later, became part of the Grand Duchy of Tuscany; decadence had already set in. Over 700 families left, preferring exile to the rule of the hated Florentines. Siena became a quiet country town on the edge of history and has remained so ever since. As a result the media-eval character of the city has been preserved. Even the passion-ate irrationality of the people survives between the old walls. The *Palio* will give the visitor some inkling of this.

On July 2nd and August 14th, ten of the seventeen *Contradi* or city districts, battle for the *'Palio'*, a silk banner bearing a picture of the Madonna; the *'Palio'* is displayed in the parish church of the victorious *'contrada'* until the next race. The event of the *'Palio'* is a barbaric, bareback horse-race around the steep, oval Piazza del Campo in front of the town hall.

There is nothing quite comparable to this in Europe with the possible exception of Spanish bullfights. Strangers are well received — and forgotten, for here Siena celebrates its own history in a two hour procession in 14th to 16th century costume, to the slow staccato of drums and pipes and whirling banners. All Siena throngs to the Piazza, or jockeys for position on rooftops and at windows all around, in a turmoil of enthusiasm, hope or disappointment.

The involvement in the *'Palio'* lasts the whole year round, dividing friends and families who live in different areas and who see themselves as members of the 'Tower', the 'Tortoise', the 'Porcupine' first, as citizens of Siena second and last of all as Italians. I know a dignified banker in Siena who refuses to eat at the same table as his sons who live in another *'contrada'*. I also know a jockey who has ridden twice in the *'Palio'*, risking life and limb. Since it became known that he had been bribed by a rival *'contrada'* to hold back his horse, he has not dared to come back to the province, let alone to Siena, for fear of being attacked.

Each of the horses selected is first blessed in the parish church, and it is considered a good omen if the horse defecates at the altar. Even a riderless horse can win — and any rider who has safely completed the course risks being torn apart by enthusiastic supporters all of whom want to carry him shoulder high. The losers are somtimes literally beaten.

For the gourmet
Of the specialities of Siena, (the most famous are *"panforte"*, a type of fruit loaf, and the sweet *"ricciarelli"* and *"cavalucci")*. I would recommend the wild boar salami and the *"pecorino"*, a particularly aromatic ewe cheese.

The best restaurants are:
'Guido', Vicolo Pier Pettinaio 7:
'Nello—La Taverna', Via del Porrione 28.
'Tullio—Tre Cristi', Vicolo di Provenzano 1:
'Renzo', Via delle Tarme 14:

'Le Tre Campane' Via Monna Agenese 5 and 'Il Campo', Piazza del Campo 50 are also good.

Excursions from Siena

The countryside south of Siena, like the Casentino in Arezzo province, is sparsely populated. Here Tuscany has remained as the 14th century artists portrayed it for us: a rough rolling countryside of silvery grey perspectives. One often has the impression that artists are still shaping the contours for us with cleverly placed groups of trees, single umbrella pines on hilltops, erect lines of cypresses climbing up a hillside. The shrewd peasants have planted the trees, however, to protect their thinly soiled hillsides from erosion.

This landscape of harmonious austerity is an excellent antidote to the narrow and noisy confines of modern life. The following tour through it is only an outline of the more interesting places, a prelude, perhaps, to more detailed exploration.

Buonconvento

From Siena take Road 2, the *Cassia,* an old Roman road, south to *Buonconvento* (30 km, 19 miles) a small walled town with a tiny but select collection of paintings from the Sienese school. These are in the *Pinacoteca* near the *Pieve* or parish church of *SS Peter and Paul,* which is also worth a visit. It was here, in 1313, that Henry VII, whom Dante refers to as the 'lamb of God', died on his way back from Rome, and with him the last hopes of the Ghibelline cause. His tomb is in the Cathedral in Pisa and there is a fine sculpture of him on the Camposanto outside.

Monte Oliveto Maggiore

Turn left in Buonconvento and drive through impressive scenery to the monastery of *Monte Oliveto Maggiore* (9 km, 5½ miles). It stands in splendid isolation in a wood of cypresses above olive groves. The white-robed monks of the Oliveto order (a strict sect of the Benedictines) follow their vows of *'Ora et Labora',* 'prayer and work', here. They will gladly show you their church, however, where you are welcome to sit in the ancient pews for a Gregorian Mass. They will also show you their great masterpiece: the frescoes in the cloisters by *Signorelli* and *Sodoma,* depicting the life of Saint Benedict.

Montalcino
From Monte Oliveto drive back to Buonconvento and from there
take the Via Cassia as far as *Torrenieri* (there is a cheap, clean
albergo with enormous rooms, on the right) for about 10km (6.2
miles) then turn right to *Montalcino* (9km, 5.6 miles). The
picturesque little town which is of Etruscan origin, sits majestically
above the surrounding hills. It has several fine palaces, a *'rocco'*
(castle) and two museums. It was the seat of the Sienese
government in exile, which was set up in 1555 by the great families
who left Siena after it fell to Florence. Four years later, Cosimo
de Medici put an end to their activities.

Montalcino (the name derives from alcium, the oak) is justly
proud of its wine, *"Brunello"*, and has carefully preserved twelve
bottles of the 1888 vintage: the corks are changed every year with
solemn ceremonial. It can be bought for 1.3 million lire per bottle
(approximately £750). One bottle is on display in the red plush
bar on the Piazza del Popolo.

In the 9th century, Montalcino belonged to the *Abbey of Sant'
Antimo* which you can visit on the way to Monte Amiata (9km,
5.6 miles to the south).

Sant' Antimo
The early Romanesque *Benedictine Abbey* in the Starcia valley
below *Castelnuovo dell'Abate* is as beautiful as its location and
the peace which surrounds it. It is listed in few guidebooks and
I have a Tuscan friend to thank for bringing me here.

Legend has it that the abbey was founded by Charlemagne. The
triple-naved basilica in the valley below the village of Castel -
nuovo dell'Abate is impressive even from a distance. More than
any other Benedictine building in Italy, it displays characteristically French architectural features: it is almost like a piece of France
implanted in Tuscany. The facade and the lofty interior are
unadorned and solemn. The superbly elegant matroneum, (the
gallery reserved for women), with its Gothic arcades, rises on
pillars and capital which are decorated with an immense variety
of relief work.

The arhcitectural ornamentaion on the pale travertine building
is of onyx. The old sacristan knows how to heighten the pleasure
of the few visitors he receives, by using the light of a candle to
make the stone looke transparent and to pick out the golden tones.
The chapter house of the monastery, which is almost totally in
ruins, dates from Carolingian times.

If the basilica is closed, as it generally is, you can fetch the
key from the custodian, Ermenegildo di Monaco, in Castel-

nuovo dell'Abate. It is better to leave your car outside the village, for, although it has three grandiose Renaissance palaces, the streets are very narrow.

Monte Amiata
8km (4.9 miles) further on you reach Road 323: turn south/right and go via *Castel del Piano* to the highest point in Southern Tuscany, *Monte Amiata*, a 1740 metres (5,700 ft) high extinct volcano which towers above the surrounding countryside. It is an excellent orientation point and landmark.

It is a popular skiing resort in winter and, in summer, a cool oasis, particularly popular with the Romans. From the iron tower on the summit, you have a magnificent view as far as the Apennines near Modena to the north, the Abruzzi Hills in the east, Monte Cimini beyond Viterbo to the south, and Elba in the west.

If you are interested in minerals, you will find an excellent selection of the ores mined on and around Monte Amiata, at the kiosks just below the summit. Take the beautiful mountain road through thick forests of chestnut trees, to the *Abbadia San Salvatore* (14km, 8.7 miles), which was founded in the reign of the Langobard king, Rachis, in 743, and became the richest abbey in Tuscany. It was first occupied by the Benedictines, then by the Camaldolesians, and from the 13th century onwards by the Cistercians who returned here in 1939. Little remains of the original monastery. The beautifully restored Romanesque church survived, however. It contains an interesting cycle of frescoes of the legend of Rachis.

The *"borgo medievale"*, the old centre of the village, is an interesting example of an almost intact walled village. There are houses from the Gothic and Renaissance periods, built from trachyte, a volcanic rock, which has aged to tones of dark grey and black over the centuries.

There is also a very winding road from San Salvatore almost to the top of Monte Amiata (12.5km, 7.8 miles).

At the weekly village market in *Abbadia San Salvatore*, you will find pretty, strongly woven baskets, strings of garlic and the huge green umbrellas typical of Tuscany, which will provide ample consolation on grey, rainy days in the North.

Road 478 leads over the Radicofani Pass, through wild isolated hills past Sarteano to the thermal springs in Chianciano.

Etruscan tombs at Chiusi (Prov. Siena)
Near Chianciano is *Chiusi* (Latin: *Clusium*), now a small busy country town. From the 7th to the 9th centuries B.C., it was one of the leading Etruscan city states.

Chiusi was occupied by the Goths, made a Dukedom by the Langobards, then decimated by malaria: it was briefly a free city state in the 14th century and finally yielded to the superior power of Florence in 1556. The layout of the Roman garrison town survived, however, above the labyrinth of underground passageways which were dug by the Etruscans.

The *Cathedral*, which was founded in the 6th century and extended in the 12th century, is worth seeing, despite the over-enthusiastic restoration work carried out in the last century. The interior is almost totally disfigured by modern frescoes made to look like moasaics. The *Chapter House* has an interesting collection of twenty-two old hymn books which are filled with exquisite miniatures.

Beneath the bell tower of the Cathedral under a dome, there is a large water container (*piscina*), dug out of the volcanic rock probably in the 1st century B.C. One of the subterranean tunnels dug by the Etruscans, which wind through the bedrock beneath Chiusi, like the holes in a Gruyère cheese, begins here. Only a fraction of it has been cleared.

Opposite the left wall of the Cathedral is the famous *Etruscan Museum*. Among the interesting items on display are an alabaster sarcophagus with a relief of the Battle of the Gauls and a sculpture of a dead man on the lid; a bronze throne decorated with fantastic animals and a palm tree: and two funeral urns, each with the figure of a woman in a ritualistic pose, surrounded by other female figures and the heads of griffins. There are also Attic amphorae decorated with black figures. The most beautiful shows Achilles and Ajax playing dice in front of Athene.

Chiusi has various old churches and palaces: the finest are in the *Via Porsenna*. On the *Piazza Vittorio Veneto*, which is overgrown with weeds, Etruscan and Roman remains lie scattered around in picturesque fashion. On the main road to Chianciano you will see enormous remnants of a wall which appears to date from the Umbrian period in the pre-Etruscan era.

The most interesting part of Chiusi is the *necropolis*, the only one in Tuscany with painted tombs. The frescoes are so beautiful and lively that they almost match those in Tarquinia, but they are fading so badly that only a few years can be left in which to see them in detail.

To reach the necropolis, take the Chianciano road, then turn off to the right shortly after you leave the town, into the Via delle Tombe Etrusche.

The first tomb, the *"Tomba della Pellegrina"* (3rd - 2nd century B.C., *i.e.* late Etruscan) has frescoes on themes from Greek mythology and is a rarity in Etruscan burial grounds. It was restored when it was discovered in 1928 and the funeral urns and sarcophagi were left in place. Immediately next to it, under a huge cypress tree, is the *"Tomba della Scimmia"*. It is the most interesting tomb in the Chiusi area because of its frescoes, though these have now faded almost completely. The name comes from a fresco of a little monkey, tied to a tree, waiting to make its entrance at the burial celebrations staged by musicians, jugglers, boxers and warriors. The dead woman sits attentively and elegantly under a parasol and looks on. From the main vault, doors lead into another three painted chambers.

The guide will indicate and explain the other important tombs: the *"Tomba del Granduca"* which has reliefs, the *"Tomba del Colle"* which has only copies of the original frescoes (the originals were removed and taken to the museum) and the *"Tomba delle Tassinaie"* which also has frescoes.

Take Road 146 from Chiusi via Chianciano where there are plenty of good hotels and spa facilities which claim to cure you of every imaginable ailment. It is open from April 16th till October 31st. This will bring you to *Montepulciano.*

Montepulciano (Prov. Siena)
Montepulciano, the birthplace of the Renaissance poet, *Poliziano* (Politian) (1454 - 1494), is said to have been founded by the Etruscan king, Porsenna: the town is first referred to as *"Mons Politanus"* in a chronicle dating from 715. It stands on a hill like an open air museum of Renaissance architecture.

As with all the towns worth seeing in Tuscany the total impression is as enchanting as the detail. You should walk about the little town and up and down its steep streets, for everywhere you will find something of interest; not least important of the discoveries you can make is the famous local wine, the *"vino nobile di Montepulciano"*....

The following are worth a visit: *Antonio da Sangallo's* finest church, *Madonna di San Biago,* at the foot of the hill; in the town, the churches of *Sant'Agnese, Sant'Agostino* and *Santa Maria dei Servi;* the birthplace of *Poliziano* in the *Via Poliziano No. 5,* and at the top of the hill, the *Cathedral* and the magnificent palazzi around the Piazza. On the left is the Gothic *Palazzo Comunale:* from its tower you can see as far as Siena in the west and Lake Trasimene in the east. Opposite is the *Palazzo Contucci,* built by *Antonio da Sangallo* and next to that the elegant *Palazzo Tarugi,* built by *Vignola.*

Since 1974, one of the best improvised festivals has been held in Montepulciano in the first half of August: the "art workshop" directed by the German composer, Hans Werner Henze fills the old street with life, music and young people. The enthusiasm of the famous soloists, conductors, choirs, actors and directors who have worked here without a fee, was so infectious that the Montepulciano craftsmen built the sets for nothing and restored the elegant little *Teatro Poliziano*, which had been a total ruin, for the operatic performances.

A good meal may be had in the *"Trattoria Riva"*, *Via del Graciano del Corso*, immediately to the left beyond the city gate, where farmers from the vicinity seem to bring their freshest produce. *"La Greppia"*, *Via Fiorenzuela 14* was also recommended to us.

Castello di Monticchiello (Prov. Siena)
8km (5 miles) South-West of Montepulciano — the road is firm though not made up — is Monticchiello, one of the prettiest walled hill towns in southern Tuscany. The past remained so intact that the whole town with its Cathedral, its narrow, clean streets and the flower pots on the steps, looks like a theatrical set. And, in fact, for the last ten years, from July 15th till July 30th, the village has been the setting for the *"teatro povero"*, which has saved the community from extinction.

With the drift of young people into the cities *Monticchiello* had become, by the 1960's, a town largely inhabited by the old. Then one of the exiles, a teacher in Rome, wrote a play based on a recent event in Monticchiello's history. The local surveyor became the director; the whole village took part and found in the play new meaning for their existence and a new sense of pride in the old grey walls of the town.

Nowadays visitors from all over the world come to Monticchiello each year. No one is leaving any more. Many inhabitants returned and each one of them is involved year in, year out, in the preparations for the new play. However the village is worth a visit whether you can go at the time of the play or not. In particular the church of SS. Leonardo and Cristoforo contains a fine *Madonna* by *Pietro Lorenzetti.*

Pienza (Prov. Siena)
From Monticchiello there is a narrow country road to *Pienza* (6km, 3.7 miles) which was the first town in Italy to be "planned" in the modern sense of the word. The town dates from 1458.

It bears the name of its founder, Pope Pius II, a member of the Piccolomini family. He sat in Rome thinking of the little village of Corsignano, where he was born, and longed to see it large and impressive. He commissioned the Florentine architect, Bernardo Rossellino, to design the layout for the town and talked some of his cardinals into building fine houses for themselves next to his palace and the newly built cathedral. In 1464 when Pius II died (just as he was about to leave Ancona at the head of a crusading army), he left behind him an incomplete city but one which is, nonetheless, full of fine buildings.

The architectural centre of Pienza is the *Piazzo Pio II*. On it stands the Cathedral which, on the instructions of the Pope, was modelled on the hall churches of Northern Europe: it is full of excellent paintings, all of which were commissioned by Pius II.

To the left of the Cathedral is the *Bishops' Palace* and next to it, the *Casa dei Canonici*, which has a small museum on the second floor containing exquisite paintings from the Sienese School and memorabilia of Pius II who has a humanist and politician before becoming Pope.

Opposite the Cathedral is the *Palazzo Comunale* and to the right of that, the *Palazzo Piccolomini*, a majestic work by Rossellino, which was inspired by the Rucellai Palace in Florence. From the path along the top of the town wall there is a magnificent view: it becomes immediately understandable why Zeffirelli, the film director, chose to film his 'Romeo and Juliet' in the peace and quiet of Pienza rather than in the crowded streets of Verona.

The food in the *"Il Prato"*, *Piazza Dante 25*, is excellent. You can either rejoin the *Autostrada del Sole* (30km, 8.6 miles) and return to Florence (you can also take the other motorway to Siena), or make the excursion to *San Quirico d'Orcia* (9.5km, 5.8 miles to the West on the Cassia).

San Quirico d'Orcia (Prov. Siena)

The little country town looks down from its hill across the wide expanse of countryside which surrounds it: the town has several important buildings. Like San Miniato al Tedesco, San Quirico was the seat of one of the Imperial Representatives in the 12th century: it was later ruled by Siena, before being swallowed up by the omnipotent Florentines.

The most important building is the *Collegiata*, begun in the 8th century and extended in the Romanesque style in the 12th century. The doorway with its caryatids standing on lions, is thought to be the work of the *Giovanni Pisano School*. In addition to the *tomb of Count Henry of Nassau*, who died here in

1451, the interior contains a series of frescoes and beautiful choir stalls.

To the left of the Collegiata is the magnificent 17th century *Palazzo Chigi* which badly damaged in the last war, and to the right, the Renaissance *Palazzo Pretorio* which has mediaeval buildings on either side.

Follow the picturesque old street to the *Porta dei Cappucini* and then continue along the Via Dante Alighieri to the Piazza della Libertà. The church of *S. Maria Vitaleta* stands on the left: it contains a fine Madonna from the *della Robbia School* on the main altar. The *Porto Nuova* on the right leads to the romantic, overgrown *Orti Leonini* park. If you wish to visit it, inquire at the Fattoria Chigi next door.

San Galgano (Prov. Siena)

The fastest route from Siena to the sea takes you through *Massa Marittima* to *Follonica*. 35km (21.7 miles) along Road 73, a yellow tourist sign will point to the left to the *Abbey of San Galgano*. The Gothic ruin which soon rises before you in the midst of deserted countryside, will seem remarkably familiar to anyone who knew Caspar David Friedrich's *"Cistercian Ruin near Greifswald"*. The ruin you see here is like a southern twin.

The Cistercian *Abbey of San Galgano* (it was a powerful influence on Gothic architecture in Tuscany) ruled wide areas of the country in the 14th century. It was frequently fought over and destroyed: its power started to decline in the 15th century and by the 16th century it had fallen into decay. The campanile collapsed in 1786, then the roof. Napoleon's secularisation of the monasteries drove out the last monks and the abandoned church was used as a source of building material.

But what remained is worth coming for. Next to the *Chapter House* and the tiny section of *cloisters* which survived and is occupied by Belgian nuns, tower the outside walls of the triple-naved church with its high pointed windows and rosettes in the transept and apse. You have to go into the ruin to appreciate the wonderful light inside. Open to the sky, it is so full of sunshine—and at night of moonlight and stars, that you are dazzled at first; but then you will appreciate as never before the lines of the Gothic pillars and arcades. Beneath you, the ground is a meadow filled with the chirping of crickets. Birds twitter above the moss-covered altars. Dark swallows' nests cling to the pale travertine of the arcades and their occupants weave patterns across the sky in its Gothic frame.

On a hill next to the ruined church is the *Chapel of Monte Sieri* an unusual example of Sienese Romanesque architecture: the church is round and its unusual shape is emphasised on the exterior by concentric strips of travertine and fired tiles. It contains interesting synopia and frescoes by *Ambrogio Lorenzetti.* You can obtain the key from the priest who lives on the farm some 300 yards from the entrance to San Galgano.

Bibliography

La Divina Commedia and *La Vita Nuova* by Dante Alighieri [*Penguin Classic**, translated by Dorothy Sayers and *Oxford Paperbacks**). The latter tells of Dante's abiding Platonic love for the legendary Beatrice whom he adored from the moment he first saw her in a street of Florence, when Dante was still a boy. The former is his vision of Hell (*L'Inferno*), Purgatory (*Il Purgatorio*) and Heaven (*Il Paradiso*), full of historical allusion and religious and philosophical speculation. It is the work that 'fixed' the Italian language, Latin previously having been used for 'serious' subjects.

The Dialogues (*I Ragionamenti*) by Pietro Aretino are outspoken, and sometimes outrageous discussions of contemporary sexual mores by imaginary people. (*A translation was published* by *Allen and Unwin in 1972*). *His Letters* (**Penguin Classics Tr. by George Bull*), are very entertaining.

The Decameron by Giovanni Boccaccio (**Penguin classics*). Boccaccio is one of the greatest story-tellers (especially of tall stories) of all time; deft, funny and moving.

The Prince by Niccolò Machiavelli (**Penguin Classics Tr. by George Bull*). A famous treatise on statesmanship and the art of politics, much abused and misunderstood, but never ignored. **Penguin* also publish a collection of his writings in *The Portable Machiavelli.*

The History of Italy and *The History of Florence* by Francesco Guiccardini have been published in an edition edited by John Hale (*R. Sadler, 1966*).

Selected Poems by Francesco Petrarca, (Petrarch) have been published by *Manchester University Press* (*1971*). He is remembered best for the popular '*Le Canzoniere*', a collection of lyrics and sonnets, though he regarded them as slight and wrote mostly in Latin.

The Lives of the Artists by Giorgio Vasari (**Penguin Classics Tr. by George Bull*). Vasari did for the artists of the Renaissance what Dr. Johnson did for the English poets. A great deal of our information about the shadowy geniuses of the 14th and 15th century comes from him, though he has been shown to be inaccurate in places, particularly in the earlier biographies.

Guides
The Companion Guide to Florence by Eve Borsook (*Collins, 1966, Fontana paperback**). A very detailed building by building guide packed with historical information and unusual anecdote.

The Blue Guide to Northern Italy edited by Alta Macadam (*Ernest Benn*, 1978, also in paperback**). Follows the painstaking and thorough formula of the series.

The Companion Guide to Tuscany by Archibald Lyall (*Collins, 1972**). More discursive than its sister guide to Florence and consequently slightly more selective.

Some books for further reading

Some of the books listed are out of print and will have to be obtained from the library. Where a current edition is available, it is marked with an asterisk.

Modern Italy
Italia, Italia by Peter Nichols (*Macmillan, 1973*). Readable account of what Italy is like today, fact-filled, and full of insights; Nichols is *The Times* correspondent in Rome.
  The Italians by Luigi Barzini. (*Hamish Hamilton, 1964, Bantam Paperbacks**). Caused quite a stir in Italy when published as Barzini can be devastating about what he sees as his homeland's shortcomings. Witty and impressionistic.

History
The standard history of the Renaissance, still not superseded, is the monumental *Civilization of the Renaissance in Italy* by the Swiss nineteenth century historian, Jacob Burckhardt. It was first issued in 1860. A two volume edition in paperback is published by *Harper and Row Torchbooks**.
  The Florentine Renaissance by Vincent Cronin (*Collins, 1967*) is a good general survey of the art and thought of the Renaissance.

The Merchant of Prato by Iris Origo (*Cape 1957*). A classic reconstruction of the life of Francesco Datini, a wool merchant who died in 1410, all of whose business papers and letters have been preserved. His relationship with his wife, his business deals, the standard of living he enjoyed and a thousand details of everyday life in the 14th century are revealed in this brilliant piece of literary excavation.

The Stones of Florence by Mary McCarthy. (*Illustrated hardback edition Heinemann, 1959, available unillustrated in *Penguin with 'Venice Observed'*). An evocative historical tour of Florence by one of America's leading writers.

The Etruscans

The Etruscans by Christopher Hampton (*Gollancz, 1969*). A good clear and thorough book, both a history and a guide to the Etruscan sites.

Etruscan Places by D.H. Lawrence (with *'Mornings in Mexico', Heinemann, 1956, Penguin*)*. As is to be expected, this is a highly poetic account of a visit to the Etruscan sites. More for lovers of Lawrence than for lovers of the Etruscans. *'Flowery Tuscany'*, Lawrence's tribute to the Tuscan countryside is to be found in *Selected Essays* (*Penguin**).

Index

accommodation 8, 20, 44-53
air travel 6
Alberti, Leon Battista 136
Ammannati, Bartolomeo 119
138, 172
Anchiano 188
Angelico, Fra 31, 130-1, 150
Anghiari 151
Agriturist 21-2, 140
architects 31-4
architectural styles 35
Aretino, Pietro 36
Arezzo 147-50
Arezzo province 147-54
Arnolfo di Cambio 119, 194

Badia a Coltibuono 26
Bagni di Lucca 177
Barga 177
beaches 21, 100
Boccaccio, Giovanni 36, 139
Boccherini, Luigi 37
Borgo San Lorenzo 29
Botticelli, Sandro 31
Brunelleschi, Filippo 31, 119,
129, 132, 135, 136, 139
Bruni, Leonardo 36, 133
Buonconvento 200

Calci 187
Camaiore 174
camping 19, 95
Capalbio 163-4
Capraia 166
car hire 13, 103
Carrara 176
Castellina in Chianti 26
Castello 93
Castello del Trebbio 30
Castello di Brolio 26
Castello di Monticchiello 205
Castello di Poppiano 27

Castello Poppi 152-3
Castiglione della Pescaia 156
Certaldo 189
Chianti 25-7, 86
Chiusi 202-4
church services 10, 96
Cimabue, Giovanni 29, 31,
133, 149
climate 19
clothing 19
cooking (Tuscan) 23-4
Cortona 150-1
Cosa (Ansedonia) 161
currency 7
Cusano 26-7
customs 7-8
cypresses 38

Dante Alighieri 36, 42, 132,
133, 137, 151
della Francesco, Piero 31, 148,
149, 151-2
della Quercia, Iacopo 33, 172,
190, 194, 197
della Robbia family 33, 132,
177
della Robbia, Andrea 33, 132,
146, 181
della Robbia, Luca 33, 152,
177
doctors 8
Donatello de' Bardi 31, 124,
133, 180, 194
drinking 86-7
driving
to Italy 6-7
in Italy 12-14
Duccio di Buoninsegna 195

Elba 167-8
Etruscan sites 26, 150, 153,
158-63, 190-1, 203-4

farm holidays 19
festivals 20, 97, 142
Fiesole 93, 144-5

Florence
  accommodation 44-53
  airline offices 94
  Automobile Club d'Italia 97
  banks 94
  bars 59-60
  Biblioteca Laurenziana 138
  Boboli Gardens 114
  bookshops 95
  buses 103
  camping 95
  car concessionaires 95-6
  car hire 103
  Casa Buonarroti 133
  churches
    Badia Church 132
    Baptistery 124
    Duomo (Santa Maria del
      Fiore) 124-9
    Medici Chapel 137-8
    Orsanmichele 122-4
    Pazzi Chapel 135
    San Lorenzo 137
    San Miniato al Monte 107
    Santa Croce 42, 133-5
    Santa Maria del Carmine
      135-6
    Santa Maria Novella 136-7
    Santo Spirito 135
    services 96
  cinemas 96
  concerts 97
  consulates 96
  courses, language/cultural 97
  eating places 54-85
   classifies by type, price
    and area 61-83
   defined 54-55
   menu explained 84-5
   recommended 56-9
   tearooms, cafes, bars 59-60
  flood (1966) 112-4, 133
  food stores 60
  football 140
  Forte de Belvedere 108
  Fortezza da Basso 114
  golf 96
  galleries see museums
  historical background 40-3

  hotels 44-53
  ice cream parlours 60
  libraries 97
  Loggia dei Lanzi 119-20
  maps 101
  museums and galleries
    Accademia 131
    Archaeological Museum 132
    Bargello 132
    Galleria d'Arte Moderna 119
    Galleria Palatina 119
    Museo degli Argenti 119
    Museo dell'Opera del
      Duomo 124
    Museo dell'Opera di S.
      Croce 133
    Museo delle Porcellane 119
    Museo di San Marco 130-1
    opening and closing times
      88-93
    Uffizi Gallery 122
  music festivals 97
  night life 99
  Oltrarno 135
  Ospedale degli Innocenti 132
  palaces
    Bargello 132
    Medici-Riccardo 129-30
    Pitti 119
    Vecchio 119-20
  petrol 99
  pharmacies 99
  Piazza del Duomo 124
  Piazza della Signoria 119-20
  Piazza San Lorenzo 137
  Piazza Santissima
    Annunziata 131
  Piazzale Michelangelo 106
  Ponte Vecchio 108-12
  postal services 99-100
  restaurants 54, 61
   by area 56-9, 62-83
  San Marco (monastery)
    130-1
  Scoppio del Carro 142
  shops 100-1
  swimming pools 101
  telephones 100
  tourist offices 101, 106

Florence Contd.
  travel agents 104
  Via Maggio 135
  villas, Florence and region
    Artimino 139
    Cafaggiolo 30
    Careggi 139
    Gamberaia 30
    I Tatti 21, 140
    La Petraia 21, 139
    La Pietra 21, 140
    Mansi 178
    Medici 144
    opening times 93
    Palmieri 139
    Poggio a Caiano 139
    Poggio Gherardo 30
    Torrigiani 178
    Vignamaggio 26
  Youth hostels 45
Forte dei Marmi 174
Futa Pass 28

Galileo 36, 133, 183, 184
Galluzzo 93, 146
Ghiberti, Lorenzo 32, 124
Ghirlandaio, Domenico 32,
  131, 136, 190
Giambologna 114, 139
Giannutri 166
Giordano, Luca 130
Giotto di Bondone 29, 32,
  124, 133
Gorgona 167
Gozzoli, Benozzo 32, 130,
  184, 190
Greve 26
Grosseto province 155-7
Guicciardini, Francesco 37
Guido d'Arezzo 37

holidays (national) 8
hotels 8, 44-53

Isola del Giglio, L' 166-7
Italian Automobile Club 13,
  97
Italian language 15-16

La Verna 152
Lago di Burano 164
Leonardo da Vinci 34, 120,
  188
Lippi, Fra Filippo 32, 130,
  180
Lippi, Filippino 32, 130, 132,
  135, 136
Lippo Memmi 32, 190
Livorno 169
Lorenzetti, Ambrogio 155, 196
  197, 208
Lorenzetti, Pietro 149, 150,
  195, 205
Lucca 170-3
Luni 175-6
Lunigiana 176-7

Machiavelli 27, 37, 133
Magliano in Toscana 163
maps 101
Marina di Pisa 186
Maremma 156-7
Marinella 176
Marsiliana 163
Martini, Simone 197
Massa Maritima 155-6
Masaccio 32, 135-6
Medici family 42-3
  Cosimo the Elder 42, 131
  Lorenzo the Magnificent 42
  museum 188
Michelangelo Buonarroti 33,
  108, 120, 129, 132, 133,
  137-8, 152, 194
Michelozzo 33, 131, 144, 180
mining 21
Montalcino 201
Monte Argentario 164
Monte Amiata 202
Monte Oliveto Maggiore 200
Monte Savino 151
Montecristo 165
Montepulciano 204-5
Monteriggioni 26
Montevarchi 26
Mugello 29
museums 9
  see also under Florence

214

Nardo de Cione 136, 137
national holidays 8

Orcagna, Andrea 33, 133, 13(

Petrarca, Francesco 37, 149
Pianosa 165
Pienza 205-6
Pietrasanta 174
Pieve di Socana 152-3
Pinturicchio 194
Pisa 182-7
Pisano, Andrea 33, 124
Pisano, Giovanni 33, 183, 19(
Pisano, Nicola 33, 184, 194
Pistoia 180-2
Poggio a Caiano 93
police 9
Poliziano, Angelo 37
Pontremoli 175
Populonia 160-1
Prato 179-80
Puccini, Giacomo 37, 174
Punta Ala 156

rail travel 6
Renaissance 42-3
restaurants *see under* towns
Romena 153
Roselle 159-60

S. Andrea in Percussina 27
San Casciano in Val di Pesa
  27
San Domenica de Fiesole
  145-6
San Galgano 207-8
San Gimignano 190
San Miniato al Tedesco 189
San Quirico d'Orcia 206-7
Sansepolcro 151-2
Sansovino, Andrea 34
Sant' Antimo 201-2
Santa Brigida 30
Saturnia 163
Savonarola 42, 131
Scarperia 29
Segromigno 178
Sesto Fiorentino 93

Settignano 30
shops 9, 10, 100-1
Siena 193-9
  cathedral 193-5
  Palazzo Pubblico 196-7
  Palio 198-9
  Piazza del Campo 195-6
  Pinacoteca Nazionale 195
  Torre del Mangia 196
Signorelli, Luca 34, 150, 200
Spinello Aretino 149
Sodoma 197-8, 200
Sovana 161-2
spas 28
summer time 10
swimming 21

Taddeo di Bartolo 190
Talamone 157
telephones 10,100
Tirli 156
topography 21
tourist offices 6, 8, 101, 106

Uccello Paolo 34, 129, 137

Vallombrosa 154
Vacari, Giorgio 135, 136, 150
Verrocchio, Andrea del 34,
  119, 124, 188
Vespignano 29
Vetulonia 159
Vicchio 29
villa tours 21-2
villas 21-2, 26, 30, 93,
  193-40, 144, 178
Vinci 188
voltage 10
Volterra 190-2

wine 22, 25-7, 86

youth hostels 11, 45